The
Lightwood Chronicles

Murder and Greed in the Piney Woods of
South Georgia, 1869-1923

Being The True Story of Brainard Cheney's
Novel *Lightwood*

Contributions from
Brainard Cheney, Caroline Gordon and Ashley Brown

And also:

Mrs. Wilton P. Cobb, Roy N. Cowart, Marion Erwin, John Goff,
Dorothy Hargrove Stoeger and Welda Davis Whigham

Compiled and Edited by Stephen Whigham

MM John Welda BookHouse
2012

ISBN: 978-0-983-9365-0-3
LCCN: 2011940232
The Lightwood History Collection: Book 1
First Edition

For more information:
www.lightwoodchronicles.com

Permissions:

Roy Neel for permission to use Brainard
Cheney's Introduction to *Lightwood*

Chattahoochee Review for "The Novels of Brainard
Cheney" by Ashley Brown

Sewanee Review for "The Novels of Brainard Cheney"
by Caroline Gordon

Southern Review and Roy Neel
for "Look-a, Look-a Yonder! I See Sunday, I See Sunday—Or A Deliverer Delivered" by Brainard Cheney

University of Georgia Press for John Goff's essays,
"The Great Pine Barrens" and "Suomi"

Roy N. Cowart for permission to reprint his "Legal
Treatise," with thanks also to Jane Walker

Dedicated with appreciation to the memory of
Frances Neel and Brainard Cheney

And to the spirit of those early pioneers of the
Ocmulgee, Oconee and Altamaha River area

To Dodge County

Vanished long since are the tribes,
That once roamed over valley and upland.
Yet lingers their speech,
in the name of the fair sister rivers,
Oconee, Ocmulgee and murmuring Altamaha.
Gone is the forest primeval, and
silent forever its sighing
Of music Aeolian, that breathed
over earth and to heaven.
And gone are the strangers who journeyed
from out of the Northland,
To gather the harvest the pines had amassed
through the ages.
Yet lingers their memory still
in the name of a county,
In the names of the cities of Eastman and
Chauncey forever.
And where Lumber City looks out over
rolling Ocmulgee,
And Normandale nestles, their work will
never be forgotten.
Instead of the croon of the pines or
the wail of the sawmill,
The song of the ploughman and
the lowing of the cattle are mingled,
And where once was solitude,
now are glad homes of contentment.
From out of the soil, men are reaping
A harvest of gold,
The past is forgotten and gone,
like a story that's told.

[From Cobb's *History of Dodge County*,
the poem's author may be H. W. J. Ham,
Eastman newspaper editor, circa 1900]

Contents

Illustrations

"The Work of a Fiend"

October 7, 1890

THE WORK OF A FIEND.

CAPT. J. C. FORSYTH, OF NORMANDALE, FOULLY MURDERED.

Andrew J. Reneau, the Fiend Who Is Supposed to Have Fired the Fatal Shot, Tracked to His Home and Shot After a Desperate Resistance.

On Tuesday night last at 6:15 o'clock p. m., Dodge county experienced one of the most dastardly crimes ever committed. Captain J C Forsyth while sitting in his room, at Normandale, at that hour was maliciously and foully assassinated by some blackhanded villain who slipped up in his bare feet placed his gun to the window glass and emptied a load of buckshot into his victim's head. Capt. Forsyth was sitting within four feet of the window when the fatal shot was fired, the whole load taking effect in the back of his head a little to the rear of the left ear. The wounded man called to his wife and daughter, who were in an adjoining room, was all that he was able to utter after being shot. Almost immediately friends and a physician were at his side, and all that medical skill could do was done to relieve him; but after lying in an unconscious state until 9:35 p. m., he died.

Early Report from the *Macon News* October 9, 1890

"The Work of a Fiend"
October 7, 1890

On the evening of October 7, 1890, Captain John C. Forsyth finished his evening meal and retired to the parlor to read the newspaper. His duties as Superintendent for the Dodge Company's extensive timber and milling operation warranted a full day's work. He looked forward to the quiet and restful evenings with his family at the end of the day. Unknown to him a killer lurked outside.

A steady drizzle fell beyond the high windows of the room overlooking the wraparound porch of the large house. It was just after 6 p.m. From the adjoining room his wife and daughter heard a loud noise and then heard Captain Forsyth call out for help. They rushed in to find him slumped over in his chair with a gunshot wound to the back of his head. He died later that night.

Investigators discovered bare footprints in the damp soil outside in the flower beds. The killer escaped down a lane into the nearby woods where pursuers found evidence of an accomplice. As darkness closed in, bloodhound trackers lost the killer's trail in nearby Sugar Creek, choosing to wait until daybreak to continue their search.

The shot fired by Forsyth's murderer crystallized in an instant the many years of discord and bitterness between the timber company and the "squatters"—those people who lived on disputed Dodge Company land holdings. Charges of dark conspiracies implicated prominent local citizens, resulting in a sensational murder conspiracy trial in Federal Court. Those convicted spent many years in prison, some dying there, still proclaiming their innocence. Nearly fifty years after the events, in 1939, the novel *Lightwood* by Brainard Cheney related this story in fictional form.

The book you hold seeks to introduce this fascinating and tragic tale told in both the novel and the historical record. The old saying, 'truth is stranger than fiction', comes to mind. In this case, both the facts and the fiction are equally strange and compelling.

The Lightwood Chronicles
An Introduction

Stephen Whigham

Map of the *Lightwood* area circa 1860

The Lightwood Chronicles
An Introduction

Stephen Whigham

The Lightwood Chronicles brings together in one volume a compendium of literary and historical material related to the novel *Lightwood* by author Brainard Cheney. The reader may consider the *Chronicles* a companion piece to the great and tragic history dramatized in Cheney's novel.

In presenting this collection, we celebrate the life and work of Mr. Cheney, who was born in 1900. His novel *Lightwood* appeared on the literary scene in the fall of 1939. Mr. Cheney based his work on historical events and the people of south Georgia who lived that history from 1865 until 1890 and beyond. *Lightwood* recounts in fiction the coming of the timber barons to the backwoods of south Georgia shortly after the Civil War ended. For more than three decades after 1868, the Dodge Company and many of the original settlers—labeled *squatters*—waged war on one another over ownership of the land. They fought their battles first through the Reconstruction-era legal system. Feeling betrayed by the courts, the squatters turned to guns and violence.

Cheney's novel rings true even today, more than seventy years later, in its retelling of this tale of corporate greed and the battles of common citizens against forces of power and wealth.

William E. Dodge and William Pitt Eastman, New York entrepreneurs, headed a group of Northern investors who secured ownership to more than 300,000 acres of virgin timber in south Georgia. For this "wooden treasure" they paid as little as five cents an acre under disputed legal title. The company operated in the area under various names, primarily incorporated as the Georgia Land and Lumber Company. Locals commonly referred to it as the Dodge Company, as will this book.

In Dodge's development and exploitation of these riches, the saga of the Dodge Land Wars originated. These events reverberate through the history of the area to this day. In the ensuing conflict, many people lost their land and their livelihoods. Others lost their freedom. Some lost their lives.

Geography of the *Lightwood* area

Dodge County is situated 150 miles south of Atlanta in the very heart of the state of Georgia. Created in 1870, the new county was named by an Act of the State Legislature for William E. Dodge, a New York entrepreneur. Dodge County was formed in large measure from portions of Pulaski and Telfair counties, with smaller parts of Montgomery also included.

The geographical area associated with *Lightwood* resides between the Oconee and Ocmulgee Rivers in south Georgia. For many years prior to 1865, the majority of Georgia's population settled along the Atlantic coast and the rivers, for the most part shunning the interior. Inland from the rivers, great forests of virgin longleaf pine timber covered most of the area, supporting a sparse population of hardworking farmers and herders. The rivers offered the sole means of transporting goods to larger towns, limiting the economy to local and minimal development. For that time period, one historian labeled it the "inner frontier" of Georgia, due to its remoteness.

The Dodge Company land purchases covered nearly 500 square miles between the Oconee River on the east and the Ocmulgee on the west. These two rivers converge below Lumber City to form the mighty Altamaha River which flows southward into the Atlantic Ocean at Darien. This area between the two rivers is often referred to as the Big Bend of the Ocmulgee and Oconee Rivers, and also as the forks. In 1865, its topography consisted primarily of large stands of virgin pine timber called the *pine barrens,* interspersed with the random clearing often occupied by farmers and herders. Census records revealed a population as small as six persons per square mile occupying the area between the rivers.

History and Economic Development

Prior to the Civil War, the scattered population of farmers and herders made their living growing corn and tobacco along with raising livestock. Some residents further supplemented their income by cutting timber, building rafts from the logs and floating them downriver to the port of Darien during the winter rainy season. They walked the 150 miles back home with their hard-earned cash.

Most of these early settlers, comprised of English, Irish, and Scottish descent, migrated from the Carolinas into Georgia. From about 1810 onward, they fashioned an isolated yet independent existence throughout the pine barrens or the "piney woods," as the locals called it. Many of them fought in the Revolutionary War and the War of 1812. This often qualified them and their heirs for land grants in the new territory in the years following the removal of the Creek Indians, circa 1810.

The first attempt to harvest the vast riches of the pine forests occurred in 1833, when Maine investors purchased extensive land holdings in the area, creating the Georgia Lumber Company. They established the town of Lumber City on the Ocmulgee River and built a large timber mill to service the 300,000 acres of virgin pine trees in their holdings. The timber mill depended on water power provided by the river. The owners planned to transport the timber downriver to the port city of Darien for shipment worldwide. Unfortunately, the investors failed to take into account that the rivers were not always navigable, prone to dwindle to a shallow stream during the long dry months of summer and early autumn. Navigating large timber rafts and steamboat barges downriver became impossible. Their grand enterprise failed.

As stated in Talley's paper, *The Dodge Lands and Litigation*:

> The end was at hand. By 1842, those in charge and most of the employees had returned to Maine. The cutting of timber ceased. The lands were abandoned. Actual possession and the title parted. The Flournoy plantation grew up in bushes, the Auchee Hatchee River flowed through the broken dam, shy swamp birds sang in the ruins of the mill, and the pines in safety slumbered, while the vagrant title wandered long in distant states.

The company abandoned its operations, setting in motion a series of legal and financial complications that questioned the ownership of the property. For the next thirty years, banks and other creditors possessed title to the land. Even the State of Indiana held title at one point. In 1867 it fell under the ownership of New York investors including Dodge and Eastman.

Prior to the Civil War, investors incorporated the Macon and Brunswick Railroad in 1856. Its charter envisioned more than 200 miles of track connecting Macon and the coastal city of Brunswick. As outlined in an article by William J. Steele in the *History of Dodge County 1932-1992*, the railroad planned to cut through the pine forests of Pulaski, Telfair and counties southward. This preceded the creation of Dodge County. Its progress slowed by the Civil War, track was laid as far south as Hawkinsville and the new town of Cochran (formerly Dykesboro) by 1866. Utilizing subsidies and tax breaks from the Reconstruction Georgia government, the Dodge investors assisted in completing the railroad. By 1868, track was completed to Station Number 13, soon to be rechristened as Eastman. In 1870, the M&B reached its final destination, the port city of Brunswick.

Probably no other single development rivaled the importance of the railroad. Its arrival transformed the forks, that area situated between the rivers, from an isolated backwater into a booming economy almost overnight. Within the span of a few years, beginning around 1868, this sparsely populated section grew from a few settlers living along the rivers and in the pine forests into a series of boom towns sprouting up alongside the new tracks. The once quiet backwoods reverberated with the hum and activity of steam engines, timber gangs and sawmills.

William Pitt Eastman settled in the area that became the town of Eastman. He chose to set up his operations at Station Number 13, buying up much of the surrounding land from William (Billy) Lee, a local farmer. The new town took Eastman's name as its own. His partnership with the Dodge companies brought him riches and prestige. Real estate speculations in the new town further increased his wealth. At his death, he owned 45,000 acres of land in the Dodge county area, worth as much as 75 to 100 million dollars in today's valuation.

Historian Mark Wetherington, in his book *The New South Comes to Wiregrass Georgia*, outlines the methods used by Eastman to gain advance knowledge of the route the new railroad intended to cover. Wetherington recounts Eastman's real estate dealings along the railroad line. These echo the stories of economic speculations, booms and busts of our own recent times.

By 1870, the new town of Eastman rivaled anything to be found in the mythical Wild West. It included mysterious strangers and imported workers, shootouts and camp meetings, rowdy saloons and proper churches, Yankee carpetbaggers and foreigners from all over the globe. New arrivals stepped from huffing steam-driven trains eager to give their luck a whirl. Others showed up on foot and on horseback, some even in covered wagons, seeking to put down stakes in the new territory or drawn by the promise of steady wages. Whites and blacks left the farms and found work in the timber mills and the pine woods. Recently freed from slavery, black workers migrated to the towns and cities seeking work. They found it in the nascent timber industry.

These new citizens created an economy and social order centered on the new railroad and the booming timber industry. The native settlers of the area first welcomed the Dodge Company.

The infusion of northern capital promised wages and prosperity for all, black and white alike.

In 1874, William E. Dodge made his sole visit to Eastman to dedicate the new courthouse he donated to the county. A handsome building costing $25,000, it stood in the courthouse circle along planned city grids laid out for the new town by an architect retained by William Pitt Eastman. An early scene in *Lightwood* recreates this event. On first seeing the new courthouse, a boy marvels to his father: "Look, Pa, it's painted!"

Mr. Dodge's investment demanded from the squatters a high price. Thirty years of discontent, legal struggles and killings followed.

Legal Battles: Who Owned the Land?

The story of *Lightwood* recounts the story of the land in both fact and fiction.

The players in this story include not only the wealthy investors—Eastman, Dodge, Chauncey and others. One must not forget those settlers already living in the area, occupying land purchased decades ago on which they made their homes, harvested their crops and raised their families.

The war between the Dodges and the squatters constituted a legal conflict over who held legal title to the land. Attorney Roy N. Cowart's essay outlines the basic underlying premise of this story, emphasizing the legal term, "chain of title." The law states that the holder of a land deed, unchallenged for seven years, having lived on and developed the property, under certain legal processes, may be deemed by the courts the legal owner of said property. Most of the disputed land—whose timber the Dodge Company wanted—was situated in northern Telfair and southern Dodge County, which was formerly in Telfair.

Current occupants of the land in question purchased their holdings from an 1844 tax sale after Telfair County officials legally determined it to be abandoned land. By 1869 and later, the new owners had occupied the land for more than 25 years, built homes there, and improved and cultivated their property. Through the years they paid their taxes. The coming of the timber companies turned their world upside down.

Eastman Attorney Luther Hall (Calhoun Calebb in the novel) played a central role in the conflict between the squatters and the Dodge Company. In the early days, he represented the squatters against the Dodge Company in the local courts, defeating the Company's "ejectment" claims before sympathetic local juries. When the cases moved into federal court, Hall's success in fighting the Dodges ended.

Although there existed many alleged squatters whose land ownership claims rested in legitimate deeds from the 1844 tax sale, a trade in falsified deeds also thrived. To make the deeds appear older, the forgers soaked the paper in coffee grounds, thus originating the term "coffee-pot deeds." Most of these bogus deeds met with quick and decisive nullification in the courts.

Perhaps in desperation, certainly in defiance, Luther Hall turned to creative legal means to secure land from the Dodges. He received information that the Dodge Company's chain of title was missing an important link. The deed transferring the land from Colby, Chase, and Crocker, agents for the 1832 purchase from Peter J. Williams, to the Georgia Land and Lumber Company, never properly cleared title. Hall took advantage of this failure through legal machinations and offered land for sale. He advertised "homes for the homeless," and initially profited from this scheme, allegedly to the tune of $15,000.00, a large sum at the time. His temporary success summoned further legal wrath from the Dodge Company, resulting in an injunction prohibiting Hall from continuing the land sales. This decision antagonized Hall, who served jail time for contempt of court.

Rightly or not, these events are considered by some as the pivotal point leading Hall and others to undertake drastic action against the Dodges, resulting in the murder of Captain John Forsyth on October 7, 1890. Luther Hall received a life term as a conspirator and died in an Ohio Federal penitentiary.

Wielding its wealth and political influence in Reconstruction-era Georgia, the timber company continued to fight the squatters in court. Multiple cases against the squatters made their way through the federal court in Macon, always favoring the Dodge Company. One notorious ejectment case cited more than three hundred defendants as illegal occupiers of Dodge land.

The very first case entered into the docket of the new county of Dodge, in 1870, was an ejectment case against an alleged squatter whose land the Dodge Company claimed. It represented the first of many, in a trail of legal actions that lasted for more than fifty years in state and federal courts, the last case ending in 1923.

To the Reader of *The Lightwood Chronicles*

The Lightwood Chronicles consists of two sections with a total of nine chapters. The first section of the book, consisting of four chapters, addresses fiction, as in the novel itself. The second section totals five chapters and relates the historical facts underlying the novel. Brainard Cheney acknowledged that his work derived from actual events occurring in the Ocmulgee River country during the struggles between the Dodge Company and the squatters.

Lightwood as Fiction

In early 1939, a publisher's notice appeared in a Nashville newspaper announcing the upcoming publication of a novel by local newspaperman, Brainard Cheney. At first, the novel was called *The Squatters*. When published several months later, the title changed to *Lightwood*, a somewhat mysterious term explained later in this article.

Author Brainard Cheney based *Lightwood* on his study of historical facts concerning the coming of the Dodge Company to the "great pine barrens" of south Georgia in 1869. The novel covers a period ranging from 1869 through 1890, with reference to events half a century earlier.

Cheney spent several months in the area researching the novel. His work included reading through a complete archive of legal materials related to the Dodge Company's struggle to establish legal precedent over the "squatters" who were living on disputed land. He chanced upon this archive in the storeroom of an attorney's former office in McRae, Georgia. Cheney wrote that he felt "fated" to have discovered this archive.

The title of the novel, the word *lightwood*, is the 'proper' spelling of a common term describing pine wood used in making fires. It is pronounced as if spelled *lighterd* or *lightard*, while accenting the first syllable. One most commonly hears this term in the phrase "fat lighter," as it would sound. In the 1990's, a play titled *The Lightard Knot* was produced based on the Dodge Lands controversy, written by Dr. Delma Presley, a prominent Georgia educator and historian.

Resources for the Novel, *Lightwood*

The first four chapters of this book highlight the fictional *Lightwood,* beginning with Brainard Cheney's short introduction to the 1984 republication of his book. Here he writes from the perspective of forty-five years since 1939, noting the continued interest in his work. He attributes this to the novel's basis in historical fact. The underlying premise of *The Lightwood Chronicles* agrees with Mr. Cheney on this point. Following Cheney's introduction is his 1976 essay from the Southern Review, "Look-a, Look-a Yonder,—I See Sunday, I See Sunday! Or, A Deliverer, Delivered." In 1971, Mr. Cheney returned to Lumber City to revisit the rivers of his youth and his fiction, traveling with a boyhood friend by boat. In this essay, he weaves the sources of his novels into the narrative of that journey along the Ocmulgee, Oconee and Altamaha Rivers.

Next follows the essay, "*Lightwood* by Brainard Cheney: the Novel and the Author," prepared by the editor. This section offers a summary of the novel itself and biographical material on the author, with background on his researches. Much of the material in this essay derives from a 1982 interview with Mr. Cheney.

As an introduction and overview to Mr. Cheney's work as a novelist, we next present Caroline Gordon's review essay, "The Novels of Brainard Cheney." This work appeared in the Spring, 1959 issue of the Sewanee Review. A celebrated novelist, teacher and respected critic, Caroline Gordon maintained a close personal and literary friendship with Brainard Cheney. By his own description, he regarded her as his mentor, as his "literary godmother."

The fourth chapter, Ashley Brown's essay, also titled "The Novels of Brainard Cheney," appeared in the Chattahoochee Review in the Spring, 1998 issue. His work follows Ms. Gordon's by almost 40 years. In the interim, Cheney had published his last novel, *Devil's Elbow*.

As friends, the two men shared many years discussing their mutual study of literature, especially southern writers. Professor Brown dissects the four novels and emphasizes the autobiographical and historical elements contained in all four works.

Lightwood as History

The editor's interest in *Lightwood* and its historical underpinnings stems from family connections to the house where Captain Forsyth was murdered and its history. My great-grandparents, Hattie Clark and John I. Hargrove, owned the house from about 1907 until 1927. Hattie grew up in Chauncey and later purchased the home. She was eight years old when the murder occurred. Her father, Hamilton Clark, counted Captain Forsyth as a friend. My grandmother, Wylena Hargrove Davis, born in 1898, grew up in the house. Several of her siblings and two of her own children were born there, including my mother, Welda Davis Whigham. These children were born in the parlor, the same room where Forsyth's murder occurred. Wylena commented to me that the events of 1890 made such an impression on the locals that they were "still talking about it" when she was growing up. And she continued discussing it as late as 1986, the year she died.

The first item in this section presents a chapter from the 1932 version of the *History of Dodge County* by Mrs. Wilton Philip Cobb. [Editor's Note: Mrs. Cobb's maiden name was Addie Davis. We follow the convention of the 1932 publication in designating her as Mrs. Cobb]. Mrs. Cobb's excerpt summarizes a paper presented by attorney J. N. Talley to a Georgia Bar Association meeting in 1925. His paper, *The Dodge Lands and Litigation*, presents a concise yet detailed study of the case.

In summarizing Talley, Mrs. Cobb avoids using names in retelling the events occurring as recently as forty years prior to 1932. Her likely reason for this attests to the animosity and ill-feelings that still existed at that late date. We offer her condensed version (rather than Talley's) first in this section for its briefer telling of the story. Mrs. Cobb refers to the case as the Dodge Lands and Litigations, in the plural, when in fact Mr. Talley's paper uses Litigation in the singular. We follow her convention here.

Next, we present two essays by John H. Goff, from his collection, *Placenames of Georgia*. Mr. Goff was an eminent economist, historian and geographer who studied placenames throughout Georgia.

His longer essay, "The Great Pine Barrens," traces the history of the great belt of pine forests stretching from Virginia through Georgia and westward to Mississippi. Here he evokes the geographic remoteness of the area before the advent of railroads.

In the second essay, "Suomi," Mr. Goff discusses the location of the headquarters of the Dodge Company, originally named Normandale. Both of Mr. Goff's essays provide useful background information to the story of the Dodge Land Wars.

The article prepared by Welda Davis Whigham recounts her memories of the Forsyth House, in Normandale/Suomi, where Captain Forsyth met his end. Written in 1995, the article addresses historical information concerning the location of the house where Captain Forsyth was murdered. Her family at one time owned the house and lived there, always referring to it as the Forsyth House. She was born in the house.

In the early 1990's, a Georgia historical marker was placed in the area of the Forsyth house, its information raising the possibility that a house still standing nearby was the scene of the murder. This article seeks to correct that information. A news item from a January, 1934, edition of the Eastman *Times-Journal* references the burning of the Forsyth House. Also included is background information from Ms. Dorothy H. Stoeger. She describes how she painted her portrait of the old house, for which no certain photograph exists.

Once the reader gets a feel for the facts from Mrs. Cobb's excerpt and the essays of Mr. Goff and Mrs. Whigham, we turn to *The Land Pirates*, a pamphlet prepared by Marion Erwin. Erwin prosecuted the Captain Forsyth murder conspiracy case in 1890. His rendition of the case brings to life the people and times in post-Civil War Georgia and the challenges they faced.

Mr. Erwin's perspective comes as no surprise, as it reflects that of the prosecution and the courts. In the legal battles in Federal court, the authorities deemed many local landowners as "squatters," or illegal occupiers of land owned by the Dodge Company. To add a touch of irony, the very title of his study, *The Land Pirates*, refers to an old southern term defining unscrupulous and crooked 'land grabbers'. Who is the villain here—the moneyed northern industrialists, represented by the Dodge Company, or the farmers who had occupied the land for the past quarter century or longer, even paying taxes on it? Although brimming with abstruse legal terms, it rewards the patient reader with a deeper sense of the charges in the case.

Completing the chapters is attorney Roy Cowart's essay on the legal intricacies of the Dodge Lands litigation. A veteran attorney, Mr. Cowart has litigated numerous cases involving the kaolin mining industry in central Georgia. Kaolin company legal actions often revolve around land titles and questions of ownership, as did the Dodge cases. Mr. Cowart's explanations of land deeds and adverse possession of abandoned land present his unique perspective as both a current litigator of similar disputes and as the descendant of Lucius Williams, a participant and victim of the Dodge Land Wars.

The final section of the book consists of Additional Material which includes: Acknowledgements, Contributors, *Lightwood*: People, Characters and Places, A Chronology of Events, and References and Suggested Reading. Consulting this section gives the reader insight into the setting of the story.

In Conclusion

The novel *Hopscotch* by Argentine writer Julio Cortazar appeared in 1963 to critical and commercial acclaim. An experimental work, its title derived from the author's suggestion that its chapters may be read in several different sequences, giving each reading a unique perspective on the story.

In reading *The Lightwood Chronicles*, we suggest that the reader move along in sequence, although you may feel free to choose your own order from the nine sections offered. The longest and most detailed of the offerings is *The Land Pirates*, which in some ways constitutes the heart of this book, along with Mr. Cowart's sterling essay. Mr. Erwin not only recounts the legal events of the trial but also presents a compelling account of the history of the Dodge story.

On the other hand, the two essays by Ms. Gordon and Mr. Brown transport the reader into a deeper appreciation for the literary merit of Mr. Cheney's novels. Truth be told, the editor has special praise for all of the work in this book, each with its own gift for the reader.

In Mr. Goff's essay, "The Great Pine Barrens," several descriptions of the ancient pine forests reach levels approaching poetry. For example, the French traveler, Levasseur, in 1825 described that "the tops of these old trees ... seem to measure the age of the world, [as they] sway over our heads." Another traveler spoke of being "lost in the gloom" of the seemingly endless forests, which to him resembled the interior of ancient cathedrals.

Fifty years later Levasseur's majestic forests fell before the ax of industrialization, ushering in our modern world. The Dodge Company purchased the land not as a long-term investment but to secure the "wooden treasure" resting upon it. They practiced what historian Mary Ellen Tripp Wilson calls the "cut out get out" philosophy. The once vast pine barrens disappeared, transported to all corners of the world. Timbers from the forests ended up in the Brooklyn Bridge, as masts for the German Kaiser's schooners and in other parts unknown. As testament to Dodge's short term ownership, the cut-over land, all stumps and sawdust piles, was sold off by the company once cleared of trees.

The reader who completes this book may emerge with an informed overview of the story of the Dodge Land Wars and the *Lightwood* area. We hope this encourages further researches and continuing interest in the subject.

If the reader discovers the novels of Brainard Cheney, all efforts invested in this project will be rewarded.

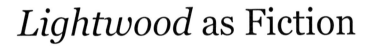

Lightwood as Fiction

1.

Foreword to *Lightwood*

&

"Look-a, Look-a Yonder—I See Sunday, I See Sunday!" Or A Deliverer, Delivered

Brainard Cheney

Brainard Cheney on the Ocmulgee River circa 1940

Foreword to *Lightwood*
1984 Edition

Brainard Cheney

The persistent trickle of inquiry for this book over the forty-five years since its first appearance, bringing about its republication, is undoubtedly due to its historical content. It is substantially a pseudonymous history of the South Georgia *Squatters War*. The enveloping action is largely factual. The dramatic action, I believe, symbolically true of the fate of these last victims of the *Lost Cause*.

I won't pretend to be unbiased in this war, but I will reveal that I changed sides during my digging into the background, in preparation for the writing. It was a personal relationship that originally inspired me. My father in his early years as a lawyer was a member of the lumber Company's legal staff. Moreover, he and my mother—his Charleston bride whom he was introducing into this wild back country, for a time lived with the Company superintendent—the *fated* Company superintendent! And, the Company story I cut my teeth on was quite different from what appears here.

But I had the accidental (I believe *fated*) good fortune to fall heir to the complete legal record of the Company's operations in Georgia. That is, all of the legal documents of that long war were left behind by the Company's last agent, for me to find and examine. And the account I give of how the Company came by its enormous holdings of Georgia land and its legal battle with the *squatters* is based on these records.

With your indulgence for my sympathies, I will add another small incident. I also learned from these papers that my father (of brief acquaintance, since he died when I was eight) in the beginning a Company lawyer—twenty years later was representing a group (twenty-five in number) of "squatters," trying to hold onto their land.

I found the relicts—the children and grandchildren—of the "squatters" (those who lost land to the Company) very reluctant to talk about it. The cause of the *Squatters* had lost respectability utterly with them. And this last battle of the Civil War was, indeed, a *lost cause*.

Editors Note: Interest in Mr. Cheney's novel continues long after its publication in 1939, now more than seventy years later. The italics used in the Foreword were Cheney's own.

"Look-a, Look-a Yonder—I See Sunday, I See Sunday!" Or A Deliverer, Delivered

Brainard Cheney

Southern Review, January 1976

A great river is both history and prophesy. The Altamaha, Georgia's largest river, though little known beyond the borders of the state, today stands revealed of a great and perhaps unique ecological destiny.

Scattered over thirty years, in four novels, I have sought to celebrate the story of the Altamaha and its people. This I have done with some sense of my role as historian. But a recent return to the Altamaha and a rereading of these forgotten novels has brought to me their prophesy, in the revelation of the river as deliverer, now delivered.

It is perhaps unknown to many citizens of Atlanta that the Altamaha rises under its pavements in three small streams, to become, before they reach Macon, the Ocmulgee—one of the river's two formative branches. The other, the Oconee, rises in the hills beyond Athens. All of which is important to the river's revealed role.

But the name of the river is important, too. The Indian word, *Altamaha,* means into *tama* country—Tama, the chief's lodge. The legendary land of Tama lies at the confluence of the Ocmulgee and the Oconee.

In the fall of 1971, at the suggestion of a boyhood and, I may add, life-long friend and fellow exile from the Altamaha, John Mobley of Atlanta, we met at Lumber City for an excursion down the river and (after a half century) up the stream of memory.

The timing of our trip happened to coincide with a topical stir over a proposal to turn the three rivers that make up the system into a twelve-foot-deep, hundred-foot-wide barge channel. It had arrayed the environmentalists, ecologists, and fisherman against the Altamaha Basin Commission and regional chambers of commerce. There had been hearings, under the sponsorship of the U.S. Army Corps of Engineers, held that spring in Macon and Jesup.

Our three days on the rivers were spent not merely in viewing their beauty and might again, but in recalling our past—the past that gave inspiration to my novels *Lightwood, River Rogue, This Is Adam,* and *Devil's Elbow.*

If the prophesy implied in the Altamaha's singular history is celebrated in my fiction, I admit at once that the foresight of which I speak is now largely a matter of hindsight—for past drawbacks of Georgia's biggest and most unaccountable stream are now recognized as that river's chief value.

There was one astonishing claim made for the Altamaha at the hearings in '71. A million and a quarter Georgians, living within the river's drainage system, send their raw sewage into it. And the old swamp-bound, variable, changeable river purifies it. If the river were turned into a chain of concrete reservoirs, this natural septic tank would be destroyed and the consequent pollution would be disastrous for everybody concerned; and extensive study, under the direction of Dr. Burbanck of Emory University, supported the claim.

"It was like looking for your lost memory in another man's mind." When those lines were first written about "the ever-

moving, yellow back" of the river some years before, I didn't fore-
see how aptly they could be used to describe the unaccountability
of the Ocmulgee, coming at us as soon as we got underway down
stream from the boat landing above the railroad bridge there at
Lumber City that Saturday afternoon.

My seventy-year-old companion of this Ponce de Leon plunge
had proposed that we name our fourteen-foot, outboard-powered
boat, *River Rogue*. And amateurishly, I had stuck the decal letters
on the side of its silver-gray aluminum hull in a running-together
rakish tilt. The novel thus celebrated is about a raftsman and
rogue who adventured upon the Ocmulgee, Oconee, and Altamaha in earlier times. "Snake" Sutton was a sort of composite of
many nameless river runners who drifted timber down to Doctor-
town and Darien during the Wooden Wealth Era—roughly 1875-
1900.

Could past drawbacks of the rivers become their future? The
dramatic terms of the four novels I had written about this country
and the rivers supporting it grew out of those drawbacks—
variable flow, variable stream bed, massive swamps. In 1844 the
first industrial enterprise in the forks of the rivers, establishing
Lumber City and giving it its name, was a water-powered sawmill
that failed because of the freshet and low water in the tributary
Little Ocmulgee. Did the intransigent old Altamaha's destiny still
lie ahead of it? I confess that the thought fascinated me. And
there was, too, the more mundane political question of whether
the skillful strategy and tactics of the engineers could be scotched
by a soft-headed motley of environmentalists. But what could two
old returning exiles from Altamaha country find out about all of
this?

True, the issue of perspective was after all the aim of our trip.
We had spent most of the first twenty, the most impressionable
years of our lives, on and about the Ocmulgee of the Lumber City
vicinity. And the Oconee, too, in fact—all the way from the mouth
to Cheney's old ferry. Sure, each of us knew these sections of the
rivers like the palm of his hand—could close his eyes and see
them plain as day, any time. In fact, many's the time we had done
just that.

But when we opened our eyes, opened them so to speak, at seventy—widened and jiggered a bit by warnings of rocks and snags

and sucks, in a small, unfamiliar skiff that rose on a current boil like a tumbleweed in a sand twister—why that familiar old face of our boyhood couldn't have looked stranger!

Nine miles further down the river the "confluence" was suddenly upon us, the Ocmulgee, the Oconee, and the Altamaha—three boiling river mouths—surrounding us like an Indian attack. A half century never seemed wider.

Eventually we circled and headed off up the Oconee. I recall vividly that moment of coming out of it, on my first raft trip of those fifty-odd years back: at nineteen, sub bow hand and cook. It was higher and swifter then, and as we obliquely approached the cross-current of a somewhat clearer hue from the Ocmulgee, I had suffered the optical illusion that our logs were going over a waterfall, and stumbled at the bow oar.

In generations past, our families dwelt on the Oconee—the Mobleys on the *white* side and the Cheneys on the *Indian*. And we now hoped, by the grace of their ghosts, to find ourselves in a more familiar environment. This, with qualifying irony, turned out to be the case. Two miles above the mouth, concrete and gleaming, the (to us) new Bells Ferry bridge thrust its geometric certitude across the muddy old stream, swamp to swamp, and we knew, for the first time, for sure, where we were.

Thus oriented, we were able, a mile further on, to pick out the mouth of Moses' old dead river. Here the fictional "Snake" Sutton, as a ten-year-old runaway, found refuge with the old mulatto, Uncle Mundy, in his swamp shanty built on stilts.

Here, too, in the fringe of the swamp, lies old Dead River cemetery, where a number of Mobley's ancestors sleep. They include the factual, though fabulous doctor, John Mobley (our John's grandfather), who for a half century, in horse and buggy, his long-stemmed pipe resting on an expansive bay window, administered pills and tourniquets, sound advice, and salty humor to a countryside.

We located White's landing on the Indian side by virtue of the wide expanse of cut-over swamp behind it. With this as a point of reference, a mile further upriver we were able to make certain of Cheney's old ferry crossing. I scrutinized the low, bush, vine, and tree covered bluff from which I once helped raft timber, fished baskets and trotlines, and took part for six weeks in a search for the body of a murdered boyhood friend, supposedly weighted and sunk under the willows across from it. I eye the once familiar river bank, bearing for five generations my family name, but to my chagrin I cannot find a single identifying mark.

We moved on to Burnt Island—by the engineer's map only a little over a mile upriver, though I'd always heard it called three miles. And river distances are altered. This was the final point of interest of our excursion on the Oconee. Here, a little over fifty years before, in the company of an uncle and cousin, I had found the decayed cadaver of my murdered friend, Robert Willcox. It lay on the point of the island, where a receding freshet had left it, caught under a sparkleberry bush. My memory of this early personal tragedy eventually inspired *Devil's Elbow*, published in 1969.

The island is shaped like a shoe. The mainstream of the river goes over the toe, up the instep, over the top, and down the heel— the cut comes under the sole the short way to the heel. There was no water coming through the cut then. But because of my familiarity with the shape of the island (and an engineer's map), I was able to identify it. We went on around to the point of the island, the toe of the shoe, and I looked for the place.

For a moment I closed my eyes and saw again graphically the trash pile of derelict logs, whitened like bones on top, brown mud clinging to their underbellies—a freshet's toothpicks, crossed crazily akimbo by the high water and left there. Suddenly the khaki sleeve of a crooked arm caught my glance through a gap in the logs, and my heart trips. Then I opened my eyes again, and there was only the seamless swamp.

The passage from *Devil's Elbow*, the first sentence of which I used earlier, came to me here in full: "It was like looking for your lost memory in another man's mind. Tonight he (Marcellus Hightower) could hear the muddy Oconee laughing. It was windy cold laughter. That ever-moving, deceptively-yielding yellow back, three hundred yards wide and thirty feet deep—yielding nothing."

That cold, windy laughter echoes, and the yielding-unyielding yellow back of the river moves throughout the four novels. The Altamaha provides an important part, not only of their enveloping action, but also of their action proper, their plots. In *Lightwood* and *This is Adam* the river is incidental to actions on

its banks—the former story being a postscript to the Reconstruction Era involving a squatter's war in the basin; and the latter an
unaccountable communion of exiles (a mulatto overseer and the
widowed white woman whom he serves) that finally brings them
to terms with the alluvial land. In the other two—*River Rogue*
and *Devil's Elbow*—the river contributes controlling action, also.
Often enough this involves the river's so-called *drawbacks*. In
these stories, moreover, the river becomes a moral force and a
mythopoeic stimulus.

In *Devil's Elbow* the river takes on a metaphysical function.

Perhaps the story behind the story here is relevant. *Devil's Elbow* presents the metaphysical unfolding of a murder mystery in
which the hero's sense of moral guilt evolves into a redeeming
love. The story is organized in Marcellus Hightower's three returns to the scene of the crime and an apocalyptic wake, or reso-
lution. The mysterious death of his boyhood friend, David Ransom, five years before the story opens, provides the catalytic and
modus operandi of the novel, rather than the action, which centers about Hightower's sexual relations with three women. The
title of the novel is supposed to suggest the form of the action,
and on several levels of meaning. The protagonist and all of the
other principal characters are fictional. However, I drew on autobiographical material for much of *Devil's Elbow*. And, in a cate-
gorical way, the fictional murder does parallel history.

But the actual murder occurred when I was little more than a
boy and it didn't appear to me as fictional material until many
years later. The circumstance of that murder that dogged me over
the years and may be said to have inspired the novel eventually
was the finding of my friend's body. That incident in the story is
factually presented. But there is a literal sense in which the hap-
pening "dogged" me that contributed to my fictional inspiration. I
had never before smelled rotting human flesh when I chanced
upon the cadaver of my friend, on the upper point of Burnt Isl-
and, six weeks after his death; "Shorty" Hightower's reaction to
this odor, as detailed in the novel, offers an exact description of
my actual experience. And it is true that the odor pursued me,
pursued me for years. It was just this thing that gave me the no-
tion for the fictional idea that delivers the action, that is—the me-
tamorphosis—in this story.

In real life when, at twenty, I came upon the decayed body of my most intimate boyhood friend, my state of excitement and devastation and horror was such that my sensorium, and specifically my intellectual reaction to my olfactory nerves refused to accept the sensible evidence for a time—perhaps, for fifteen or twenty minutes. I was there, in the presence of—indeed, enveloped in—the dread odor, without smelling, that is, without comprehending it for this length of time. Then, I must say, after its significance broke in upon me, I was never able to forget it. For fifteen years or more after the event and when I was far removed from the scene, the smell came back to me so vividly on occasion that I suffered nausea from it. It was this factual circumstance that gave me the idea of using the smell of my fictional dead man as a sort of psychic Banquo's ghost, a moral monitor, a conscience out of my hero's unconscious.

This turning of the physical into the metaphysical is, of course, the dramatic hocus pocus of the book. It is for Marcellus Hightower an intrusion of the muddy old river. But it is more. It becomes for him the *tama* of Altamaha!

Our talk that evening, under a ripe river moon, turned to the day when sturgeon spawned in the Oconee. I had heard stories of it in my childhood. My father and his brothers, when they were boys, had harpooned the big fish on the shoals, not far from where we were camping. They did it for both sport and gain. They weren't interested in caviar, if they'd ever heard of it. But they rendered the blubber for the oil which brought two dollars a gallon back there in the 1860s and 70s. This lore has found its way into an incident of one of my novels.

We spoke of Devil's Elbow, which we were to pass through in the morning. I recall the excitement of the action on the raft of my first trip down (in April of 1920, I think it was) though I wasn't allowed to take part in it. Our pilot was notorious old Tobe Vaughn, six-foot-six and as fierce looking as Giant Grim, with his bristly mustache and short-stemmed pipe, the brim of his weathered wool hat pulled down over his bobcat eyes—though actually he was a clown and wit and teller of tall tales. At the bow oar was a redheaded cousin, older and taller than I, who moved agilely despite a clubfoot, and a stout, squat colored man named Henry. I was too green to be allowed to get in the way; for this was serious business. But I can hear now the hollow quiet of Tobe's voice, going suddenly sharp and incisive, from the stern of the raft, as that swinging lope of the boys at the bow oar grew furious. The larboard prow of the raft had hit the bottom of the hairpin turn, and the raft was bouncing off toward the onward side of it.

Or, as it was re-created in *River Rogue*:

> "We gonna slam! Be ready to hold 'er out!" Poss shouted. His mouth stayed drawn open, a black hole between gleaming blades of sweat. Ratliff heard a thud and crackle of limbs behind him. Logs wobbled, lumbered up on each other. The raft shuddered. But they made the turn..."Ole Devil snap he arm at us, but he didn't git nothin'. De water wuz just right."

Next morning, in our sprightly motorboat, the hazards of a century had vanished into air, into thin air.

Ah me, there hasn't been a raft on the Oconee river in forty years! As I was crossing the highway at Lumber City the afternoon before to get to the boat landing, I was almost run over by a diesel truck, highballing it along the interstate at sixty miles an hour with a load of thirty-foot long pine saw logs on it!

Yet would a barge channel bring them back to the rivers? Or will the ecological future of the Oconee return the sturgeon to spawn?

In almost no time we were back in sight of the confluence once more, with the big, ambiguous Altamaha below us, and I raised my voice in the old raft-hand's refrain, "Look-a, look-a yonder! I see Sunday, I see Sunday."

The stretch of river we were moving into a few miles further on was very handsome and high-walled in dense, trackless swamps. The trees were towering cypresses and gums and pines and magnolias, with dark corridors between them into the distances of the woods. It was along here somewhere on the white side that we saw a hog bear on my first journey a half century before. He eyed us curiously from the water's edge. Old Tobe said he was trying to thumb a ride. Even now, between the brown and the gray boles of

those bearded pines and cypresses, a bear might have just disappeared in the timeless mystery of the timber.

On that memorable first trip we had tied up our raft for the
first night's camp at Gray's landing. Just as we were coming off
the logs with our croker sacks of groceries, coffee pot and skillet,
and our blankets, a hard rain hit us. Tobe led us at a run up the
bluff and back into the woods to a scattering of abandoned derelict board-and-batten shanties. We got there a little wet and
winded, but feeling very fortunate, and we picked out one that
still had a chimney and put a roaring fire in the fireplace, for the
weather was sharp.

Our meal of fatback, black-eyed peas, sweet potatoes, corn-
pone, and coffee seemed sumptuous there before the blaze, the
rain outside still falling. And afterward we lay back on our blankets and listened to Tobe's tall tales. And I thought what a fine
thing rafting could be as I fell off into bottomless sleep.

About two o'clock in the morning I was torn out of sleeping
senselessness by an enveloping torture. Throwing a chunk on the
fire, I yanked my clothes off to find myself literally black with
fleas, the hungriest I had ever encountered. I had to abandon my
underwear, and the shack, too, for the river where I took a pre-
dawn scrub with water and sand. Wild hogs had been scratching
their backs on the sleepers that underpinned our night's swamp
haven.

There were a couple of acres of cleared bluff to assemble logs
for rafting, on Gray's landing back there, but the jungle overhung
it like the rococo frame of a baroque picture. On our recent return
we found a covered concrete-walled marina with a dozen power
boats in it, and from some unseen source, music blaring forth
over loudspeakers. Back on the bluff there was a large sporting
goods store, a grocery store and, where logs once lay, a large playground with slides, swings, and a merry-go-round. In the background was a picnic shed and a settlement of trailers and camp-
houses.

John and I ate our tins of Vienna sausage, crackers and cheese,
and scuppernong grapes from a table of concrete on the river-
bank, while across the playground from us a full-fledged picnic
found shelter under the new shed and listened to the shouting of
disembodied, tuneless country music.

Before we knew it *River Rogue* was alongside Piney Bluff, at the head of the Narrows. Here the river sucks in and straightens out into its longest reach. This section used to be feared by raftsmen in high water, but at a moderate stage it is relatively simple to negotiate if you keep away from the rocks.

John recalled a raft trip of his youth, in which he and another youngster manned the bow oar on a raft piloted by Mack Tillman, an old Negro river runner, known for his raftsmanship and big feet. As they were coming into the four-mile stretch, Mack pulled the raft close to the bank and John and his fellow oarsman jumped ashore with their shotguns. They hunted the swamp for squirrels while old Mack handled the raft by himself in the reach and, with a bag full of game, they rejoined him where he had tied up just below the easy river. Thus, the raft lost no drifting time. Mobley remembers their pot of squirrel stew that evening as one of the finest game suppers of his life.

The Narrows is no less with me! We had turned loose from Gray's landing before day, on my first trip, and the rim of the sun was just edging up even with the tree line at the bottom of this river as we came into it. For almost an hour I sat on the front binder of the raft, my boy's senses absorbing that amazing river full of sunrise. There was a play of all the tender colors of hope and glory in the sky and on the water, as a stately sun approached me between the numb lines of wild swamp trees. It was a blazing mirror of expectation and belief that still lends a little of its light to the transcendent reality of this world for me.

Lost again! This time we beach our boat and get out our bale of maps. A fisherman at Gray's landing had told us that in the crooked river below the Narrows it wasn't so much a matter of navigating the river as knowing which river to navigate. "You'll come to two rivers," he said, "and the one to take is the one that looks like it couldn't be the right one." This was what we thought we'd done. A motorboat appeared in the nearer stream below us and I waded out into the shingle, waving my arms and shouting at them. They (there was a boatload of them) cut down their motor and pointed out the Altamaha. Mobley carefully, for it was very snaggy, turned into the nearer river. When we had moved a couple of hundred yards, we came upon a third river, piling in upon us from our left. The Altamaha was no longer a dilemma but a maze!

We were glad to call it a day and beach our boat on a sandbar across from the mouth of the hydra-headed Ohoopee. As we were crossing the bar to pick out a spot for camp, we came upon an alligator track. This was exciting, the first we had seen. Then it came over me. Here we were at the mouth of the Ohoopee, nearly fifty miles down the Altamaha and we hadn't seen a single alligator. What had happened to the old river?

On that first trip fifty years ago, I had sighted a half-dozen 'gators along the way by the time we reached the Ohoopee. We had come close enough to two of them, floating along with their eyes and nostrils skimming the surface, for me to take a shot of them with my box camera. A couple of days later, passing the mouth of Alligator Congress, I saw a mud hole full of them. I counted seven big rusty 'gators.

Alligator Congress is the scene of the fictional "Snake" Sutton's wrestling match with a 'gator. The basis in fact for this incident was a tale told me by an old Negro ferryman about an uncle of mine, Drew Cheney.

As a joke on the boy, Ratliff (Snake) Sutton, Bud True jerks a corner of their raft into a rubble of alligators sleeping along the edge of the bank, and one is pitched onto the logs.

Ratliff's hands drew slowly back from the oar handle, his eyes fixed on the long, lunging head. Imperceptibly, he drew into a crouch as the head came on. It was at his side, in front. On his toes, hands out before him like a cat's claws, he plunged.

The 'gator's stubby legs shot outward and he grunted. Ratliff was on his back, knees clamped to his belly, hands about his neck. In the fragment of time while the 'gator lay still, sprawled upon the logs, Ratliff's hands slid swiftly along his throat. Fingers went under his jaws, over his eyes. The big reptile bellowed and bowed upward, then left the logs in a spasm of flapping that made his tail a black blaze of motion. He landed with a bellow, rose up on his hind legs and leaped, bucked like a horse. Ratliff was still on him, riding behind his forelegs.

The 'gator's head bent upward toward Ratliff's face. The wide mouth rounded into a barrel. Foam and a bellowing scream shot from it. The long jaws clamped shut like a bear trap and he rose up on his hind legs and tail. With a whirling motion, he lunged forward into the air, off the raft, Ratliff still leeched to his back.

The river's surface split in butter-colored waves, spume rising. It crumpled into a whirlpool with a dark, dizzily spinning core. The men on the raft could see the hump of Ratliff's shoulders. The vortex spun a zigzag course out into the river and disappeared. Water boiled, foam, mud, bubbles rose to the surface. They kept rising for what seemed like a long time to the men who stood watching.

Suddenly Ratliff's head appeared near the boom log, he swam in and pulled himself up on it. He leaned over on his knees and gave himself up to breathing. His face was blue and he sucked in air in great gasps.

Bud came close to him and bent down. "Jesus Christ!" he said. Then he lapsed into silence with the others and watched Ratliff breathe.

After a time Bud asked, "Yuh hurt anywhere?"

Ratliff shook his head. In the same motion, he threw wet hair back from his face and braced himself on the log with his hands.

Bud looked at them. "What's that in your fingers?"

"I gouged his eyes out," Ratliff said.

Snake Sutton's drama, as presented in *River Rogue*, wears the mask of the naturalism current in fiction of that day. There were such runaways, such rogues, such raftsmen, such rough and ruthless men who crashed Darien's tight mercantile ranks. Snake Sutton was potential in the genius of the timber running community of the final years of the last century. But he is mythic, too, in the sense that he was potential to the life of that time and place, rather than actual. He is the creature of the prophesy as well as the history of the Altamaha.

I found when I reread the book that I'd forgotten how it ended. I found, too, that I'd fumbled Sutton's ill-fated romance with Robbie, daughter of Darien uppercrust, in the next to the last chapter. I failed to get out of my head and onto the page his Garden of Eden image of his mother that was what he really saw in Robbie, was really in love with.

But the ending of the book is right. The Tama of the Altamaha for Snake Sutton lay back up river at the confluence—lay in the ever-moving yellow muscle that makes up there—lay in its prophesy as well as its history.

I have spoken of the river as both prophesy and history. I have intimated that there is a mythical quality in a character of one of my books—Snake Sutton—in *River Rogue*. In another, *Devil's Elbow*, I have borne the travail of the river into the realm of the moral and the Altamaha become metaphysical.

In this recognition of things about us and things that have gone before, I have suggested the role of deliverer for Georgia's intransigent river. But what of the engineers? What of the threat of the concrete reservoirs? Has the deliverer been delivered?

Recently I talked with the chief of research and planning for the engineers of the Savannah district to find out the score. He told me that for all practical purposes the barge channel was dead. He said the promotional organization, the Altamaha Basin Commission, had dissolved, that the state government and the river, as well, were jumping with ecologists. "Of course *we* were always for *balanced development*," he assured me, which I interpreted to mean that the engineers weren't going to try to upset the ecological balance of the Altamaha, after all.

For a quarter of a century I served a newspaper, a senator, and a couple of governors as a "TVA man," in that damnedest state in the union, Tennessee. But we know now even in Tennessee that you can't hem up happiness. And those symbols of the Modern Age, the concrete dam and the reservoir, have lost their ethical significance. There is surely a poetic justice, if not indeed an inscrutable wisdom, in the circumstance that the old Altamaha that has baffled the engineers—in truth, baffled us all for so many years—should turn out to be the hidden Providence of the health of a million and a quarter of my fellow Georgians!

I can hear Snake Sutton saying now, "Yeah, 'bout the time them engineers could get their dams built, the old river would have shed her skin and come up somewhere's else—a new reptile, in another swamp!"

2.

Lightwood and Brainard Cheney
The Novel and The Author

Stephen Whigham

John Stamps Insurance office in McRae, Georgia, where Cheney
researched the Dodge Company archives in 1936

Brainard Cheney arranges lodgings for his first *Lightwood* research trip
(Courtesy of Ann Clements Clark)

Lightwood and Brainard Cheney
The Novel and the Author

Stephen Whigham

The Novel

The year 1936 found Brainard Cheney determined to write his first novel. He took extended leave from his Nashville newspaper job and journeyed to his hometown of Lumber City in south Georgia.

He was pursuing the story of the timber wars that occurred deep in the piney woods of Georgia in the decades following the Civil War. He planned to fashion these epic yet obscure historical events into fiction. By a stroke of luck—and assistance from relatives—he gained access to the complete records of the Dodge Company's legal struggles with the local landowners.

Sitting in the back room of the old Stamps insurance office building in downtown McRae, Georgia, he pored over thousands of pages of material outlining legal actions that began as early as

1880 and continued until 1923. He discovered for the first time that his own father, as an attorney, had represented both sides in the litigation. He first represented the Dodge Company, and later, the so-called squatters who fought the Dodges. This change in allegiance intrigued the author.

Interviewed in 1982, Cheney recalled his researches from nearly half a century earlier. He roomed in a small hotel in downtown Lumber City owned by LeRoy and Sarah Clements. Mrs. Clements took an interest in the project. She directed Cheney to locals who recounted tales of the Dodge Company. He traveled to sites in the Dodge and Telfair area related to the events, seeking connection to the landscape and the geography. He visited places like the village of Suomi, near Chauncey, the timber camp ruins near Milan, and the former home of Luther Hall in Eastman.

Using these personal accounts, in addition to his researches of the Dodge Company, he began writing the novel. Mrs. Clements protected his privacy as he typed away. For $30.00 per month, he secured a room with lavatory and three meals a day. He volunteered to chop wood each day for exercise. In time, the manuscript began to take shape. He created two main protagonists, who as characters were also distant relatives—Micajah Corn, farmer and unsuspecting squatter, and Calhoun Calebb, an ambitious young attorney.

The novel begins circa 1874, when Micajah Corn first hears about the Dodge Company. The timber concern is claiming ownership to land occupied for decades by families in the area, including Micajah's.

Micajah and his family then travel to Lancaster (a fictionalized Eastman) in Coventry (Dodge) County. They make the day-long journey to attend a speech by Mr. Coventry (William E. Dodge), the northern investor and reputed "merchant prince of New York." Coventry and Company is transforming the once sleepy area by establishing a burgeoning timber industry. As a gesture of his good will to the citizens, he donated funds to build a courthouse for his namesake county.

The speech takes place in a festive atmosphere, with the locals excited by the continuing prospects of the jobs and prosperity Coventry promises. "River Road rich folks" jostle alongside the farmers. Horses and mules swell the edges of the new town. The men folk sneak out behind recently constructed buildings to take snorts of home brew liquor.

Among the crowd, Micajah spots his distant relative, the lawyer Calhoun Calebb. Calhoun is not an easy man to miss, even in the crowd. He stands more than six feet tall and dresses as a gentleman of prospects. They greet each other warmly.

Calhoun Calebb cuts a striking figure. As Calhoun praises Coventry and the progress he brings to the area, Micajah thinks of his face as looking like a "gnarled and burnt catface," referring to the gash cut into a pine tree trunk to gather turpentine. When only a child, Calhoun had been burned severely, scarring his face. He sports a black patch over one eye. Yet the force of Calhoun's charisma marks him as a man on the way up. He speaks kindly to his relatives and promises to see them again. Their meeting foreshadows the story of greed, tragedy and murder that is the novel.

Lightwood is not a straight fictionalized retelling of the events, as Cheney creates composite characters and in places shapes the truth to dramatize the story. Yet one can distinguish real places and events from the fiction. For example, Captain John Forsyth is embodied in the character of Ian McIntosh. Calhoun Calebb portrays a version of Luther Hall. In the story McIntosh's daughter, Kathleen, is much older than Forsyth's teenage daughter, Nellie. Calhoun's attraction to Kathleen enters into the novel's plot with consequences both psychological and real. In history, Calhoun's counterpart Mr. Hall was married with several children.

Micajah Corn may be based loosely on Lem Burch. The novel's opening scene relates the story of Jere Corn, Micajah's father. As a young boy, Jere and his father were scalped by Indians. Jere survived, his father did not. Such an event actually occurred, near Abbeville, on the Ocmulgee River. Joseph Burch was the slain father, Littleton Burch the son who survived. This story appears in Mrs. Cobb's *History of Dodge County,* along with other actual events that subsequently appeared, in fictionalized form, in *Lightwood.*

Cheney recounted that his novel of the Dodge Company story may have taken a simpler form had he not addressed the legal issues at the heart of the story. Many legal observers considered The Dodge Lands and Litigation, so called, to constitute one of the most complicated and controversial legal actions in United

States history. As an admirer of Charles Dickens, Cheney knew the great man's work, including *Bleak House*. As in Dickens' novel, one finds in *Lightwood* echoes of a similar labyrinthine legal quagmire.

The theme of legal wrangling and the nightmare it brings to the characters' lives flows through *Lightwood*. Micajah Corn, his family and his peers, the people of the piney woods, live simple lives as farmers and herders. These pinelanders, as historian Mark Wetherington labels them, occupied a part of the world remote from the money centers of New York City. Even within the state of Georgia, they lived an isolated existence, raising crops for food and occasionally for money. Land holdings rarely exceeded 212 and a half acres, the size of a land lot. Their meager sources of cash derived from growing cotton and tobacco, along with livestock herding. The only other cash transaction consisted of the occasional timber raft made from logs lashed together and floated out of the swamps into the river, bound for Darien.

Most of the farmers and herders depicted in this novel migrated to the area from North Carolina, with some earlier settlers coming directly from Scotland and Ireland. They brought their culture with them. Before the railroad came, the population congregated along the rivers. Their isolation fostered independence, in both production of their staple foods and in their social and political outlook. First, the Civil War, and then Reconstruction, altered their world. *Lightwood* tells this story of radical transformation and illuminates the lives of the characters. In telling this tale, Brainard Cheney preserved a lost time and way of life in a historically obscure section of the country's past.

In the novel, the decades from 1870 up to 1890 bring a cascade of events escalating the conflict between the squatters and the Coventry Company. The squatters grow weary of legal and perceived intimidation at the hands of the timber company. People die. Property is sabotaged. Finally, Calhoun Calebb and others conspire to eliminate the superintendent of the timber company.

One of the most intriguing and mysterious characters in the novel is Trigger Fowler, the "mixed-breed" man who fired the fatal shot, killing McIntosh. The character derives from Rich Lowry (alternately spelled *Lowery* and *Lowrie*) also known as Rich Herring. Lowry, referred to as a "Scuffletonian" in some historical records, allegedly hailed from an area in Robeson County, North Carolina named Scuffletown, 'known for' the rough and ready ways of its inhabitants. Many early settlers of Dodge and Telfair counties, both white and black, hailed from Robeson County.

Lowry's origins may trace from the Lumbee Indian group, who in turn are descended possibly from the famous lost colony of Roanoke and Sir Walter Raleigh fame. Historian Malinda Maynor Lowery has researched the Lumbees, describing the migration of some of them to Bulloch County, Georgia, near the Ocmulgee area, to work in the turpentine industry. A connection may exist between this migration and Lowry's subsequent arrival in Dodge County, located ninety miles southwest of Bulloch. The novel portrays the fictional Rich Lowry/Trigger Fowler as a cold-blooded killer who boasts that killing a man was "but a breakfast to him."

The murder of Captain Ian McIntosh sends Calebb to a life term in federal prison. Micajah Corn, mourning the deaths of his family members in the struggle, tries to make things right with the world. In the end, he too is forsaken by the timber company, in what Cheney labeled "the final betrayal."

The Lightwood Chronicles introduces the facts of the story, or versions thereof, providing the reader the historical background informing the fiction of Brainard Cheney. The oft-quoted maxim attributed to the painter Pablo Picasso that "art is a lie that tells the truth" applies here. Brainard Cheney's art penetrates through time. More than a century after the events depicted in his novels, one experiences a connection to the ghosts of those times, long since departed from the piney woods.

The Author

The author of *Lightwood* was born in Fitzgerald, Georgia in 1900, although he soon relocated with his family to Lumber City. His father and namesake, Brainard Bartwell Cheney, who practiced as a successful attorney, inherited extensive land holdings in the Lumber City area of Telfair County. He assigned the administration of the estate to overseers while he pursued his legal career.

In Brainard's eighth year, his father died unexpectedly, leaving his widow to raise their children on her own. Cheney's mother,

Mattie Mood, came from an old and prominent Charleston family. Though a long way from Charleston, she chose to remain in Lumber City to administer the estates. Brainard remembered an idyllic childhood living in the small river town. His days included school work and playing and swimming in the Ocmulgee River—a boyhood he recalled as not unlike that of Tom Sawyer, one of his literary heroes.

A childless couple took young Brainard under their wing and introduced him to the world of literature. In a 1982 interview, Cheney remembered visiting their home and enjoying free rein to borrow books from their library. The house contained books in every room, he recalled, even in the closets. He read Mark Twain and Charles Dickens, and then Thackeray, George Meredith, Trollope, along with many others. One must consider the time, circa 1910, and the place, a very small town hundreds of miles from any large city, to fully grasp the isolation a child may have experienced. Cheney recalled a striking image. He remembered his literary patron reading on the front porch, pacing back and forth while holding a book. Because of a back injury, he was uncomfortable sitting down. Looking back on this time, almost a century in the past, one marvels at the transformations wrought by the modern world. Those days of leisurely reading oneself through the private library of one's own, or of a friend, absorbing as a young person the great literature of the age, conjure images of a lost and golden time vastly different from our own.

Cheney's mother administered the family estates, depending on Robin Bess as overseer. Mr. Bess, a black man, occupied a farm located on the holdings. This arrangement, with Robin as overseer, was unusual for those times in the segregated South. Cheney regarded Mr. Bess as an essential influence in his life, tantamount to a father figure. He recalled their fishing and hunting trips. They often traversed the river swamps and cypress forests belonging to the Cheneys, known as the Cheney Woods. Cheney's third novel, *This is Adam*, is based on Robin and the professional relationship between Mr. Bess and Cheney's mother. It celebrates the friendship between Brainard and Robin. He dedicated the work to Mr. Bess.

As a young teenager, Cheney considered training as a steamboat captain on the Ocmulgee River. A lively steamboat transport system plied the Ocmulgee and Altamaha Rivers as late as the 1930's, reaching as far north as Macon—that is, when the river's water level was high enough to accommodate the boats. Cheney sought an apprenticeship with a local steamboat captain. That captain, Mr. Ashburn, discouraged him, correctly foreseeing the coming demise of the steamboat era.

World War I began in 1914 just as Cheney entered the Citadel in Charleston, with vague notions of pursuing a military career. He counted his time there as the unhappiest period of his life. Small in stature, he was hounded by upper classmen and officers. He recalled being addressed incorrectly as "Cheeney" by one particularly unpleasant teacher. Military life and discipline aggravated the young man, who rose to the occasion and transformed his frustration into rebellion.

An English professor at the Citadel encouraged Cheney's interest in writing, an interest destined to lay dormant for a few more years. The War ended before Cheney finished the Citadel and by the same token deflated his ambitions for a military career.

After the Citadel, he attended one quarter at Vanderbilt University. Family financial straits required that he return home to Lumber City. He went to work in the family farming and timber business, at one time running a timber camp with some success. He also worked as a school teacher, functioning as an educator at three successive "one-room" schools in as many years. His teaching career ended when he decided to return to college at Vanderbilt University.

Vanderbilt offered the young man a new world of possibilities. There, through chance connections and a lot of hard work, Cheney became a writer. He worked as a journalist while attending classes. One of those classes was taught by the renowned poet, John Crowe Ransom, who introduced him to the Fugitive and Agrarian literary movements of southern writers. Another important mentor was Caroline Gordon, a professor and author. When he first tried writing fiction, Gordon steered him away from journalistic prose and into the creation of literature, as Cheney related in 1982.

At this time, Cheney also became friend and roommate with the young poet, Robert Penn Warren, known as "Red" among his friends. Warren later published the acclaimed novel, *All the Kings*

Men. On many occasions he acknowledged Cheney's critical assistance with some of the political speeches contained in the famous work. Robert Penn Warren went on to become an eminent poet, author and teacher, as well as Poet Laureate Consultant in Poetry at the Library of Congress. Their friendship endured until Warren's death (one year before Cheney's) and included not only literary collaboration but also field trips for research to local rivers and rural areas.

Brainard married Frances Neel, a young woman just then embarking on a prominent career as a librarian and author. They settled in Nashville. Among their friends, Frances was known as Fannie, and Brainard was called Lon, after the silent movie star Lon Chaney. Many of Cheney's autographed works are signed "Lon."

Cheney left Vanderbilt before graduation to forge a career as a respected newspaperman in Tennessee and later worked for various political figures as a speechwriter and advisor. Frances began her career in the library world, becoming an eminent librarian, respected professor and author of a famous textbook on librarianship. During World War II, she worked as Allen Tate's assistant when he accepted the post of Poet Consultant at the Library of Congress.

In 1936, Cheney took a year off to write a novel. He embarked on a journey to his home town of Lumber City. An old story of the timber wars in the area drew him back and he commenced work on the novel which became *Lightwood*, his fictional retelling of that story.

Fortune presented Cheney with a cousin whose insurance office once served as the last office of the Dodge Company. Those tenants left behind a mass of papers documenting the complete record of nearly half a century of legal wrangling. Cheney recalled sitting in this office, situated in a back room, reading through thousands of pages of musty legal papers. From his study of this archive and additional research, he created *Lightwood*, the story of an epic battle between the proverbial haves and have-nots, the timber barons and the land squatters. Published in 1939, the book sold respectably and this encouraged him to write his next novel, *River Rogue*.

Lightwood was reviewed nationally, including in the New York *Times*. The November 5, 1939 issue contains a favorable review by Edith H. Walton, who called the work a "superior novel of the South, exceedingly well written." *Time* magazine summed up the novel as having "the unimpeachable honesty, goodness, flatness, of a mouthful of cold excellent corn bread."

Cheney traveled to the south Georgia area and signed many copies of the novel for local friends and family. These autographed copies of the original 1939 hardcover edition surface in the area periodically. They usually contain dates ranging from late October to early November, 1939.

In 1941, Cheney received a Guggenheim Fellowship. This enabled him to research the novel *River Rogue*, which is also based on events and people he knew from the Ocmulgee area. The book sold respectably and garnered a movie option from MGM, though it was never produced. After 1941, Cheney concentrated on his journalism career, later moving to speechwriting, working for Tennessee governor, Frank G. Clement, among others.

Fannie Cheney inherited a family home near Smyrna, Tennessee, which they called Idler's Retreat. There they hosted many prominent literary and political figures through the years. Through Caroline Gordon's introduction, the Cheneys befriended Georgia novelist Flannery O'Connor in 1953, with whom they exchanged visits and letters until her death in 1964. Selections from this correspondence were collected into the book, *The Correspondence of Flannery O'Connor and the Brainard Cheneys*. They shared common interests in both literature and Catholicism, to which the Cheneys had converted. O'Connor is on record as saying that Brainard Cheney is the only reviewer who 'got the meaning' of her first novel, *Wise Blood*. Over the years they discussed and critiqued one another's work.

Cheney published two more novels, *This is Adam*, in 1959, and *Devil's Elbow*, in 1968. Both of these works take place in the Ocmulgee area, based on autobiographical events in Cheney's life. He continued to work on additional fiction, but no new titles appeared during his lifetime.

In 1982, Dr. Delma Presley, of Georgia Southern University, conducted Project RAFT, also known as the Restoring Altamaha Folk Traditions project. This grant-funded project gathered together the few surviving timber rafters of the area. The events rekindled interest in the works of Brainard Cheney, specifically at that time, *River Rogue*, whose main protagonist was a timber raftsman.

In the spring of 1982, Dr. Presley and other project personnel actually built a timber log raft and navigated it down the Ocmulgee and Altamaha rivers to Darien. They recreated the experience of many of the old piney woods settlers who rafted timber for supplemental income. Brainard Cheney participated in the festivities, even traveling on a portion of the raft trip. He was 82 years old at the time. Through the efforts and support of Dr. Presley, a new edition of *River Rogue* was published to coincide with the project. This renewed interest in Cheney's work led to the republication of *Lightwood* in 1984, spearheaded by his nephew, Roy Neel.

Brainard Cheney remained an author to the end, passing away at age 89 in January of 1990. Several unpublished works, primarily fiction and plays set in his native Georgia, remained. Fannie Cheney passed away in 1996 also at age 89. These two remarkable people bequeathed a rich legacy of literature, authorship and teaching, and left many friends.

3.

The Novels of Brainard Cheney

Caroline Gordon

Brainard Cheney's first and third novels

The Novels of Brainard Cheney

Caroline Gordon

Sewanee Review, Spring, 1959

This Is Adam is Brainard Cheney's third novel. With its publication, the pattern—and the vision—that shaped his previous novels becomes discernible. The people in Mr. Cheney's novels live
on the banks of the Oconee River in Georgia—on "wild, rough
land." The Oconee flows into the Ocmulgee which flows into the
Altamaha, which, in turn, flows into the sea. Dark swamplands
stretch for miles on each side of the river. The great trees that line
its banks are hung with moss and lean so close over the water that
the current, except when in flood or freshet, gleams as gray as
steel. There are dangerous shoals in the river and "sucks" that test
the skill of the most experienced raftsman and a haunted island
which bears the name of a woman who died there after being
raped by soldiers during the Civil War.

Cheney's characters lead lives which seem to mirror the ebb and flow of the tidal rivers. All of his characters, whether they live in the swamps in houses raised on stilts, like Uncle Mundy of *River Rogue*, or behind wrought iron gates, like Oxford-educated Geoffrey Dale of the lumber firm of Dale and Coventry, or on what is left of a vast tract of fertile river bottom land, like the Widow Hightower, are subjected in one way or another, to the hazards of life on the river.

In each of Mr. Cheney's novels these hazards are embodied in a conflict, a conflict, which, in the end, reveals itself as the perennial conflict between good and evil, but which, on first sight, seems to be the puny efforts of the weak and lowly to overcome the strong and highly placed. In each novel the action centers on litigation—or the threat of litigation. These maneuvers make hard reading: Mr. Cheney does not spare his readers the exertions or the tedium of legal processes. There are times when the reader feels that if the hero doesn't abandon the suit, he will have to! It is at such times that the spell of the river makes itself felt. A raftsman, drifting down stream, will throw "a chunk of fire" to fellow raftsmen who all night long have been taking their turns at mauling the same log to keep from freezing, two boys on a "pick-up raft" will have their first sight of the masts of the tall timber schooners of Darien or the cotton bolls in the Widow Hightower's "Wyche field" will show white so suddenly that they might be blossoms left there by receding waters. If the reader perseveres he is rewarded by a picture—a vision—of contemporary life which he will find in the work of no other contemporary novelist.

Cheney's heroes have something else in common besides their hard lives and their bondage to the river. The struggle in which each one engages is, from a worldly standpoint, for life and death. But in each case his hero is bent on something more than survival. He is battling towards a goal which he, himself, envisages only dimly. In each of the novels it is the hero's realization of the intangible forces which have motivated his actions that provides a powerful climax.

Lightwood celebrates man's dumb, almost blind hope in the face of seemingly insuperable obstacles. Micajah Corn does not win his suit against the powerful lumber companies; they outmaneuver him by getting the suit transferred to another court, in faraway Macon, where he will stand even less chance of winning than in the local courts. Micajah, when he gets the news, expresses no regrets for his loss or animosity against his victors. He merely says, "Macon...?" and we know that he will go back to his river farm, where, Antaeus-like, he will renew his strength and take up the struggle again.

Ratliff Sutton, of *River Rogue*, is landless and, he fears, nameless. It is in a desperate quest for his own identity that he turns back to the dark roots of life and takes refuge in the swamp with kindly old Uncle Mundy, who, in his fashion, is fleeing, too: "I thought when us come down heah in de swamp us 'uz through with white people." But flight does not avail Ratliff any more than Uncle Mundy; every man he meets on the river twits him with having turned his back on his own race, with being "a white nigger." Revenge is the motivation of his early years. He proves his prowess by gouging out an alligator's eyes and in a "fist and skull" fight, bites off the thumbs of Diggs McMillan, the man who aspersed his mother's honor, becomes a real river runner under the tutelage, first, of Uncle Mundy, and later under that of the giant raftsman, Bud True—"Raft yuh logs right and you'll git there with 'em"—and finally becomes such a figure on the river that, as his mistress, China Swann, puts it, he makes Darien, the city of his boyish dreams, his "son of a bitch."

China is "a career woman," a "madam" of a house of prostitution at twenty-one. But it is Robbie, the daughter of the blue-nosed Presbyterian, MacGregor, who is to be the chief influence in Ratliff's life. There is something reminiscent of Theodore Dreiser's clumsy power, of his unabashed, elephantine tread in Cheney's presentation of Robbie. Frail, long-nosed, with fine eyes, wearing "a grey squirrel pelisse and wine-red skirt," she moves about, doing good so persistently that the unregenerate reader is likely to sympathize with old Bud True, when, embittered by the loss of his leg and sodden with whiskey, he finds her at the bedside of his sick wife and is so enraged by what he considers her invasion of his privacy that he raises his crutch and deals her a fatal blow.

Robbie is actually a less engaging figure than the red-haired China Swann. But it is in looking through her eyes—eyes which seem to him "window panes" of the soul—that Ratliff sees his life in a new perspective. *"What has happened to me and why?"* he asks himself as he rides to the court house in Darien to prosecute Bud True for the murder of his wife. The answer comes to him in a vision:

> There on Clayhole Bluff, with the darkness coming on, and it had seemed that he, Ratliff, stood watching the raftsmen turn one by one to leave him, their faces strange, livid, sightless. Then suddenly, with great soundless detonation, a light came up the slope from the creek and he looked up and saw that it was Bud—not broken or crippled but towering high—billows of smoke whirling from his short-stemmed pipe and over his shoulders. And Bud came on, with giant strides, and the sun was at his back. Nearer, nearer he came. And Ratliff had awakened in cold sweat and shaking.

He concludes that:

> "Power is not enough—here, or anywhere." You quit the river and came to town. But you never did join with Robbie, but you never did accept her—what she stood for. You tried to make her yours; what you stood for....And what was that? Nothing....You had no crowd. You had no rules...you broke your bonds with every one—and self, blind self, swallowed you.

The more one considers Cheney's work the more one is struck by its likeness to Dreiser's. It is not that one novelist seems to owe anything to the other—if Cheney has read Dreiser the latter's influence is not actually perceptible. It is, rather, that the two novelists share the same preoccupations. Both writers turn their backs on the hero who, as R. P. Blackmur has pointed out, has been increasingly popular since the days of Byron, or indeed since the Renaissance: the hero *manqué*, the *poete maudit*, the man of exacerbated sensibilities, in short, the artist himself—and consider the plight of the ordinary man, that is to say, the man whose imaginative faculties are not exercised professionally. Likened with this, in the case of both writers, is another preoccupation: Woman as an archetypal figure.

Robert Graves, in his *The White Goddess*, and Philip Wylie, in his *Generation of Vipers*, have popularized a theme that has for mankind a perennial attraction: the death-dealing attributes of "The Great Mother" or, as Mr. Wylie calls her, "Mom."

William Troy has pointed out that we find one of the most dramatic interpretations of this archetypal symbol in the work of a "realist." Zola's Nana cannot sing very well or dance very well and she is not really beautiful but she passes Mr. Graves's test of a "white goddess"—it is, interestingly enough, the same test that Housman used for good poetry!—all the men who are to be ruined through their association with Nana, at first sight of her, register their awareness of her presence—and perhaps the apprehension of their own dooms—by physical manifestations. The truant school boy, Georges, who is to drown himself for love of Nana, is half lifted out of his seat by his passion when she comes on the stage; the Count de Vandeuvres, who, bankrupt, will shut himself in his stable and burn to death with his horses, pales and his lips look pinched. The fat banker, Steiner, grows purple to the verge of apoplexy, Daguenet's ears turn blood-red and twitch and in the box of the Count de Muffat "the Count was sitting straight upright, with mouth agape and face mottled with red, while close by him in the shadows, the restless eyes of the Marquis de Chouarc had become cat-like, phosphorescent, full of golden sparkles."

Zola began writing *Nana* in 1879. Theodore Dreiser, writing half a century later [in his novel *Sister Carrie*], follows the familiar and ever fascinating patter. The men who will come to grief—and in Hurstwood's case, death—from knowing Carrie all sense in her the same power, the same mysterious, disturbing charm. Only Ames, the Bostonian, whose pride of intellect enables him to remain aloof from her, succeeds in putting it into words:

> "It's in your mouth and eyes," he went on abstractedly. "I remember thinking that the first time I saw you, that there was something peculiar about your mouth. I thought you were about to cry....The world

is always struggling to express itself. Most people are not capable of voicing their feelings. They depend upon others. That is what genius is for. One man expresses their desires for them in music; another one in poetry; another one in a play. Sometimes nature does it in a face—it makes the face representative of all desire. That's what happened in your case."

He goes on to say:

"That puts the burden of duty upon you. It so happens that you have this thing. It's no credit to you....You paid nothing to get it. But now that you have it you must do something with it....You can lose it, you know. If you turn away from it and live to satisfy yourself, it will go fast enough...The look will leave you....Nature takes care of that. If I were you I'd change."

But the effect of this speech "is like roiling helpless waters." (Dreiser went in no awe of Ruskin's "pathetic fallacy"!) Carrie, who is as insensitive and as good-natured as Nana does not—or perhaps cannot—change and Hurstwood goes to his death.

Mr. Cheney gives us the other side of the picture: Woman, the archetypal figure, as the regenerative force in the life of a man. She is seen first, dimly, in *Lightwood*. But it is, primarily, a man's world which Cheney portrays there. The heroine of *Lightwood* has the virtues of the pioneer woman but she does not sway men's lives as do the heroines of the later novel.

It is in *River Rogue* that this symbolic figure emerges from the shadows and takes the center of the stage. Robbie is actually not as attractive a woman as China Swann; but China is an inmate of a house of prostitution and Robbie, with her habit of looking down her long nose, her "old glass goat" of a father, nevertheless has access to the world of the spirit, a world whose existence Ratliff has heretofore only envisioned. When she tells him in her "Sunday School voice" that she is willing to defy her father and elope with him he registers the impact of his fate in much the same way as Nana's victims:

> He shut his eyes and his body grew rigid. A thin, implacable chill, a fire moved in his veins: it had been years since he had had the feeling but it was unmistakable.

But Robbie is a frail embodiment of the great archetype. In *This Is Adam* she attains her full stature. Ratliff Sutton doubts his own paternity. Adam Atwell knows who his father is but he bears another name—the name of the white man who brought him up. We see him first approaching the back steps of the Hightower house "as assuredly and almost as ceremoniously as an actor advancing to take a bow" and then, when he has offered his tribute, the last shad of the season, lingering at the foot of the steps to talk with the widow.

Adam's fate is linked with that of the widow by ties of both gratitude and responsibility. When Adam was nineteen a miscarriage of justice sent him to the penitentiary. The young lawyer whom the court appointed to defend him told him to "go up to the Mines and be a good boy and I'll get you out." The Colonel is better than his word. He not only gets Adam's sentence commuted but he gives him the fertile "Wyche Field" to tend. "Stay with me, Adam, and I'll make us both rich." Four years later, the dying colonel tells Adam that he counts on him to advise his widow and "look after the place": "There are others more properly placed to take this responsibility but I confess that I don't have confidence in them."

The colonel has something else to say to Adam:

> "There are things that count more than money, Adam. There are things worse than not having enough to wear and to eat—and I've known want...when you come to die....I know now that where I made my mistakes was in not taking *it* into my calculations."

What "it" was that the Colonel had failed to take into his calculations is the theme of the novel. It is through the Colonel's widow that Adam makes the discovery of what it is. But the relationship is by no means one-sided; he gives as much as he gets. The white woman and the Negro man, bound together by their common interests and her husband's dying request, set out together on a spiritual pilgrimage. The two pilgrims' movements, as far as outer sight goes, are prescribed as strictly as if they were stepping off a *minuet*. The conversations between Mrs. Hightower and Adam actually constitute the main current of the action and these conversations always occur at the same place and the man and the woman always stand in the same position: Mrs. Hightower at the top of the steps, Adam at the foot.

In our first glimpse of Mrs. Hightower we are reminded of Robbie; her garments have the same ritual air: a black skirt, a black cape over a white shirt-waist and pince-nez, which, to Adam, at least, giver her countenance "a formidable intellectual glitter." Their conversations are ostensibly about Mrs. Hightower's business affairs which are, indeed, complicated. A big lumber company has offered what seems a good price for her land. She is tempted to accept the offer, partly from her own desire to go back to Charleston to live and partly because she does not want her son to grow up in the backwoods. She tells herself that her boy needs a father and has promised to marry her old suitor, Edward Louthan. It is during her brief engagement to Edward that she lays aside her black garments and appears all in white—a significance which is not lost upon Adam.

Aware of some of her anxieties, he has already assumed the role of foster father to young Marcellus and reassures her:

> "Mrs. Hightower, you wouldn't know it, of course, but boys Marse's age—and I kin tell you color don't make no difference 'tween 'em at 'leven and twelve—I tell yuh, a boy at dat age, he ain't quite a beast and he ain't quite a man...Don't take it too serious if'n he acts scandalous! Against Nature, even!"

But Marcellus Hightower's waywardness is only one problem that confronts Adam. He knows that Osbert Paley, a protégé of the late Colonel, has conspired with "the Yankees" to defraud her of valuable clay deposits under the guise of buying her timber land. He uses against the conspirators every ruse and sleight with which, from time immemorial, the weak have sought to combat the mighty but he suspects that the widow wants to sell out. And his fortunes are bound up with hers. He leans on the rail fence and gazes at the field which the late Colonel had promised him he could tend as long as he lived. "But the Colonel wasn't here. His word didn't count any more...If he could only *talk* to the Colonel!"

Ratliff Sutton, at a critical moment in his life, kills a young turkey gobbler and sees in it a "token." Adam, too, has recourse to a sign from the natural world. He watches a turkey hen cross the road followed by her brood, and realizes that the widow "sometimes *prayed* over her troubles." That night he dreams of the ghost that haunts "Hannah's Island," "naked, the color of a scraped pig, with smoke pouring out of her belly," running towards him and crying, "The lighthouse! The lighthouse!"

> Then he heard Mrs. Hightower's voice crying, "I'm going to sell out lock stock and barrel!" And, it seemed, he looked up, and there she was, climbing up the outside brick wall of the lighthouse. And he was scared. And it seemed to him that he looked across the water to the mainland and saw eyes shining from a tree.

The eyes are the eyes of his son's "little pet coon." The coon tells him "there is a green boat hid under the bow oar of your raft. Get in that boat and paddle over here.

And when Adam has paddled over to the other bank, the coon "gnaws tenderly at his hand" and says:

> "Trouble with you, Adam, is, you went to the island without a boat to get back to the mainland, we can't help you..."

Adam succeeds in thwarting the conspirators only to have victory snatched from his grasp: the widow informs him that she has

written Osbert Paley a note, telling him that she will not prosecute him and returning the letters which establish his guilt.

Adam, seeing the Wyche field slip from him, cries out in his
anguish: "Oh, Mrs. Hightower, Mrs. Hightower, Mrs. Hightower,
Whut you gone and done!...You done ruint me! Ruint me!"
whereat the city-bred woman, knowing that now she will have no
Indian summer, that "the wild land on the banks of the Oconee
carried for her an irrevocable commitment," cries out:

"You've ruined me, too. Charleston's gone!"

They confront each other. The Negro man sees that all the time
he has been leading her to what he thought was victory she has
been leading him to what a moment ago seemed defeat but now
seems another kind of victory. He feels himself washed clean of
anger and hate in the current of their mutual dependence and
"sees now what the Colonel saw, lying so close to the door."

And he realized that there had been behind him
all of the time, through the storm, like a mooring
mast, the dim shadow of a black-caped and -skirted
woman—a blackness that somehow cast a light
through his balloon-like transparence, now shrive-
ling and expiring.

If Gibbon is right and all narrative prose styles are only "means
of subduing the reader," Brainard Cheney's style may be likened
to one of those "fist, gouge and skull" fights in which his backwoodsmen—survivals of pioneer days—engage so frequently. The
author, like Dreiser again, stands up to each sentence as if it were
the first and the last he would ever write. In his strenuous efforts
to convey his full meaning he lays hold of words as if they were
weapons. It might be better if he were less well read or had a
smaller vocabulary. In his zeal, the combatant often lays hold of a
weapon that is too ponderous for the task at hand; his prose ab-
ounds in sonorous words of Latin derivations, used often at a
juncture where a one-syllable Anglo-Saxon word would be more
effective. And the combatant does not confine his choice to those

weapons that are strewn about him on the ground but sometime plucks one, as it were, out of the air; he uses a great many metaphors. They are often too violent to be effective: "His blood-shot eyes strained in their sockets like chained bears." Indeed, in Cheney's prose, metaphors are not employed for their usual purpose—the extension of the dimensions of a scene by a sudden illumination. They are, rather, called upon to carry the burden of the narrative, a task at which—to change our figure—they are, as a rule, as inept as the lion, which, when put into an ass's harness, is traditionally incapable of drawing his load—unless disciplined by grace.

Grace—natural and supernatural—and its manifestations in the life of men and women is, however, Mr. Cheney's subject; and grace seems to come to his aid often in passages which a warier stylist would never have embarked upon. He writes about the backwoodsmen of southern Georgia because he knows and loves them and he tells us things about them—and mankind in general—that no other writer tells us. One hears that he contemplates the writing of two more novels, in which characters from his previous novels will figure—in particular, young Marcellus Hightower. Presumably, these novels will develop the theme stated in the first two novels and expanded in *This Is Adam*: a relationship between the two races in which they are co-equal because the bond which holds them together is forged by love and mutual understanding. It is, certainly, a timely theme and one that has been essayed by other novelists. Cheney's treatment of it is, however, I think, both powerful and unique.

Editor's Note: Brainard Cheney published one more novel in his lifetime, for a total of four. *Devil's Elbow*, which appeared in 1969, brought together characters from his previous novels, as Ms. Gordon foresaw in the preceding review piece.

4.

The Novels of Brainard Cheney

Ashley Brown

Advertisement for *River Rogue*, Cheney's second novel, a "picaresque" tale of the mythic river raftsman, Snake Sutton

Cheney's last published novel, *Devil's Elbow*, a tale of redemption.

The Novels of Brainard Cheney

Ashley Brown

Chattahoochee Review, Spring, 1998

Brainard Cheney, born in 1900, was the least noticed Southern novelist of his generation. One reason may have been that he was not the thoroughgoing literary man that some of his friends were; he spent much of his career on the edges of public life in Tennessee, where he was well known. From 1928 to 1942 he was a political writer for the Nashville *Banner*. During the war years he moved to Washington as executive secretary to Senator Tom Stewart of Tennessee, and he served on the staff of Governor Frank Clement for much of the 1950s.

Now and then he was able to buy the time to write his novels and, in later years, his occasional essays on literary and theological subjects. Like some of his friends, he was involved in regional theater; two of his plays were produced in Nashville and elsewhere. But his novels, which number only four, stand at the center of his work. One might suppose that his long experience in the ways of Tennessee politicians would offer him an easy ready-made subject, but he shunned politics when he turned to fiction, as though he were looking for something more permanent than the fluctuations of power that he knew only too well. This is rather curious in a sense. The South as a cultural entity was partly created by the public voices of the preacher and the politician, especially during the long period between the Civil War and the First World War when Brainard Cheney was growing up. Although something of their old-fashioned rhetoric survived when the region came into its great literary period after 1920 (one can hear their voices in a few of Ransom's poems), the politician has seldom attracted the modern Southern writer as a character suitable for fiction.

Cheney in fact already had his subject before he went to Tennessee in 1924; he attended Vanderbilt briefly during the heyday of the Fugitives and remained in Nashville for the rest of his long life. He was born in Fitzgerald, Georgia, and grew up in Lumber City on the Ocmulgee River; the country of his boyhood is the setting for all that is most authentic in his fiction. The Cheney family had lived here since 1813. It is a countryside of considerable grandeur dominated by its great forests and its rivers: the Oconee, which joins the Ocmulgee, which in turn flows into the Altamaha, which eventually reaches the sea at Darien. During the 19th Century this part of Georgia was what some historians call an "inner frontier": a stretch of territory that lies between the old towns and settlements along the coast and the newer towns (Macon, Milledgeville, Atlanta) in the center of the state. It was for a few generations almost a region unto itself, with Darien its main outlet to the world. Here the timber that had been floated down the rivers was loaded onto ships from Europe and the North; the yellow pines of the remote Georgia backwoods became part of an industrial enterprise (chiefly architecture and shipbuilding). This was, locally, a kind of heroic age. As a teenager Brainard Cheney made the trip down the Altamaha on a timber raft. More than half a century later he recreated his experience with a boyhood friend, this time in a small motorboat called "River Rogue"; and during 1982 he was present at a public celebration called "Project Raft," largely inspired by his novels.

Brainard Cheney's mother came from a Charleston family named Mood, who had a place in the history of that city during the 19th Century. One of his ancestors was a friend of Paul Hamilton Hayne at the College of Charleston. Cheney himself attended The Citadel from 1917 to 1919; Charleston is part of his background. It is somewhat remote in his novels, because it stands for the settled formal society that was only intermittently realized in his home country, but it is still a point of reference in his larger fictional image, especially in *This Is Adam* (1958).

The four novels take place over approximately half a century, from the last years of Reconstruction to the 1920s, and together they compose a chronicle of this part of the South. *Lightwood* (1939) begins in 1874 and ends in the early 1890s, but in recollection we sometimes move through a tangle of history that lies back of the events in the foreground. The patriarch Jere Corn, whose descendants make up most of this family tragedy, remembers when he first came to this country in 1820. He was scalped by Indians, but he survived, fathered a family, and held his ground. This sturdy backwoodsman and his son Micajah, the central figure, live by a simple but deeply felt code of honor; in this post-Reconstruction society they already represent a point of view that was somewhat antiquated, and the final irony of the novel is based on this. The Corns, father and son, have a powerful sense of tradition; they know instinctively that only by perpetuating its property, however small, can the family remain intact. Cheney rendered in fiction what his friend Frank Owsley would later document in an important work of historiography called *Plain Folk of the Old South* (1949).

If the Corns occasionally look to the past for sustenance, others look to it with a calculating eye, because the main issue here is the ownership of the land which the Corns and their neighbors have occupied and paid taxes on for two generations. To the agents of the northern lumber company which has moved into the country, the Corns are simply "squatters" who have never established title to the property. Micajah Corn and his sons react to the presence of the company forces, directly and then violently. This is a familiar subject in American history, the revolt of the dispossessed against the large remote forces protected by their expensive legal talent, and it has sometimes been used by our novelists. (Cheney's

friend Robert Penn Warren published his first novel, *Night Rider*,
at the same time, also through Houghton Mifflin; it deals with a
somewhat comparable situation in Kentucky c. 1905.) Appearing
when it did in 1939, *Lightwood* might have been taken as a work
of "social protest"; but the situation as Cheney has developed it is
much more complicated. Micajah Corn is perhaps too simple, or
at least too predictable, to be a modern hero. He lives by his code
and resists adverse circumstances, but by himself he isn't interesting enough to carry the action of a longish novel. Cheney, however, has set up another post of observation through the lawyer
Calhoun Calebb, who is quite another matter.

Calhoun Calebb is himself complicated. His mother was dis-
tantly related to Micajah Corn's wife and he is thus associated
with the plain folk of south Georgia, but his father, a graduate of
Amherst and a schoolmaster, deserted his mother; he is remembered as just a "runaway Yankee." Calhoun's face is permanently
disfigured from a childhood accident; no woman can overlook
this flaw. But his superior mind and presence have earned him a
certain eminence in the community. Now, in 1876, he has defended the "squatters" and won nine suits against Coventry and
Company; he has become their champion. His advantage is that
he has a considerable social range; he can talk "local" to the juries
who decide the cases in his favor, or he can assume an easy familiarity with Micajah Corn. His first legal successes lead him on to
larger ambitions; he supposes that he can gain a financial victory
over Coventry and Company, and eventually he seeks the political
power that would make him master of the situation. He is defeated at the polls. Meanwhile he had become emotionally involved with Kathleen McIntosh, the daughter of the general superintendent of the company; this is hopeless, and her rejection
of him is almost needlessly cruel. After this moment he seems to
lose his bearings. As the countryside gradually becomes a battle-
field, almost a guerilla war between the farmers and company
agents, Calhoun descends to ruin. He loses a lawsuit and is sentenced to five months in a Savannah jail for swindling. Released
from jail, he returns and decides to run for the state senate; he
has great confidence in his oratorical abilities. But he loses the
election, probably because Coventry and Company had financed
his defeat.   And he complicates his life otherwise: Micajah's

daughter is pregnant; Calhoun is the father; and Micajah finally turns on him.

As the novel approaches its climax it becomes a sort of revenge tragedy for Micajah's family, set within the larger action of the farmers resisting the lumber company. His older son Zeke is shot by Zenas Fears, an unscrupulous company agent. Calhoun Calebb pays Littleton Corn, the younger son, to assassinate Ian McIntosh, Kathleen's father and the general superintendent of the company. The murder is actually performed by "Trigger," Littleton's black accomplice, in the finest chapter of the novel, where the point of view moves from the murderers to Kathleen to Calhoun. When Micajah realizes the full extent of his family's involvement in the disaster, he is overcome by his feeling of being betrayed and has a stroke. He partially recovers, goes to the company lawyer, and unburdens himself of his terrible story. This prepares for the climactic scene, a courtroom drama done with great economy. Calhoun loses whatever poise he has had, and Micajah sits in judgment on him as well as his son, Littleton. The company lawyer has virtually promised him the title to the farm, but at the end he learns that he will face an ejection suit along with his neighbors. This is the final betrayal.

When *Lightwood* was reprinted in 1984 (by Burr Oak Publishers of Washington), Brainard Cheney in a brief forword revealed that his own father, in his early years a lawyer, had originally been on the lumber company's legal staff, but eventually he championed the "squatter." Cheney in fact had access to the entire legal record of the company's operations in Georgia and made use of it in writing the novel. Although his work is fiction, it is based on actual circumstances that are described by Delma Presley of Georgia Southern College in a very useful introduction. Clearly Cheney, in the course of writing the novel, came to sympathize with the "squatters" who lost their farms: "And this last battle of the Civil War was indeed, a lost cause," is his succinct judgment on these events. As Delma Presley suggests, Cheney had brought to life a segment of southern history that has seldom been treated by novelists. And he seldom wrote better.

In the spring of 1940, after publishing *Lightwood*, Cheney returned to the Altamaha River region and spent some six months on and about the rivers before he began *River Rogue*. A photograph of him taken in 1942, on the book jacket, had him looking the part, jaunty in his riverman's cap. In 1941 he received a Guggenheim Fellowship to assist him in completing the novel, which was published in 1942. If *Lightwood* is a kind of revenge tragedy, *River Rogue* is picaresque; indeed *picaro* means a rogue in Spanish. In traditional picaresque (for instance *Lazarillo de Tormes*, the original novel in this genre, published in 1554) the central character goes through a variety of adventures and may even advance to a higher social level, but essentially he doesn't change. Hence picaresque had often been used for satire. Cheney isn't a satirist at any time, but his central character, Ratliff Sutton, certainly moves through a surprising range of social situations on this "inner frontier." He is called Ratliff or "Snake" or Sutton according to circumstances. But, like Augie March or Felix Krull, he doesn't change in any fundamental way; in the end he simply returns to the Oconee where he started out. Cheney, like Faulkner and other southern novelists, was an heir to the tall tale of the Old Southwest, and some episodes in *River Rogue* are almost in that genre, especially the scene where "Snake" wrestles a twelve-foot alligator on his raft.

Cheney himself, of course, had made the trip on a timber raft as a teenager, and in *Lightwood* he drew on this experience for a scene in which Micajah Corn and his sons go down the river to wreck a raft train belonging to the lumber company. The river, however, isn't central to *Lightwood* in the way that it is to *River Rogue*. The great forest, always in the background, is a natural setting that can be subdued or at least exploited, but the river, as T.S. Eliot remarked about Mark Twain's Mississippi, is a "treacherous and capricious dictator." Cheney's first paragraph sets up the forces that will dominate the novel:

> The unaccountable Oconee River was at flood stage on a late May day of 1884. A dugout, bearing a boy in its bow and paddled by a Negro, moved over the muddy water of its swamp. Out of the woods the boat crept into the opening of an old course, marked only by the trunks of funnel-shaped trees. The woods and stream alike were now part of the giant Oconee. Moss-trailed boughs still overshadowed

their way giving the water a cream-and-coffee color. Ratliff Sutton, the boy, cocked an ear to listen to the soft, growing roar ahead of him. An inlet from the swollen body to the branch came into view. He tilted his head to gaze through the gap and beyond, across the flat, seemingly still surface of the main stream. Its yellow plain stretched off to a far wood, and disappeared in dim tree-framed caverns.

Ratliff is a white boy who ran away from home and took refuge with a family of blacks in this Georgia swamp. He has already adapted himself to the life of the river, and now he and his friend Poss are ready for the trip down the Oconee and the Altamaha to Darien. In his little world becoming an expert riverman is about the only way of being successful, and this boy is already ambitious. Life is often brutal, but Ratliff wins the respect of the tough raftsmen. The episode of the alligator, cruel though it is ("Snake" gouges out the creature's eyes) occurs on this rafting trip.

Darien, although only a small port, is an opening to a larger world—not only the great northern and European cities whose ships move in and out, but a world with a degree of sophistication, corrupt though it may be. The brothels and taverns that cater to the rivermen offer possibilities of behavior unknown back in the swamp where Ratliff grew up. He becomes a friend of China Swan, the madam of a brothel called the Bird Cage, and eventually he has a successful tavern in partnership with her. This isn't exactly respectable. Then another friend turns up, Geoffrey, the son of an owner of one of the big lumber companies. This young man, educated at Oxford and Yale, finds Ratliff more interesting than many others and takes him into his world. This includes Geoffrey's cousin Robbie, whom Ratliff (now called Sutton) marries. Like Lazarillo and other picaresque heroes, he would seem to have been successful at last. Then things begin to go wrong; his wife loses her child; she is accidentally killed by an old friend of Sutton's. And *River Rogue* ends somewhat as *Lightwood* does, in a courthouse. Sutton refuses to prosecute his old friend, who, according to Sutton's statement, was insane. The novel ends with Ratliff (as he is again) leaving the courthouse "and into the sunlight."

This novel complements *Lightwood* in various ways. Ratliff
had lost his new family, wife and child, but at least he is not in the
hopeless situation that Micajah Corn is at the end of *Lightwood*.
Robert Penn Warren, in an introduction to the Burr Oak edition
of *River Rogue* (reprinted in 1982), says simply that "He is going
back to the Oconee to try to find something he had lost."

Brainard Cheney himself made a comment on the novel in a
fine essay published in The Southern Review 12 (Winter 1976).
The essay in fact is a review of his life's work in fiction and the
importance that the Altamaha had for him:

> Snake Sutton's drama, as presented in *River
> Rogue*, wears the mask of the naturalism current in
> fiction in that day. There were such runaways, such
> rogues, such raftsmen, such rough and ruthless men
> who crashed Darien's tight mercantile ranks. Snake
> Sutton was potentially in the genius of the timber
> running community of the final years of the last cen-
> tury. But he is mythic, too, in the sense that he was
> potential to the life of that time and place, rather
> than actual. He is the creature of the prophecy as
> well as the history of the Altamaha.
>
> I found when I reread the book that I'd forgotten
> how it ended. I found, too, that I'd fumbled Sutton's
> ill-fated romance with Robbie, daughter of the Da-
> rien uppercrust, in the next to the last chapter. I
> failed to get out of my head and onto the page his
> Garden of Eden image of his mother that was what
> he really saw in Robbie, was really in love with.
>
> But the ending of the book is right. The Tama of
> the Altamaha for Snake Sutton lay back up river at
> the confluence, lay in the evermoving muscle that
> makes up there [sic] lay in its prophecy as well as its
> history.

This Is Adam (1958) is probably Cheney's best novel, and it encouraged him to write a successor, *Devil's Elbow* (1969), and plan
a third novel to compose a trilogy, unfortunately never finished.
He had drawn upon his experience and that of his family to some

extent in the early novels, especially *Lightwood*. In his second pair of novels the central character, Marcellus Hightower, is a version of himself when young. Cheney's father, a Confederate veteran, died in 1908 when his only son was eight years old. Brainard and his two sisters had to be brought up by their mother, a Charleston lady who had somehow learned to cope with life on the "inner frontier," but circumstances were not always easy. She was aided by Robin Bess, the mulatto overseer of the family's land, and the novel is dedicated to his memory. He is the Adam of its title. I often heard Cheney (who, incidentally, was known as "Lon" to his numerous friends in Tennessee) talk about Robin Bess with affection and gratitude.

Cheney's success in this novel is partly based on its structure. There is a double post of observation, immediately established, involving Lucy Hightower, recently widowed, and Adam Atwell, her overseer. This would be around 1910. We move from one to the other, usually in alternating chapters, and the boy Marcellus or Marse is the focus of the drama. His late father, "Colonel" Marcellus Hightower, a lawyer, hoped on his deathbed that his widow and his overseer would be able to perpetuate his holdings for his son and daughters. Since we are close to both Lucy Hightower and Adam, we gradually explore the complications of their lives. Adam, when still youthful, became drunk at a camp meeting and was arrested on a false charge of murder with many others and sent to prison. Refusing to join a group who tried to escape, he was released through the aid of "Colonel" Hightower. The real unhappiness in his life was caused by his wife, who, becoming dangerously insane, had to be committed to the asylum in Milledgeville. A former raftsman like Ratliff Sutton, Adam gradually becomes a surrogate father for Marse, and Lucy Hightower depends on him at crucial moments.

Although Lucy has accepted the limitations of this small backwoods town, she is still something of an outsider. Now she receives a letter from Edward Louthan, a former suitor in Charleston; his letter deliberately evokes the life that she knew there as a girl. They were very close in those days, and in fact were caught together in the Charleston earthquake of 1886—a brilliant scene. Edward proposes to her again, and she seriously considers accepting him as a solution to the problems that have emerged since the death of her husband. Meanwhile, like Penelope in the *Odyssey*, she is besieged by bankers and land speculators, mostly unscrupulous, with only Adam to protect her. As a mulatto, he is always at a disadvantage, even though he makes them respect him. In the end she has to reject her Charleston suitor:

> ...for twenty years, she had endured her Georgia exile by the light of her dream of returning to Charleston. The celestial city! ... Her youth? Her throat constricted, and she shut her eyes to the rising image of Edward. There was to be no Indian summer for her. Her title to wild land on the banks of the Oconee had carried an irrevocable commitment! This was Hightower country, father and son, and Marse must grow up in it. Raw, rough, dark land, but somehow it was vital. And not the least of its vitality was, in the illiterate mixed Negro before her, torn from the womb of sin and slavery and curiously shaped in God's image, the only man alive she had complete confidence in, her son's foster father!

And the novel ends with the two principals confronting each other as they did at the beginning, "an unaccountable communion of exiles," as Cheney calls them in his essay.

In *This Is Adam* we know Marcellus only through his mother and Adam; their lives are determined to some extent by his presence. *Devil's Elbow* (1969) has him established as an adult and the central intelligence; he is now responsible for his actions in ways that he wasn't earlier. The structure of the novel is based on his three "returns" to his boyhood home, which was the scene of a murder. His closest friend, David Ransom, disappeared during a hunting expedition several years earlier; he was shot by one of a group of low bootleggers who actually tried to blame Adam for the crime. The most ghastly aspect of the affair was that the body wasn't discovered in the river for six weeks, and then Marcellus was obliged to be present at the autopsy. Although much in the novel is fictional, Cheney states in his Southern Review essay that this incident was only too actual; he was haunted for years by the odor of the putrefying corpse in the back room of the drugstore where the local doctors did their work. The novel could have been a murder mystery and a very exciting one at that level.

But Cheney insists that he wanted to turn the physical dimension of the novel into something metaphysical. Marcellus's guilt about his friend's disappearance (he had told David to look for turkeys in the woods) complicated these things. And he is no longer the boyish innocent that he was in *This Is Adam*. The novel has him involved with three women, whose names supply the title for the three "returns": Judy, Melanie, and Sheila. Judy is his youthful love during a brief period when they are students at the University of Georgia. She becomes pregnant and he turns her over to an abortionist; the affair doesn't end with that. Five years later, during his first "return," he actually proposes to her. But now he is a police reporter in Nashville and has fallen in with a racy set of young people there, one of whom, Melanie, a Vanderbilt student, becomes the subject of his ardor. They are hastily married and drift into a long, often indifferent relationship as he attempts to write novels and break out of the journalistic world. Meanwhile, he has lost his interest in the Hightower properties in Georgia. With his mother long dead, there is only Adam to guide him. During the Second World War he joins the OSS and is sent to Dublin, where he has an affair with a Roman Catholic woman, Sheila. She withdraws from him with the sharp comment, "But you're not religious. And you can't be. You don't believe." He abruptly turns and runs from her. This episode anticipates the end of the novel.

Brainard Cheney and his wife Frances had become Roman Catholics during the early 1950s. As converts and friends of Caroline Gordon Tate and Flannery O'Connor (among other literary associates), they took their new religion very seriously. His aim as a novelist here was obviously affected by this. Caroline Gordon had already dealt with the problem of religious conversion in *The Malefactors* (1956), a novel much admired by Cheney. He tries to do something like that at the end of *Devil's Elbow*, where, after a final pilgrimage to Adam, Marcellus assumes a humility that he hasn't known before. David Ransom, dead for twenty-five years, is the catalyst in this process, and Adam tells Marcellus about the decayed body of his friend, "Hit was a sad but saving smell to me. Has been ever since." After this, he is reunited with Melanie on Saint Simons Island along the Georgia coast. They both seem to have found their way to the verge of a religious conversation, and his emphatic comment is, "For the murdered hero burdens his followers with the crime—as Adam understood. It's their way to salvation."

The literary problem of religious conversion remains here. Is the sudden change entirely credible? We haven't seen Melanie for a long time, and she has good reason to be suspicious of her husband, whose treatment of her hasn't been exactly honorable. This last novel of Cheney's has tried to take in a lot of territory. The Nashville scene of the 1920s is thinly rendered. Much of it is ephemeral and later we quickly go through Washington and Dublin during the war. It is when Cheney returns to his familiar territory along the Ocmulgee and the Altamaha that the novel gains its substance—as in his earlier fiction. One doesn't want to call him simply a regional novelist, but certainly he writes his most powerful scenes out of his knowledge of one segment of his native state. One would say the same thing about most of the best American novelists from Hawthorne on.

Lightwood as History

5.

Dodge Lands and Litigations

Mrs. Wilton P. Cobb

Mrs. Wilton P. (Addie Davis) Cobb
Author of *History of Dodge County*
(1932)

The Dodge Lands and Litigations

Mrs. Wilton P. Cobb

from *History of Dodge County* (1932)

We are indebted to Judge J. N. Talley of the Federal Court in Macon for the story of the Dodge Lands and Litigations. Judge Talley was connected with the Federal Court and participated in the trials had before that body during all the years of litigation, he having been appointed by the court as commissioner to receive evidence in the different cases submitted.

Before going into the story of the long years of litigations we wish to state that the people against whom these cases were brought had purchased these lands in good faith, believing the transactions legal. Many of the people had purchased the lands, lived on them for years and reared families, only to find that they were really not in legal possession of same. This naturally caused them to feel bitterly against the Dodges, because they felt that they were being cheated out of their rightful claims to the property bought and paid for by them. But to understand the technicalities of the laws regarding the titles to these lands we will have to read the court decisions through. We give in part a speech prepared and read by Judge Talley before the Forty-Second Annual Session of the Georgia Bar Association at Tybee Island, Georgia, June 4, 1925.

Judge Tally says:

> At a session of the United States Court held in Macon on May 28, 1923, Judge William H. Barrett signed an order disposing of the case of Norman W. Dodge vs. Lucius L. Williams and three hundred and eighty other defendants. This judicial act marked the end of the Dodge litigation which had been pending in that court during forty years.

To discover its remote fountainhead and as well the more immediate causes of the great controversy, we must go back in time ninety-two years, in distance journey to the Pine-tree State, and trace for half a century the story of the Dodge Lands.

In 1832 Stephen Chase, a distinguished lawyer, was living in Fryeburg, Maine. The substantial colonial house which he built and occupied in that historic village is yet standing, and across the street from it is still pointed out the academy in which Daniel Webster first taught school.

Chase was also a Democratic politician, and among his friends were Augustin S. Clayton, a Congressman from Georgia, and Joseph M. White, a delegate in Congress from the territory of Florida. Through these Southern statesmen, the New Englander became convinced that the timber lands of south Georgia and Florida offered a splendid opportunity for investment and speculation.

The following year he came to the capital of Georgia, and there met Peter J. Williams, to whom had been granted by the State two hundred and seventy-five thousand acres of wild land in what was originally Wilkinson County. Chase was entertained by Williams at his residence, which is today one of the most notable of the many imposing homes in the city of Milledgeville that survive from the antebellum times. Enthusiastic over the contemplated purchase, the visitor returned to Maine.

At Portland was soon formed an association, known as the Georgia Land Company, and it was agreed to invest not over forty thousand dollars in the purchase of pine lands in Georgia, at a price not to exceed ten cents an acre.

The promoters sent to Georgia as their agents, Abram Colby, gentleman, of New Hampshire, Samuel E. Crocker, merchant, of Portland, and Stephen Chase, Esquire. Three hundred thousand acres of land were purchased by them from Peter J. Williams, who, to complete the necessary quantity, had acquired an additional twenty-five thousand acres.

The fifteen hundred lots embraced in the purchase then lay in the counties of Laurens, Montgomery, Telfair and Pulaski, and were widely dispersed over that mighty primeval forest lying between the Oconee and the Ocmulgee and extending to the junction of those rivers to form the Altamaha.

At that time water afforded the principal means of heavy transportation, commercial fertilizers were unknown, and cultivated fields were usually confined to alluvial bottoms. So we find in this, as in other sections of the State, large plantations adjacent to the rivers.

It is perhaps not generally known that many of the planters living in the four counties named were among the outstanding men of that day.

General David Blackshear, in Laurens, held almost feudal sway upon his country estate, "Springfield," overlooking the Oconee. The memory of the planter is perpetuated by the capital of Pierce, while that of his estate is preserved in the county seat of Effingham. On the Oconee also lived Governor George M. Troup, the name of his famous plantation in Laurens is now borne by the beautiful city of Valdosta. On the Ocmulgee, in Telfair, was the home of General Mark Willcox, and that of his father-in-law, General John Coffee, who, when a member of Congress in Washington, lived at the White House with his friend, Andrew Jackson.

The great expanse between the two rivers was sometimes called the "pine barrens." It was then very sparsely settled, except in a few localities in Telfair and Montgomery where the pasturage afforded by the wiregrass of the upland and the cane in the creeks

had early attracted settlers from Scotland because of their continued loyalty to the House of Stuart. Of them the historian, George
C. Smith, says:

> They were a thrifty people and were independent
> from the start. They had their kirk and their schools,
> and had services in their native Gaelic. There is no
> part of Georgia where there are so many Highland-
> ers, and there was nowhere a more contented and
> well-to-do people than those who dwelt in these pine
> forests. A finer type of people than the Scotch who
> settled so largely Telfair, Tattnall and Montgomery
> counties was not to be found in America. (From *The
> Story of Georgia and the Georgia People)*

The deed from Williams, dated February 28, 1834, was taken in
the individual names of Colby, Chase and Crocker. By another
purchase was acquired a tract of twenty thousand acres in Telfair
County. This included the Robert Flournoy plantation on the Auchee Hatchee River and a mill near the mouth of that important
stream, now more generally known as the Little Ocmulgee.

Upon the application of Chase and others, a charter was
granted to the Georgia Lumber Company by the Legislature of
this State on December 17, 1834, and in the following month all of
the lands in question were conveyed to that corporation by Colby,
Chase and Crocker, as its agents.

Superintendents and experienced lumberman were sent down
from Maine. The old Flournoy mill was put in operation and became, it is said, the largest sawmill in the South. Between two and
three hundred people were employed. Lumber was drifted down
the Altamaha. The old steamboat "Macon" was purchased in
1835. Cottages were erected about the mill and to the colony was
given the name Lumber City. The present town of that name is
not far from the original site. The capital stock of the company
was increased to $200,000 and its shares were freely sold in Bos-
ton and New York. For several years there was the appearance of
great prosperity.

Abram Colby, one of the promoters, visited the mills, but spent
much of his time about Brunswick. He knew that the waterpower

at Lumber City was insufficient and uncertain, and became interested in a movement to construct a canal from Darien to Brunswick. His plan was to raft logs down the Altamaha to Darien, and thence through the proposed canal to Brunswick, where it was designed to erect steam sawmills. In order to encourage and give publicity to this project, Colby joined with Messrs. Dexter, Rice, Davis and Thomas P. Carnes and established the first newspaper published in Brunswick. Upon his suggestion, Charles Davis, of Portland, Maine, was engaged as editor. In the language of the Georgia Gazetteer, "The Brunswick *Advocate* sent out its first rays of light in June, 1837."

The contemplated canal was not constructed. The Lumber Company was heavily indebted to the Bank of Western New York at Rochester. It became increasingly difficult to finance the mills. The Flournoy plantation showed an enormous loss. Brooks, its manager, had been "highly recommended," but appears to have had no experience in farming, his previous occupation having been that of a leather dresser in Boston.

By an amendment to its charter in 1838, the Georgia Lumber Company was given many banking privileges, and the right to transfer its property as security for debt. This last power was quickly and fully utilized. All of its property was soon conveyed to the Fund Commissioner of the State of Indiana to cover obligations that could not be met.

The end was at hand. By 1842, those in charge and most of the employees had returned to Maine. The cutting of timber ceased. The lands were abandoned. Actual possession and the title parted. The Flournoy plantation grew up in bushes, the Auchee Hatchee River flowed through the broken dam, shy swamp birds sang in the ruins of the mill, and the pines in safety slumbered, while the vagrant title wandered long in distant states.

Title passed out of the lumber company, and during nine years Indiana owned, of the territory of Georgia, five hundred square miles. From the Governor of Indiana the title passed through several links to William Chauncey and others of New York. There, caught by the outbreak of the War Between the States, it remained for a time captive in the enemy country. Peace restored, it went to William Pitt Eastman, of New Hampshire, who became owner in 1868.

In that year, A. G. P. Dodge, William Pitt Eastman, William Chauncey and others organized the Georgia Land and Lumber Company, under the laws of New York, and established an office in Georgia, at Normandale, so named for Norman W. Dodge. The president of the corporation was William E. Dodge, the father of A. G. P. Dodge, George E. Dodge and Norman W. Dodge. Born in Connecticut, he had become a wealthy merchant of New York, and about this time purchased the famous country estate of John Couper at Cannons Point, on St. Simons Island. He was a Republican in politics and had represented New York in Congress.

Dodge and his associates proposed to develop on a mammoth scale the timber resources of the lands purchased by Eastman in Telfair, Laurens, Pulaski and Montgomery Counties.

The coming at this time of these capitalists was hailed by the war-impoverished people of this section as the harbinger of an era of peace and prosperity. A village was called Chauncey. A town was laid out in the heart of the pine belt and named for William Pitt Eastman. A county was created, and the Legislature, in 1870, added to the gilded roll of heroes, statesmen and benefactors memorialized by the counties of Georgia the name of William E. Dodge. (A letter communicating to William E. Dodge the action of the Georgia Legislature was couched in the following language: "Appreciating your successful efforts, as chairman of the Chamber of Commerce of New York, in inducing Congress to remove the burden of taxation from the great staple of our State and of the South; mindful also of the great interest taken by yourself and friends in the commercial prosperity of our State, Georgia has, by an Act of the Legislature, given the new county your name." Mr. Dodge erected at his own expense a court house at Eastman, the county seat, and presented it to the county authorities.)

The lands in question were formally conveyed to the Georgia Land and Lumber Company, and the great development began. Gigantic sawmills were erected on St. Simons and supplied by timber rafted down the Altamaha. Others were built on the recently completed Macon and Brunswick Railroad, and logs were brought in on tramways extending for miles out into the forests. Large distilleries were constructed for the production of turpentine and rosin.

At once claimants under tax deeds sprang up in every direction to dispute the title of the corporation. The State of Indiana had failed to pay its taxes for the year 1844. A *fi fa* against the Georgia Lumber Company had been issued by James Boyd, Tax Collector of Telfair County. It had been levied upon the entire acreage formerly owned by the company, and hundreds of lots were sold, many at private sale, the usual price being about six cents a lot.

For relief the Georgia Land and Lumber Company, a foreign corporation, in 1876 appealed to the United States Court at Savannah. Through Richard K. Hines, as solicitor, a bill was filed against Josiah Paine and twenty others. Paine was claiming thirty-one lots under a tax receipt of $1.95. The defendants were represented by John M. Guerard and W. W. Paine. Two similar suits were filed, one being against W. W. Paine, who, himself, was claiming sixteen lots. On the final hearing the tax sale was declared void by Judge Erskine.

At the next session of the Legislature, in 1877, an act passed requiring all foreign corporations holding more than five thousand acres of land in Georgia to incorporate under its laws within one year. Two days before that law became effective, the Georgia Land and Lumber Company conveyed all its lands to George E. Dodge, a citizen of New York, but a natural person. The title remained in the name of George E. Dodge, and his successor, Norman W. Dodge, also a citizen of New York, but the development continued to be carried on by foreign corporations.

The turpentine and lumber industry were now assuming large proportions throughout southern Georgia, and hordes of squatters poured into all those sections where grew the long leaf pine.

Dodge sought the state courts, the small amount involved in the individual cases not being sufficient to give the Federal court jurisdiction. Beginning in 1877, more than two hundred and fifty ejectment cases were filed in five counties. His local attorney was John F. DeLacey.

Appearing for the defendants, frequently, was Luther A. Hall, of Eastman. He had been a school teacher, was a lawyer of ability and skillful in ejectment practice. Opposing a New York plaintiff, before a local jury, Hall was seldom at a disadvantage.

In this litigation, Dodge relied upon what was known as his "short chain of title." An important link extending from 1834 to 1875, consisted of deeds from the executor and heirs of Peter J. Williams to William Pitt Eastman, conveying the same lands sold by Williams to Colby, Chase and Crocker.

Oliver H. Briggs, from Massachusetts, a clerk in the office of Dodge's land agent, knew that the deed from Colby, Chase and Crocker to the Georgia Lumber Company had been lost, that it had not been properly executed and was not entitled to record. This information was imparted to Henry G. Sleeper, a lawyer, also from Massachusetts, but then living in Eastman. Hall himself had discovered, as he thought, many defects in Dodge's recorded title, and also believed that the State of Indiana could not hold lands in Georgia.

Hall, securing the co-operation of Briggs and Sleeper, ferreted out the heirs of Colby, Chase and Crocker and procured from them deeds conveying their supposed interest in the Dodge lands to Silas P. Butler, of Massachusetts, a clerk in the office of J. L. Colby, a son of Abram Colby. The three hundred thousand acres of Silas P. Butler were then advertised for sale at low prices and on liberal terms. The slogan employed was "Homes for the Homeless." Eager buyers thronged the land office opened in Eastman by Butler's land agents, Briggs, Hall and Sleeper. Luther A. Hall became the hero of the hour, and at the crest of his popularity in 1883 was elected to the Legislature by the people of the county named for William E. Dodge.

The rival title drove Dodge to his long chain of conveyances, but at the same time delivered his adversaries into the equity jurisdiction of the dreaded Federal Court.

In 1884 George E. Dodge filed his bill in the United States Circuit Court at Macon. The defendants were Briggs, Hall and Sleeper, fifty persons who had purchased from them, the heirs of Colby, Chase and Crocker, and Silas P. Butler.

The plaintiff set up his title through Williams, Colby, Chase and Crocker, the Georgia Lumber Company, and the State of Indiana, and prayed that it be declared valid, that the deeds to Butler be cancelled, and that the defendants be perpetually enjoined from asserting the rival title or in any way interfering with plaintiff's possession and ownership of the lands in dispute. The plaintiff was represented by Robert S. Lanier, Clifford Anderson, and R. K. Hines, the principal defendants by Hall, Sleeper, C. C. Kibbee and John H. Martin.

John Erskine was District Judge, but the early orders were signed by Judge J. W. Locke of the Southern District of Florida. Before the final hearing John Erskine retired and Emory Speer succeeded him as judge. The hearing extended over five days. The voluminous testimony, taken by deposition, showed that the lands had been purchased from Williams by Colby, Chase and Crocker, as agents and with the money of the promoters in Maine, who subsequently organized the Georgia Lumber Company. It was held by the court that title vested in that company regardless of the defectively executed deed.

In disposing of the contention the State of Indiana could not hold lands in Georgia, Judge Speer said:

> It must be understood that when the State of Indiana bought these lands, it came as a subject and not as a sovereign. If the State of Indiana is to be regarded as an alien, it is laid down in Washburn on Real Property that an alien may purchase and hold lands against all the world except the State: and Briggs, Hall and Sleeper may not say with Louis XIV: 'I am the state.' (27 Fed. 160).

On April 5, 1886, a final decree was entered granting the relief sought by the bill and perpetually enjoining the defendants, as prayed.

Alex N. Sexton, the land agent of Dodge, had printed thousands of handbills, and Ed McRae, just entering his long service as woodsman, traveled throughout the five counties posting and distributing the circulars proclaiming that Dodge had the true title and quoting the injunction order signed "Emory Speer, United States Judge."

The bill in this case was the beginning of the Dodge litigation in the Federal court at Macon, but the final decree was not to mark its end.

A few months later, on the ground of local prejudice against the plaintiff, Dodge vs. Dodson, et al., was removed to the Federal court from the Superior Court of Dodge County. Luther A. Hall was attorney for the defendants. Judge Speer, by decree, rendered in 1886, declared defendants' entire chain of title to five lots a forgery, cancelled the deeds, and enjoined the Clerk of the Superior Court, a defendant, from recording certain deeds forged by Dodson.

Among the important cases filed in the Federal court during the succeeding eight years were Dodge vs. Vaughn, Dodge vs. Woodward, et al., Dodge vs. Laurens Lumber Co., et al., Dodge vs. Powell and twenty others, Dodge vs. Cadwell and eighty-nine others.

The litigation was not confined to the Federal court. In many cases the State court was of necessity the forum. There Luther A. Hall contended that the final decree of the Federal court was not admissible in aid of Dodge's title, as against defendants not parties to the decree. The weakness of Dodge's "short chain" had already been exposed to Hall. It was impracticable in each case for Dodge to rely upon his long chain of conveyances and submit the elaborate proof, upon which the final decree of the Federal Court was based, in order to show a perfect equity himself as plaintiff. The serious difficulty confronting Dodge was soon removed by a decision of the Supreme Court of Georgia.

Upon the trial in 1889 of Dodge vs. Spiers, ejectment in Telfair Superior Court, the plaintiff introduced his "short chain" of title, which included a deed from the heirs of Peter J. Williams to William Pitt Eastman. Spiers, through his attorney-at-law, Luther A. Hall, tendered a copy of the deed from Peter J. Williams to Colby, Chase and Crocker, thus breaking plaintiff's chain. Plaintiff in rebuttal offered the decree of the United States court in Dodge vs. Briggs, Hall and Sleeper, the heirs of Colby, Chase and Crocker, et al. Judgment was for the defendant Spiers. It was reversed, the Supreme Court saying:

> The court below held this record and decree of the United States Court did not show title in Dodge; and this ruling we think was error. We think the effect of the decree was to put into Dodge a perfect equity, and as to the heirs of Colby, Chase and Crocker his

equity was complete; so that he could maintain and recover upon his equitable title. (85 Ga. 585).

Dodge's title had been recognized by both the State and Federal courts, but the fight against him continued. Parties to the suit of Dodge vs. Briggs, Hall and Sleeper, and bound by the decree of the Federal court, did not long cease their activity. Luther A. Hall, the chief counsel for the defendants, became the leader of those defying the court's injunction. At the instance of John C. Forsyth, agent of Dodge, rules for contempt were issued. A sensational trial was had before Judge Speer in March, 1890. Dodge was represented by R. K. Hines, Hill and Harris, and Lanier and Anderson, while for Hall appeared as counsel, Marion Erwin, Alexander Proudfit and James A. Thomas. Hall was adjudged guilty and sentenced to five months' imprisonment in Chatham County jail.

Growing out of the contempt proceeding was an indictment by the grand jury of the United States court charging Hall with perjury. He was later tried and convicted, but sentence was deferred. The prosecution was conducted by John L. Hardeman, special United States Attorney, the defense by Bacon and Rutherford and Dessau and Bartlett. (U. S. vs. Hall, 44 Fed. 864.)

Released from jail, Hall again announced as a candidate for the Legislature. In the active campaign he posed as a martyr who had suffered imprisonment in the cause of the people. He denounced Dodge, his agent, Forsyth, and the Federal court.

There were some eight or nine who had gotten themselves so deeply involved in the land troubles that they seem to have come to the conclusion that something desperate had to be done to overthrow Mr. Dodge in the successful assertion of his rights, or they themselves would be overwhelmed when their trespasses on the Dodge lots were brought to light.

Hoping that by striking terror into the hearts of Mr. Dodge and his agents, the former would be forced to abandon the prosecution of the rules then pending in the Federal court, desist from further proceedings to carry the decree in favor of his title into execution, and make terms and concessions at their dictation, sprang the most diabolical, cold-blooded conspiracy and murder that has ever blackened the annals of our State. John C. Forsyth,

Dodge's agent, was the victim. These men hired for this dastardly deed, a Negro by the name of Rich Lowery or Rich Herring, a notorious outlaw and desperado who had come to this section from North Carolina to work turpentine. He belonged to a peculiar mixed race of people who have their principal habitat at a small town or village in North Carolina known as "Scuffletown" from the characteristic disorders of the population. They are said to be a mixed race of white, Indian and Negro blood and are usually designated as "Scuffletonians."

> Lowery, when employed to kill Forsyth, did not know him by sight. During the period he was at the home of one of these plotters waiting for the word to go on his mission, it was learned that Forsyth would be at Chauncey on October the first. The farmer loaded up a wagon with a supply of eggs, butter and country produce and, in company with Lowery, set out for Chauncey. Before reaching there the Scuffletonian separated from him and they went into town apparently as strangers to each other. The farmer found Forsyth, and going up to him, made some remarks in the nature of pleasantry and touched him on the arm. Lowery, who was standing near, understood the signal, the victim was known, and the object of their visit was accomplished.
>
> — *The Land Pirates,* by Marion Erwin

On the evening of October 7, 1890, John C. Forsyth was in his comfortable home at supper, his wife and children about him. (This home was in Normandale, now Suomi, and the home is the large two-story residence near the highway and is at present owned by Mathias Burch.) Having finished the meal, he arose and, lighting a cigar, walked into the living room, where he sat down in an easy chair. Outside a gentle rain was falling. The dark Scuffletonian stood peering through a window, and leisurely aimed his gun at the designated victim. Startled by the report, young Nellie Forsyth rushed to her stricken father, then braving the near presence of his assassin ran out into the night for a physician. Within a few hours John C. Forsyth was dead, and the immediate object of a great conspiracy had been accomplished.

The identity of the murderers for a time remained a mystery. A month passed, when a relative of one of them casually and unwittingly divulged the details of the conspiracy and the names of the assassins to one whom he thought knew much of the murder and was in sympathy with its purpose. After consulting his father and his friend, Judge W. L. Grice, this man communicated the information to R. Oberley, the agent of Dodge, although in so doing he ran counter to his business interest and imperiled his personal safety.

The first man arrested was taken to the office of the District Attorney in Macon. Overcome by remorse, this man confessed his part and told all about the plot, naming those who had taken part in it. True bills were returned by the grand jury of the United States circuit court against ten. A large reward was offered for Rich Lowery, who had fired the fatal shot, but he could not be found. Marion Erwin, in his account of the conspiracy trial, says that after the murder Rich Lowery went to Montgomery County, deposited two hundred dollars with an old colored man, and "sporting a new suit of clothes and a fine gold watch, he cut quite a swell among his fellows," that he was engaged to carry a raft down the river, and returning stopped at Jesup where, in a barber shop, he saw a copy of the Macon *Telegraph* giving an account of the arrest of the men involved in the conspiracy, that he made his way back to the colored man in Montgomery County, received his money, and "plunging into the thicket he disappeared, and that is the last authentic account we have of Lowery."

Indictments framed under 5508, Rev. Stat., charged that a conspiracy had been formed by the defendants to injure, threaten, oppress and intimidate Norman W. Dodge who had succeeded George E. Dodge as owner of the lands in question, because he had exercised and was exercising his right to prosecute in the United States court rules for contempt for violation of the injunction granted by the final decree in Dodge vs. Briggs, Hall and Sleeper. It was further charged that in pursuance of the conspiracy Lowery had murdered Dodge's agent, Forsyth, and that the other defendants were accessories before the fact to the murder. (See U.S. vs. Lancaster, 44 Fed. 885.)

The defendants at once moved in the U. S. Supreme Court for permission to file a petition for a writ of habeas corpus on the ground that the matters charged in the indictment did not make an offense cognizable by the circuit court. The motion was denied. (137 U.S. 393)

The trial began at Macon on December 8, 1890. The court room was crowded. One hundred and forty witnesses were in attendance. Four hundred jurors had been summoned. Friends of the prisoners from five counties struggled for a look at the trial or a word of the proceedings.

The prisoners were in a group. Near them were their attorneys, A. O. Bacon, Washington Dessau, Charles L. Bartlett and C. C. Smith. Hugh V. Washington represented the one who accompanied Lowery a part of the way when he went on his murderous mission.

At the desk of the District Attorney was Marion Erwin. On the second day of the trial he was joined by the special counsel of the Government, Fleming G. duBignon, who had just completed his service as President of the Senate and shortly before had ended a brilliant term as Solicitor-General of the Eastern Circuit.

The gravity of the offense charged, the novelty of the jurisdictional questions involved, and the widespread public interest the case had aroused, were to stir to the highest pitch of effort, all these eminent counsel engaged. Not attorneys in the case, but representing Norman W. Dodge, were Walter B. Hill, later to become Chancellor of the State University, and his law partner, N. E. Harris, a future Governor of Georgia.

Judge Emory Speer was on the bench. Distinguished as a lawyer and speaker, as a prosecuting officer in both the State and Federal courts, and a Congressman, now in the prime of his splendid mental and physical vigor, for five years he had been District Judge.

All preliminaries disposed of, the fight now centered on the jury.

The first important witness was young Nellie Forsyth, whose description of her father's death was calculated to give to the prosecution's case from the outset a tone of tragedy. Coming into the court room she was somewhat confused by the gaze of so many men, and seeing two girls, she took her seat beside them.

They were the motherless daughters of one of the prisoners. This accidental association of the innocent victim of the crime and the equally innocent victims of its consequences perhaps diminished the dramatic effect of her appearance as a witness. But on the stand, her modest demeanor and the simple story of her awful experience created a profound impression, and as she walked away there seemed to follow a wave of sympathy that so winsome a girl should have been orphaned in so tragic a manner.

Witness after witness was called during a period of sixteen days. The attorneys were constantly on the alert and no vantage point escaped them. Always an interested audience keenly followed the proceedings. Three days were consumed in arguments to the jury. Marion Erwin opened for the prosecution. Hugh V. Washington, Charles L. Bartlett, C. C. Smith and A. O. Bacon followed for the defense, and Fleming G. duBignon closed. The facts and circumstances were variously assembled and presented according to the genius and skill of each of these masters of forensic oratory and fused by the fire of eloquence into an image of the truth as he beheld it. The concluding argument of duBignon has been termed the most eloquent jury speech of his career. As he marshaled the evidence and went from one flight of oratory to another, it was easy to perceive that he was fast brushing from the minds of the jury all lingering doubts of the guilt of the accused. He was interrupted. An attorney for the defense, after squirming under the onslaught, arose and made some objection. The courtly duBignon, turning toward the ruffled attorney, raised his hand and, as he let it slowly fall with a movement of graceful agitation, said, "The wounded pigeon flutters." The angry scene and subsequent apology have been forgotten, but duBignon's cameo-like profile, exquisite poise and elegance of gesture have converted that trifling incident into an enduring memory.

In concluding his able and comprehensive charge, Judge Speer deprecated *thise ad captandam* observations of counsel which "drop the poison of prejudice into the mind of the unsuspecting juror and thus palsy and paralyze his best and most honorable efforts in the direction of a stern and inflexible performance of duty." (44 Fed. 896.)

All the defendants on trial were convicted except one, and all those convicted were sentenced to imprisonment in the Ohio

State Penitentiary. One was given ten years, three were sentenced to imprisonment for life, and one received a sentence of six years.

It was commonly believed that Rich Lowery would never suffer for the crime he had committed, but years later the truth became known that, far from escaping punishment, he had been the first of the guilty to meet his doom. Some of the conspirators, who, mistrusting and fearing the hired assassin, had again turned murderers. This time they did their own work and under the black water of a stagnant pool deep in a cypress swamp they left the body of the Scuffletonian.

The criminal cases having been disposed of, attention was again directed to the many civil cases pending in the courts.

The easy current of that litigation in the State courts however was obstructed in 1894 and diverted to the Federal court. On the 29th of August of that year the Supreme Court of Georgia, in Bussey et al. vs. Dodge, 94 Ga. 584, argued at the October term, 1893 in effect overruled its former decision in Dodge vs. Spiers, and virtually sustained the contention made in the latter case by Luther A. Hall, on the occasion of perhaps his last appearance as counsel in Georgia's highest court.

Dodge had filed in the Superior Court of Dodge County a suit against Bussey et al. and relied upon his title traced through Colby, Chase and Crocker and the decree of the Federal court. The defendants were represented by E. A. Smith. There was a judgment in favor of Dodge. This was reversed by the Supreme Court, and it was held:

> If the case of Dodge vs. Spiers was correctly decided, it was because the defendants therein, by introducing and relying on the deed to Colby, Chase and Crocker subjected himself to be treated as in privity with their heirs, who were parties to the decree and against whom the decree itself established a perfect equity by requiring them to convey to plaintiff.
>
> Except in so far as that case is supported upon this distinction between it and the present case, it cannot be adhered to or followed.

This decision was to afford no comfort to the many persons trespassing upon and setting up claims to Dodge lands, for after Bussey vs. Dodge had been argued and two months before it was decided, Norman W. Dodge undertook in one proceeding in the Federal court to bring in as parties all those, so far as known, who claimed to hold adversely, and on June 25 1894, filed a bill of peace, naming as defendants three hundred and eighty-one persons.

It was alleged that the title and lands of Dodge were well known, and that a general scheme had been formed by the defendants to deprive him of the lands, by means of forged deeds and supported by false testimony as to possession. The jurisdiction of the court was seriously questioned by an able array of counsel. Particularly was it urged that the plaintiff could not join in one proceeding so many defendants, scattered over so great a territory and relying upon separate and unconnected claims of ownership. The bill, however, in effect charged a combination on the part of the defendants, thus raising an issue of fact rather than of law. After lengthy arguments, the jurisdiction was sustained.

The record of the pleadings alone covers twenty-two hundred pages. The evidence was taken by a commissioner appointed by the court. Hearings were had by him at Macon, Dublin, Eastman and McRae. In addition to a mass of documentary evidence, the commissioner's report was filed in seven volumes.

Decrees *pro confesso* had been taken as to a number of defendants. With others settlements were made and consequent decrees taken. A final decree was entered in 1902 generally sustaining the contentions of the plaintiff.

The bill of peace was filed through Hill, Harris and Birch, and Marion Erwin, as solicitors for plaintiff, with whom were associated John F. DeLacey and James Bishop. Among the attorneys for the defendants were A. O. Bacon, A. L. Miller, William Brunson, Olin J. Wimberly, Clem P. Steed, Walter M. Clements, E. A. Smith, Tom Eason, B. R. Calhoun, F. R. Martin, J. W. Preston, and B. B. Cheney.

So great was the bitterness aroused by the conspiracy trial, so many the defendants and parties interested in the civil litigation, and such the supposed hostility to the Federal court on the part of the people who lived in the counties where the lands were si-

tuated, that for twelve years prior to 1907, there was placed in the
jury boxes of the United States court at Macon the name of no
man who resided in any of the great and populous counties of
Laurens, Dodge or Telfair.

The decrees on the bill of peace were not fully observed. Dodge
had writs of assistance issued. A multitude of applications were
made to the court to enjoin their enforcement by the marshal.
The usual ground was that the party sought to be ousted was for
some reason not bound by the decree. For the purpose of having
complicated claims of this character determined, the executors of
Norman W. Dodge, in 1908, filed a bill against several persons.
The case was referred to a master. His reports were made from
time to time over a period of six years. No exceptions were taken,
and the conclusions of the master were embodied in decrees of
court.

For the record we will state here that the commissioner who
heard and reported the evidence on the bill of peace, and also the
master in the litigation last mentioned was Judge J. N. Talley, of
Macon, the author of this article.

A few years after the filing of the bill of peace, Walter A. Harris
was admitted to the bar and became associated with Hill, Harris
and Birch, the general attorneys for Dodge. Before the final announcement in that case was made by him as leading counsel for
the plaintiff, he had achieved distinction at the bar and served
through the World War as Brigadier-General.

By 1917 the magnificent growth of long leaf pine had been removed. For years past as titles were settled by the decrees of
court, the cut-over lands had been sold by Dodge in small parcels
and to many purchasers. In that year the remainder of the Dodge
Lands was sold to Judge John S. Candler, of Atlanta. He in turn
sold a large part of it to Walter M. Clements, J. H. and Paul Roberts, of Eastman, but also made gifts of substantial tracts to
Wesleyan College, of Macon, and the South Georgia College at
McRae.

This was not the first contribution made to education and religion from the wealth of the Dodge lands. Many years before, A. G.
P. Dodge, Jr., of New York, a youth of about eighteen, while visiting the pine forests of Telfair County, decided to enter the minis-
try of the Episcopal Church. Soon afterwards his marriage to a

first cousin was the culmination of a youthful romance. The happy couple went abroad. In far away India the young wife died. She was buried at old Frederica, on St. Simons Island, and Christ Church there is her memorial. Her fortune was left to education and religion. To it was added that of the husband, who devoted his life to the service of the church. It was authoritatively stated in 1910 that of the fifty-two mission stations in the Diocese of Georgia, thirty-nine owed their existence to the Dodge fund, and many of them to the personal exertions of that consecrated man.

In Conclusion

Husband and wife, the grandchildren of William E. Dodge, now sleep on St. Simons by the sea. Near them also lie the murdered agent, John C. Forsyth, and his daughter, Nellie, who became the wife of Major Ernest Dart, of Jacksonville, formerly of the Brunswick bar. From beneath the gray moss of the live oaks, their last resting place looks across the Marshes of Glynn, immortalized by the poetic genius of Sidney Lanier, whose father, as counsel, signed the original bill which commenced the Dodge litigation.

All of the lands had passed from the ownership of Dodge. The occupation of his agents and woods-riders was gone. Thomas J. Curry and Ed McRae for twenty-five years had been on guard. They were men of high courage and character. The bill of peace had been verified by Ed McRae, he being the agent most familiar with the alleged trespasses of the hundreds of defendants. His father, John F. McRae, for forty-four years Clerk of the Superior Court of Telfair County, had, as a very young man, taught the children of the little Maine colony at old Lumber City. Oberley, the general agent, and Curry promptly obtained other employment.

Judge Emory Speer died in 1918. The Dodge litigation had extended over his entire judicial tenure, and it is a remarkable fact that throughout its long course there was never an appeal from any decision he made and no final action of the court, when he was on the bench, was ever carried to a higher court for review. When Judge Speer was appointed in 1885, the Federal court was to the masses of the people of the Southern District a foreign, an unknown and an unpopular court. Speaking in the parlance of the business world, Judge Speer "sold" the Federal court to the people, and it is a tribute to his distinguished service when it can now be declared that there is perhaps no district court in the United States where the people are more attached to the Federal court than in the Southern District of Georgia, and that nowhere is the office of District Judge regarded as one of so much honor as by the people of the district over which Judge Speer presided for a third of a century.

The last contested case was on trial before Judge Beverly D. Evans who had resigned as Presiding Justice of the Supreme Court of Georgia to become District Judge of the Southern District. This was the case of Clark vs. Dodge, an aftermath of Dodge vs. Clark litigated many years before. Clark was represented by Charles Akerman, of Macon, and Judge R. Earl Camp, of Dublin, the nominal defendant, Dodge, by Walter A. Harris, John B. Harris, and M. J. Whitman, and the real defendants, the purchasers, by John R. L. Smith and Grady C. Harris. The decision of Judge Evans, rendered in 1920, was affirmed by the United States Circuit Court of Appeals. (260 Fed. 784.)

When in May, 1923, Judge Barrett made the formal order removing the litigation from the dockets of the court, Judge Erskine, and Locke and Speer, and Lamdin, and Evans had passed away, and of the great lawyers whom, in their prime, had appeared for the parties contending in the original equity suit, in Dodge vs. Dodson, in the Hall contempt case, in the perjury case, in the great conspiracy case, and in Georgia vs. Kelly, only four— Nathaniel E. Harris, Marion Erwin, Charles L. Bartlett and James A. Thomas—accompanied by honor and "troops of friends," remained to "counsel and advise."

Jurors were again being returned from all parts of the district, and the United States Marshal who called them in court was George B. Mcleod, of the old county of Montgomery.

A great population scattered over six counties had been made secure in their homes and lands by the effective decrees of the once hated Federal court, and upon the Dodge lands, so long in controversy, had descended the harbingered era of peace and prosperity.

6.

Essays:

The Great Pine Barrens & Suomi

John H. Goff

Placenames of Georgia

Sawmill in Telfair County. Note the sparseness of the trees in the photograph's background, the oxen and mules and the outsized wheels on the
logging wagon. (Courtesy of Hubert Evans, Jr.)

The Great Pine Barrens

John H. Goff

from *Placenames of Georgia*

One of the most interesting geographic features of this country in its primeval state was a vast pine forest that swept in a great crescent from the lower Chesapeake Bay to the Mississippi River. This belt of trees was approximately 1,000 miles long and from 60 to 200 miles wide. It ranged over the eastern portions of Virginia and the Carolinas, and, in its widest part, spread over upper Florida and lower Georgia, Alabama, and Mississippi. The immense pineland occupied a substantial part of what is known today as the Atlantic-Gulf Coastal Plain, an area that is characterized along the coastal margins by flat sandy lands and inland by gently rolling sandy or sand-clay hills that gradually rise to merge with the higher country of the interior.

Some eight or ten species of the so-called yellow or pitch pines composed this pineland, the most important types of which were the short-leaf, loblolly, slash and long-leaf pines. The last variety, the most distinctive of the trees, tended to favor the lower or more southerly parts of the belt. By means of deep tap roots and a moist climate these pines were able to flourish in the relatively infertile sandy soils of the sun-drenched Coastal Plain.

In their virgin state the pines did not grow thickly, but were scattered about with considerable intervening space between the trees. The trunks of the original stands rose like superb shafts to a height of 50 to 70 feet before the first spreading branches were reached. These great arms then stretched out and often touched the boughs of neighboring trees, thus forming a canopy for the ground below. This covert, in conjunction with the indifferent soil, caused the pinelands to be singularly lacking in underbrush, thereby permitting the view, over great reaches, to fade into a wall of arboreal columns. Possibly the only place left in the country today where one could find comparable vistas would be in the great ponderosa pine forests on the eastern slopes of the Cascade Mountains in our Pacific Northwest.

The first whites to traverse the expansive pines and leave a record were the chroniclers of De Soto. They mentioned the pinelands numbers of times and referred to a part of them, in probably what is now middle south Georgia, as being a "desert." During the three centuries following the Spaniards' expedition this term was to be used many times in referring to the great pine belt. Even William Bartram, the noted botanist, who made a tour through the Southern colonies just prior to the Revolution, wrote of the pine woods, paradoxically, as "desert forests," and noted that birds were not numerous there. Much later, in the middle of the last century when Richard Cuyler and a group of Savannah citizens were trying to promote a railroad from that place to the Gulf of Mexico, via what are now the flourishing Georgia cities of Waycross, Valdosta, Quitman, and Thomasville, the area to be served by the proposed road was hooted at as Cuyler's Desert.

While the pinelands were often referred to over the years as deserts, and occasionally as sandy wastes, in time they became known from one end of the belt to the other as the pine barrens, or simply, in the vernacular of early settlers, as "pine barr'ns."

As time passed, roads were cut across the pine belt by the early settlers, who, as will be seen, were principally interested in pushing on to the higher and more fertile regions beyond. With the opening of these roads greater numbers of people traversed the forests and more writers recorded their impressions of the immense woods. These reports nearly always reflect the same reaction, by harping upon the themes of interminable pines, the sterile soil, and the monotonous levelness of the barrens. Today one can well imagine that a trip through the region was tedious, considering the slowness and difficulties of early travel. Certainly a journey lengthwise of the forest from Norfolk to New Orleans, for example, might well have taxed the hardiest and most patient traveler. Furthermore, a person making such a trip would have gathered an odd idea of the southeastern part of the country, if he did not know by hearsay or personal experience that the region was endowed with mountains, plateaus, and valleys as well as with a seemingly boundless forest of pines.

American travelers across the belt were in the main phlegmatic in their comments on the pinelands. Apparently most of them knew what to expect before visiting the region, and they dismissed the barrens with customary comments on the sterility of the country and the tediousness of travel through the forest.

The reactions of foreign visitors, on the other hand, tended to be much more distinctive, since the great pinelands were totally unlike anything known to western Europeans.

The comments of English visitors are especially interesting and descriptive. Captain Basil Hall, a British naval officer, in his *Travels in North America* left an unusually effective impression of the forest as it was in 1828. In describing the stems of the tall pines between Charleston and Savannah, he wrote: "The eye was bewildered in a mass of columns receding far back, and diminishing in the perspective to mere threads, till they were lost in the gloom. The ground was everywhere perfectly flat, and the trees rose from it in a direction so exactly perpendicular, and so entirely without lower branches, that an air of architectural symmetry was imparted to the forest, by no means unlike that of some gothic cathedrals."

Later, en route to Macon, Georgia, he noted: "Our road, on the 22d of March—if road it ought to be called—lay through the heart of the forest, our course being pointed out solely by blazes, or of slices, cut as guiding marks on the sides of the trees. It was really like navigating by means of the stars over the trackless ocean!"

Curiously enough, Captain Hall did not tire quickly of the vast and lonely barrens. After explaining that he and his family must have travelled at least 500 miles in the South, by carriage, he continued:

"I don't know exactly what was the cause, but it was a long time before I got quite tired of the scenery of these pine barrens. There was something, I thought, very graceful in the millions upon millions of tall and slender columns, growing up in solitude, not crowded upon one another, but gradually appearing to come closer and closer together, till they formed a compact mass beyond which nothing could be seen." He goes on to say, however, "These regions will probably be left for ages in neglect."

The reaction of Charles Joseph Latrobe, another Englishman, to the tiresomeness of plodding through the sand-bed roads of the pinelands was more like that of most observers. This writer made a circuit of the lower south in 1833 as far down as Florida. By the time he reached St. Marks in that state, he reports in *The Rambler in North America* that he had had seen enough of the monotonous level of the long-leaf pine barrens to produce "complete satiety." Unhappily for Latrobe, this satiation was reached half-way around his tour; he still faced the long return across the virgin pine regions of south Georgia! On the other hand, another Britisher, Sir Charles Lyell in *Travels in North America*, in 1841 found the pine barrens interesting *because* of their uniformity and monotony.

Fannie Kemble, the English actress who married a Georgia planter and resided in the winter of 1838-1839 at a plantation on the Altamaha River, left a striking but overdrawn picture of the great forest. Endowed with a lively imagination, an acid pen, and obsessed by a dislike of her sojourn in Georgia, she describes an excursion into the pines in her *Journal of a Residence on a Georgia Plantation*:

> The road was a deep, wearisome sandy track, stretching wearisomely into the wearisome pine forest—a species of wilderness more oppressive a thousand times to the senses and imagination than any

extent of monotonous prairie, barren steppe, or boundless desert can be; for the horizon there at least invites and detains the eye, suggesting beyond its limit possible change; the lights, and shadows, and enchanting colors of the sky afford some variety in their movement and change, and the reflections of their tints; while in this hideous and apparently boundless pine barren you are deprived alike of horizon before you and heaven above you.

Miss Kemble goes on to comment upon the blue-green expanse under the dark green umbrella formed by the pines' foliage. But, curiously enough, neither she nor other early observers of the pines make mention of the purplish tinge which is so noticeable in the bark of present-day pine trees. A number of the writers, however, were as much impressed by the sighing and murmuring of the yellow pines as are the people of today. For instance, Levasseur, who accompanied LaFayette to the United States and reported on the trip in his *Lafayette en Amerique, en 1824 et 1825,* in speaking of Macon said:

> She has sprung up as if by magic in the middle of the forests. It is a civilized point lost in the still immense domain of the first children of America. Within a league of there we are in the bosom of the virgin forests; the tops of these old trees, which seem to measure the age of the world, sway over our heads; the wind stirs them with that murmur in turn low and sharp which M. de Chateaubriand calls the voice of the desert.

Sir Charles Lyell was affected in much the same way as Levasseur, stating in his *A Second Visit to the United States of America,* during 1846, that the sound of the wind in the "long-leaved" pines reminded him of waves breaking on a distant seashore, and that it was agreeable to hear it swelling gradually and then dying away as the breeze rose and fell.

Many of the early accounts of the great pine belt leave the no-
tion that the pines stretched in unbroken array across the region.
As one early account stated it, "There was nothing but pines."
This same impression may also be gathered from some of the
original and official surveys of south Georgia lands after they
were acquired from the Indians. In mapping these areas the sur-
veyors were required to write on the different land lots the types
of trees growing thereon. On their maps often the only trees
named over wide areas were: pines, pines, pines.

This impression of a complete continuity of the forest is not
correct, however, since the reaches of pines were often interspersed with other types of vegetation. Occasionally, and especially
back from the coasts, there were areas, often gentle rises, which
the pioneers came to know as hummocks, hommocs, hommocks,
hammacks, or hammocks. On such spots hardwoods grew, and
since their presence was an indication of a soil change for the better over the sandy pinelands, the hammocks were early sought for
homesteads by those who settled the pine woods.

Then too, here and there, the somber pines were occasionally
enlivened by open glades or natural meadows which the pioneers
called savannahs. Such spots were relatively low and moist, and
were consequently avoided by the pines. But native grasses grew
lushly in such localities, and they were much frequented by deer
and the settlers' stock.

There were also low spongy areas scattered throughout the forest which the pioneers named bay galls. These spots, which were
quite common in Georgia, Alabama, and Mississippi, were left by
the pines to myrtles, small bay trees, and gallberry bushes.

In addition to these breaks in the great pines, numerous
streams, some of them quite large rivers, traversed the pinelands.
Here the pines gave way to dense canebrakes and thick swamp
forests of hardwoods and cypress.

With the exception of the narrower and older portions of the
forest in Virginia and the Carolinas, the great pine belt was settled
relatively slowly. The soils of the pinelands proper were infertile
when compared with those of the rich bottomlands along the rivers, or with the lands of the Piedmont plateau beyond the barrens. As a rule then the settlers sought sites for farms or plantations in the river-bottoms of the Coastal Plain or pushed on to the

higher hardwood lands across the pine belt. There were those who appreciated the value of the great pines for timber and naval stores, but transportation facilities were poor, and the forest seemed so endless and the supply of trees so inexhaustible that few dared to predict the great future which was eventually to materialize for the region.

Chief among the first who did settle in the pine barrens were stockmen, who ranged their cattle on the wiregrass which grew among the trees as well as on the savannahs and extensive brakes of reed cane that were found here and there in the forest. Occasionally, too, a farmer who did not object to the solitude of the pine wilderness would carve out a home for himself and family among the pines. When he settled in a hammock area, he prospered in a limited fashion, but if he selected a spot out in the barrens, he was likely to have only a meager livelihood and an humble economic status. In early years the people who made this last choice were called pinelanders. Later they became known generally as piney woods folks, although in Georgia and upper Florida they were often referred to as crackers.

Around the beginning of the last century [i.e., the 1800's] and up to the time of the War Between the States, parts of the pine barrens developed economic importance as places of refuge from the seasonal diseases which beset the coastal cities and the low-country towns and plantations. With the onset of summer, the sickly season, town residents who could afford it removed to the sandy regions of the pine barrens. Likewise, the rich planters of the fertile lowlands along the rivers and coast found it healthier to migrate with their families to temporary summer abodes or resorts amid the pines, leaving plantation operations in charge of overseers. In turn, with the advent of the cool weather in the fall, these groups would then venture back to their permanent homes. In Georgia such places were referred to as the sand hills, the desert, or the piney woods.

By experience the seasonal migrants had learned that the pine barren areas were more salubrious than the lowcountry, but they did not understand why. They speculated much on the reasons for the difference and advanced several theories to explain the superior healthfulness of the pines.

The chief reasons offered to explain the salubrity of the barrens rested upon a belief in the purity and elasticity of the air among the pines as contrasted with the atmosphere of the marshy and swampy sections surrounding the lowcountry homes. It was commonly held, for instance, that the low areas produced dangerous exhalations which bore miasmatic fevers. It was also thought that the heavier foliage of the hardwoods in the swampland sections held down these contagious vapors sufficiently long for them to afflict the people residing in the lowland communities. On the other hand, the same pernicious gases rising among the towering pines were able to dissipate their noxious effluvium without serious risks to dwellers in such areas. Others argued, however, that the healthfulness of the pines should be attributed to resinous particles from the pine needles, which purified the air of the pinelands by increasing the amount of oxygen in the atmosphere, thereby divesting it of any infectious material or virulence which it might bear for human beings. There were still others who insisted the very sterility of the soil in the barrens rendered it incapable of generating vapors which were uncongenial to the human body or noxious for respiration.

Such explanations as these disclose serious misapprehensions under which intelligent people used to labor. Today with our knowledge of the nature of contaminated water and understanding of the transmission of malaria and yellow fever by mosquitoes, the answers to the questions which puzzled those folk seem elemental. The simple explanation of the superiority of the barrens as far as mosquitoes were concerned lay in the fact that the sandy soils of the pinelands soaked up the rain and minimized the dangers of mosquito-breeding in stagnant waters.

Many of the spots of seasonal refuge, or "summering places" as they were known became famous, and a stay at one of them was considered a delightful social experience, comparable to a present seasonal sojourn at the seashore or in the mountains.

Certain sections of the sand-hill area along the Great Fall Line Belt where the Coastal Plain and Piedmont Plateau meet were particularly noted as healthy summering places. Especially was this true for the area north and west of Augusta, Georgia. Grovetown, sixteen miles from that place, was such a spot, and so were Bon Air and Bel Air which were nearer. Not far from Bel Air was

Sahara, a name which reminds one again of the use of the term desert in connection with the piney woods section. And, interestingly enough, the words Bon Air and Bel Air take on a different connotation from that which we would give them today when one recalls the old beliefs about contaminated atmosphere being the cause of the malarious and bilious season.

Walthourville in Georgia was another prominent summering place. It was used by rich planters from the area around Riceboro. Summerville, South Carolina, was likewise a notable refuge spot in the barrens for Charlestonians. Summertown, in Emanuel County, Georgia, was also a well-known resort for Georgia plantation and coastal families, and Salubrity, northwest of Tallahassee, was a similar asylum in Florida. There were still other but lesser-known places. They bore names like Pine Retreat, Pine Bowery, Pine Head, Pine Ridge, Pine Rest, etc. Today we should be prone to think of such appellations as merely the result of prosaic, backwoodsy placenaming, but terms such as these were once deliberately selected to carry appeal to would-be summer residents, just as nowadays resort names like Highlands and Little Switzerland are dangled before the public to attract those who would flee oppressive summer heat.

Summering places in the pines have long since lost their importance, although the Mississippi Gulf Coast may be cited as an exception. In that area, because of the absence of sand dunes, the pine barrens once came right down to the beach, and visitors sought refuge there to avoid the risk of fevers in New Orleans, Mobile, and other cities. Nowadays, however, the section is frequented by summer visitors who come to enjoy the gulf breezes, with never a thought of avoiding pestilential vapors back home.

Curiously enough, in the change of things over the years, some areas which were once prominent summering places for escaping lowcountry afflictions have evolved into well-known winter resorts. This change is particularly notable for points in the Carolinas and in the sections around Augusta.

The eventual development of the pine barren region came with a rush. It took the magic of the railroad, as in so many other instances of American economic growth, to unlock the potentials of the great pinelands. Such a vast reservoir of trees was a paradise for lumbermen and naval stores operators when they were assisted by means of cheap transportation in exploiting the forest. The railroad gradually threaded the region following the War Between the States, and by the 1890's, the section, especially in Georgia, Alabama, and Mississippi, began to boom. It became the chief naval stores-producing region of the world, and by the turn of the century was the leading lumbering belt of the nation. Towns sprang up overnight. In this rush the expression "pine barrens" was quickly forgotten. One Floridian said the name was all wrong anyway, because he thought the term was a corruption of "pine bearing," an expression which was more descriptive of the true potentialities of the area.

But exploitation of the pines was swift, ruthless, and wasteful. By 1910 there were beginning to be ghost communities here and there when sawmills closed down and moved their activities elsewhere, leaving thousands of acres of cutover lands in the recent scene of their operations. It was out of this exigency, however, that the region began to develop the prosperous agriculture for which it is noted today. The soil, which had for so long been considered poor and mean, proved remarkably productive in many localities when farmed with the aid of mixed fertilizers. The land was generally level and easily worked and the climate was favorable to a variety of crops. In these developments, however, there was relatively little effort to raise cotton, because, with the exception of the famous sea-island variety along the coastal fringes of Georgia and Florida, the staple had never thrived in the areas of the pines. Rather the people turned to melons, cane for making syrup, vegetables, fruits, nuts, tobacco, peanuts, and eventually a variety of new products which ranged from cut flowers to tung nuts.

The livestock industry also went through a regeneration, with scrubby piney woods horned cattle giving way to better stock. At the same time improved types of hogs were substituted for the once ubiquitous razorbacks and pine rooters.

In the meantime, however, the pines were coming back. Fortunately for the region, the trees reproduce easily and grow fast if given an opportunity. With this great advantage the pinelands were able to retain a place as an important lumber and turpentine-producing section. In the last two decades [i.e., circa 1930s-1940s] a big new industry, the pulp and paper business, has settled in the area to offer further outlets for the forest resources of the region in the form of pulpwood.

Thus we find the section which was formerly known as the great barrens. Today it is a prosperous region sprinkled with thriving communities and pretty towns. Few people living there nowadays have heard the name and would be reluctant to believe that it was ever applied to their locality. Here and there one may yet encounter infertile spots, and a few stretches of the country are still monotonous to ride through, but one no longer thinks of the pinelands as either a desert or barren.

—Originally published in the *Emory University Quarterly*, March 1949

Notes by Mr. Goff

1. Hall's reaction in this case is interesting, and is analogous to that of present-day people who view America's Great Plains or the desert sections of the western United States for the first time. They too find themselves fascinated by such scenery, and will often stare for hours at the landscape from train windows not knowing exactly the cause.

2. It is interesting that a century later, the Americans themselves were to regard another variety of trees—the huge sequoias of California—as the *premiers enfants* of America.

3. On a visit to the South during his second trip to America, Lyell, who was a keen observer, took the occasion while waiting during a change from a stagecoach to train at Chehaw, Macon County, Alabama, to measure the stumps of some newly felled virgin pines. One stump was 2 feet 5 inches in diameter 3 feet from the ground. On it he counted 120 rings of annual growth. A second stump with 260 rings was only two inches greater in diameter. A third with 180 rings was 2 feet across, and the stump of a fourth fallen giant measured 4 feet through and showed 320 growth rings. The height of the trees varied from 0 to 120 feet. He added the comment that no such trees would be seen by posterity after the clearing of the country, except where they happened to be preserved for ornamental purposes.

Suomi

John H. Goff

from *Placenames of Georgia*

Suomi is a small community located a mile below Chauncey on US 23 in Dodge County. At a glance the word appears to be Indian, but actually it is the native and official name of the country which most of the world calls Finland. Except perhaps for philatelists who note the word Suomi on Finnish postage stamps, few people are familiar with the designation since gazetteers, geographies, and dictionaries usually refer to Suomi as Finland. The latter name, so the Finns say, was applied to them by the Swedes.

The Dodge County Suomi is locally pronounced "*Sue oh' mee,*" and interestingly enough this form is virtually identical with the pronunciation used in Finland. Some American dictionaries depict the sound as "Swo' mee," but when Finns say the word one hears a "*sue*" or "*soo*" and not a "*swo*" sound as found in English terms swollen or sworn.

Suomi and Finland mean the same thing because both expressions signify fen and refer to low, moist ground or swampy land. These descriptive terms could well apply to parts of Finland but not to the area about our Dodge County Suomi. One must, therefore, look elsewhere for a reason to explain why the name was applied here. The people of the community do not recall how the place received the name, but they generally agree it was first used in connection with a siding or station on the present Southern Railway line that runs nearby. When this road was originally constructed in post-Civil War years it was built to tap the great timber reserves between the Oconee and Ocmulgee (rivers.) Large sawmills sprang up in the section, and since Finns are noted lumbermen, it seems likely some of them were brought here to work in these mills or to cut timber. These possible workers may well have named Suomi in honor of their former homeland.

—*Originally published in the Georgia Mineral Newsletter, #18, 1964*

Notes by Editor

1. The community was created as the headquarters for the Georgia Land and Lumber Company (often referred to as the Dodge Company). Initially it was named Normandale, in honor of Norman Dodge, son of William E. Dodge. The Dodges were the controversial owners of large tracts of timber resources in the area. Suomi (as Normandale) was the site of the murder, on October 7, 1890, of Captain John Forsyth, Superintendent of the Dodge Company. Forsyth was allegedly the victim of a conspiracy of land "squatters" who were at odds with the Dodges over the rights to their land, from about 1870 through 1900. For a short time it was also named Missler (alternately spelled Misler).

2. Mr. Goff is likely correct in his reference to Finnish workers. After the Dodge Company ceased operations, another company imported large numbers of Finnish workers and their families to the area to work the timber. Annie (Evans) Chavous (b. 1894), a

child in 1900, recalls the Finns, remembering vividly an image of them walking down the road wearing knee-high boots. She also recalled them attending school with her, remarking that they were grown men, and speculating that they were learning English. Another story notes that a large number of the Finns—men, women and children—died as a result of consuming poisonous mushrooms.

7.

The Forsyth House in Suomi

Welda Davis Whigham

&

My Portrait of the Forsyth House

Dorothy Hargrove Stoeger

The Forsyth House in Suomi (Normandale)
Painting by Dorothy Hargrove Stoeger

"Four Residences Destroyed by Fire"

"The residence near Chauncey, occupied by Mr. Mathias Burch and family was destroyed by fire on December 27 [1933]. Most of the furnishings were saved. The fire caught on the roof from burning soot. The building was owned by a loan company, and it is not known whether or not it was insured. Mr. Burch carried no insurance. He and his family have moved to Atlanta.

The burned building was the one in which Capt. John C. Forsyth was killed about 45 years ago for whose murder Col. L. A. Hall and a number of others were sentenced to the penitentiary for life."

—Excerpted from the Eastman *Times-Journal*, January 4, 1934

The Forsyth House in Suomi

Welda Davis Whigham (1995)

More than a century ago, on the evening of October 7, 1890, Captain John Forsyth was murdered in the parlor of his home in Normandale (now Suomi), Georgia. Captain Forsyth was the Superintendent for the Georgia Land and Lumber Company. The company owned huge tracts of timber land throughout the area now comprising Dodge, Montgomery and Telfair counties. In 1994, a state historical marker was placed near the former site of the Forsyth House commemorating the murder and its tragic circumstances.

John Forsyth's murder resulted from a conspiracy of disgruntled landowners (referred to as squatters by the timber company) who felt they had been forced off their land by the Dodge Company. Litigation between the landowners and the Dodge Company dragged through the courts for more than half a century. Forsyth's murder trial resulted in convictions for several people—"conspirators"—including attorney Luther Hall, a prominent opponent of the Dodge Company. Details of the controversy can be found in Mrs. Wilton Cobb's *History of Dodge County*, as well as in the novel *Lightwood* by Brainard Cheney, a native of Lumber City, Georgia. Additional resources include the novel *Beloved Invader* by Eugenia Price and assorted pamphlets published contemporaneously with the events.

Captain Forsyth is buried at Christ Church on St. Simons Island, Georgia, a church pastored by William E. Dodge's grandson, Anson G. P. Dodge, Jr..

The historical marker we are discussing resides in front of a large, beautifully restored home owned by members of the Tommy Bland family. A common misconception holds that the current house is the scene of the murder. This is incorrect. There existed a house approximately 50 yards north of the current dwelling, which is the home in which Captain Forsyth resided and where he met his end. This article addresses that misconception.

Many citizens still living [in 1995] remember the Forsyth House, including me. I was born in the room where Captain Forsyth was murdered. During the early 1900's, my grandparents, Hattie Clark and John I. Hargrove, owned the house. Our family always referred to it as the Forsyth House. My grandmother, Hattie, was born in 1882. She grew up in Chauncey and admired the impressive, two-story house. She knew of the events surrounding the Forsyth murder case as did all of the citizens of Chauncey and Normandale (later named Suomi), events that occurred in her lifetime. Later, she used an inheritance to purchase the house for her family.

Five of the eight Hargrove children were born in the house. In addition, my brother and I were also born there. All of these births occurred in the parlor, the room where Forsyth was murdered—"assassinated" was the term used at the time. My family and the other locals constantly discussed the murder and its many mysteries. One topic always drawing attention in our family was the bloodstained parlor floor. These stains proved impossible to remove—the floor being heart pine and untreated—which required my grandmother to cover the floor with a large carpet. Two of those born in the room are still living, my aunt, Dorothy Stoeger of Kansas City, Missouri, and myself. (My aunt Dorothy and I are only two years apart in age.) My late brother, Charles Otis Davis, Jr., was born there as well, in 1924. Soon after my brother's birth, my parents moved to Tampa, Florida, where I grew up and attended school.

Every summer, my family traveled to Georgia to visit with my grandparents at the Forsyth House. I remember it as a very large two story building with a porch that wrapped all of the way around the house. Inside were high ceilings, some of which were embossed with gold leaf crown molding. A large set of mahogany sliding doors, reaching nearly to the ceiling, divided the dining room and the parlor. Even as a young child I was impressed by the moldings and especially by the sliding doors, which Dorothy and I played with endlessly.

During the Depression, my grandparents lost the Forsyth House. They moved, with their youngest child, Dorothy, to Tampa, Florida. On December 27, 1933, the house burned. At the time it was occupied by Mathias Burch and his family, who rented the property. Witnesses to the fire remember the conflagration produced large clouds of smoke billowing into the sky, due to the burning of the heart pine timber used to construct the house. To this day, many of the old time residents feel there is a ghostly or haunted aura associated with the location.

Because of the recent interest in the house, and the placing of the historical marker, many people have wondered if a photograph of the house exists. If one does, I have never seen it. However, my aunt, Dorothy Stoeger, has painted a portrait of the house from memory. I remember the house vividly and I think that her painting is a remarkably accurate rendition of the house as it was. I have provided a photograph of the painting for this article for others to see. All that remains of the property from those distant days is a grove of pecan trees planted by a local nursery for my grandfather, John Hargrove. During the 1940's until about 1960, Weeks Motor Court stood there. Its cinder block buildings no longer exist. A modular home now rests on the spot where the house of murder once stood.

My family has been involved with the Forsyth House history for more than a century. We would like people to know what the vanished house looked like. I am especially grateful to my aunt Dorothy for her kindness in providing the painting and for her artistic skills in creating it. Although it was long ago that I last visited the Forsyth House, I still retain memories of those times with warmth and fondness.

My Portrait of the Forsyth House
Dorothy Hargrove Stoeger

During our correspondence over a span of many years, the memories that my sister Wylena and I seemed to cherish the most were the glory days when our parents were prosperous and we were enjoying comfortable lives in the Forsyth house in Suomi. Our life in that grand old residence came to an abrupt halt in my eighth year when the bank foreclosed on our home. My sister was twenty-four years older than me. Her recollections of those years circa 1905 to 1929, during which our family owned it, were more extensive than mine. However, I remembered details relating to architecture, the floor plan, interior features and the grounds. In our letters we often regretted that no photographs survived after the upheaval in our household that resulted from the Great Depression.

Several attempts were made by artist friends to capture a good likeness of the Forsyth house but none were considered accurate by our mother, Hattie Clark Hargrove. I had no formal training as an artist but I had painted a number of watercolors and oils, including one of Parkerson Church, which I had done for her. So, as a tribute to my sister, I committed myself to rendering a likeness of our old home that would be as close as possible to our shared memories and to complete it for her eightieth birthday. I chose to duplicate the appearance of the house as it appeared when it was built by the company for John C Forsyth, the Superintendent for the Dodge Company. Additionally, a second, similar but smaller executive home was built next door. Several additional houses were built across the railroad in Suomi, then called Normandale. Essentially, all of the buildings were "company houses" that varied in size and architecture but were identical in color and trim.

I disclosed to my sister that I was working on a painting but was vague about my inspiration for doing it. She was enthusiastic and wrote a series of detailed letters and enclosed our mother's sketches along with her own. She was emphatic about my finishing it for myself. I completed the painting, had it framed and shipped it to her in time for her eightieth birthday on April 17, 1978. Her praise and gratitude were profuse and she was satisfied that my portrayal of our beloved home was exactly as she remembered it. During her last years she left explicit instructions for her family to return the painting along with the one of Parkerson Church to me after her death. They are hanging on my family room wall where they remind me of my dear sister every day.

8.

The Land Pirates

Marion Erwin

William E. Dodge Statue, New York City. Originally located in Herald Square, moved to Bryant Park, behind New York Public Library.

William Pitt Eastman (Painted by his granddaughter, Caro Ogden)

THE

LAND PIRATES

A NARRATIVE

——— OF ———

THE GREAT CONSPIRACY AND MURDER CASE
RECENTLY

TERMINATED IN THE FEDERAL COURT

——AT——

MACON, GEORGIA

By MARION ERWIN

(1891)

The Land Pirates

Marion Erwin

Preface

The history of a great crime, premeditated and accomplished by concerted action, the dark secrets of the conspirators, the details of the plot, the manner of its execution, the means taken to prevent discovery, the clues by which the officers of the law follow step by step the faint trail, until the converging lines of evidence lead to a full discovery, the bringing of the criminals to justice, and the vindication of the law, have ever excited the liveliest interest in the public mind. On contemplating the aberration from the normal intellect, which must exist in the perpetrators of a long meditated murder, the very enormity of the crime, upon first blush, makes the law-abiding citizen waiver in fixing the guilt upon any intelligent human being. By following step by step, however, the road traveled in the downward career, we comprehend the evolution of the criminal instinct in the human heart, and understand the power for evil, which exists in misdirected ambition, when supplemented by motives of revenge and hate springing into existence against those who seemingly stand in the way of its accomplishment.

The conspiracy and murder case just terminated in the United State Circuit Court, at Macon, Georgia, while full of those dramatic incidents which naturally catch the first attention of the public, moreover presents to the student who considers the development of crime from a scientific standpoint, one of the most interesting studies.

For the purpose of preserving in convenient form a true account of the great case, to the successful termination of which I had the honor, in part at least, as United State District Attorney, to contribute, but more particularly to have in convenient form a ready answer to the numerous inquiries I have received from all parts of the United States relative to the facts and law of this case, I have prepared and now present to the public in narrative form, a brief sketch of the events which culminated in the assassination of Captain John C. Forsyth, and the consignment of his murderers to the penitentiary of life.

As being of especial interest to the profession and those general readers who take an interest in the details of a criminal trial, and in the great principles of law that stand for the protection of the rights of the citizen, I have appealed the ruling of the Court on the question of jurisdiction, and the charge to the jury.

MARION ERWIN, Macon, Georgia, February 7, 1891

ORIGIN OF THE CASE

History of the Land Troubles in Georgia

To better understand the causes which have led up to the bloody drama, which has been so graphically described by the witnesses who have testified upon the stand, in the great conspiracy and murder trail which has just been brought to a close in the United States Circuit Court, at Macon, Georgia, and which has resulted in a life sentence to the Columbus, Ohio, penitentiary for each of three defendants, and terms of imprisonment of six and ten years respectively for two other conspirators, it will be necessary to refer briefly to events which transpired some fifty-eight years ago.

On the eighteenth day of October, 1833, a number of capitalists of Portland, Maine, formed a co-partnership association for the purchase of extensive landed interests in Georgia, a section of the State then but sparsely settled, and possessing a wealth of the finest pine forests in the world. They sent out three agents, Abram Colby, Stephen Chase, and Samuel E. Crocker, who visited Georgia in the interest of the Company, and purchased large tracts of land in originally Wilkinson County, Georgia, but now being in the counties of Dodge, Telfair, Laurens, and Montgomery, since created. The purchase amounted to some three hundred thousand acres of land, which covered a very large part of the counties above named. Colby, Chase, and Crocker took the deeds to these lands in their own names, but shortly afterwards, having obtained a charter for their Company from the Georgia

Legislature, incorporating them as a land and timber company under the name of the "Georgia Lumber Company," they executed a deed from themselves to the Company for which they had noted as agents in making the purchase, and with whose funds the purchase was made. This deed was claimed by adversaries of the title to be defectively executed from a strictly legal standpoint, but it appears that the defect was not discovered, or at least no serious importance was attached to it, until some fifty years afterward, when the original actors in the old Georgia Lumber Company had long since been dead.

The originators of the Georgia Lumber Company did not long enjoy their landed possessions and their dreams of wealth from the products of their rich timber lands in Georgia. The Company became indebted to the Western Bank of New York, at Rochester, and the lands of the Company, which were held as security by the bank, were passed by transfer and deed to the State of Indiana. The lands were afterwards sold by Act of Legislature of Indiana, and by successive links in a long chain of title, passed finally in 1877 into the ownership of Mr. George E. Dodge, of New York.

In the meantime, the late civil war and the disorders incident to it had, for many years, made it impracticable for the true owners of the land to do more than pay taxes on it, and they were either powerless to interpose, or in a large measure ignorant of the inroads which had been made upon their possessions by a set of land squatters who had penetrated to every corner of the pine forests of South Georgia, and had established their homes with little regard to the legal rights of others. Under the laws of Georgia, mere possession by residence, or fencing or cultivation of a lot of land for twenty years, under claim of ownership, will give the squatter the prescriptive title; and a mere color of title, a deed from a man who has no title at all, with possession under it for seven years, will give, in its practical operation, a prescriptive title superior to that of the true owner of the legal title, unless the true owner, when he brings his suit against the squatter, can show that the latter actually knew that the person from whom he bought had no title or other fraud—facts which it is seldom practicable to prove.

In the meantime a railroad line had been built connecting the railroad system of upper Georgia with the ports of Brunswick and

Savannah, Georgia, and tapping the rich timber and turpentine region of Dodge, Telfair, and Montgomery Counties, affording means of transportation and outlets to these ports for an immense export of lumber and naval stores to Europe and South America, besides opening up an extensive business with the interior in the opposite directions. Mr. Dodge and his predecessors in title had after the war proceeded to work the turpentine and lumber interests of their lands on an extensive scale. Saw mills of immense capacity were erected, railroads running out twenty or thirty miles into the pine forests were built and maintained merely for the purpose of transporting timber to the mill. Besides the large influx of population, due to the development of the country, and made necessary by the extensive timber and turpentine business, quite a large portion of the native population of these counties found lucrative employment in cutting and supplying timber under contracts with Mr. Dodge or his agent. The immense development of the naval store business in Georgia, the growing demand for Georgia yellow pine timber, the development of the export trade from Brunswick and Savannah to South America, all conduced to the rapid advance of the value of timberlands in Georgia, and Mr. Dodge now found himself the owner of the legal title to four hundred and sixty-eight square miles of land, yielding a rich income and growing in importance and value.

The Land Grabbers

Mr. Dodge's right of ownership was not, however, left undisputed. He soon found it policy in those cases, which fortunately for him were not numerous, where a squatter had been in possession of a lot of his land for twenty years, and where the possession met the legal requirements of prescriptive title, to make no contention for it; but the development of the country had caused a more recent influx of a horde of squatters from adjoining counties, who scattered themselves over his lands and began to look for some means, fair or foul, by which they could keep their unlawful holdings.

Gathering courage from numbers, a class of land sharpers began to ply a lucrative trade with the squatters, providing deeds to a particular lot desired by a squatter, which were antedated and probated by some Notary Public in the scheme, to get seven years color of title; they were forged outright and, as was developed in the trial of the conspiracy case, there were men, like Renew and Williams, whose business it was to furnish for a consideration an entire chain of forged deeds to a lot desired.

Whenever Mr. Dodge's agents found a squatter of this class in possession of a lot of his land, he would have to bring an ejectment suit against the squatter in the local county with the chances of losing the case, by means of antedated deed operating as color of title, or a cleverly executed chain of forged deeds, or perhaps have the case worn out by mistrials, by reason of the fact that someone himself engaged in the land-grabbing business would get on the jury.

For many years past this land-grabbing fraternity seems to have looked to Luther A. Hall, a lawyer of Eastman, Georgia, as their chief counselor, promoter, and attorney. Hall, although he had in his childhood suffered the misfortune of having his face horribly burned, causing the loss of one eye and giving him an appearance painful to look upon, yet possessed considerable personal magnetism and a shrewdness and mental capacity so far beyond the class of petty land-grabbers through whom he operated, that he naturally maintained a commanding influence over them. He had accumulated the snug sum of twelve or fifteen thousand dollars by sharing the spoils with his clients for the successful defense of suits of the character mentioned.

Luther A. Hall's Great Land Scheme

Whatever may be said of his methods, it is possible that if Hall had been willing to follow the old maxim, "Let well enough alone," he would have continued in a small way to fatten at the expense of Mr. Dodge and other non-resident land owners, and would have gone on in what the world at least would have called a prosperous career. But in an evil hour for him his attention was called to the fact that Colby, Chase and Crocker, who purchased this immense body of land in 1833, had taken the titles in their own names, and that the deed from them to the old Georgia Lumber Company was to him apparently fatally defective in execution. It occurred to him that in law the legal title to these lands was still in the heirs at law of Colby, Chase and Crocker, and if he could acquire the right to such heirs, the whole of this vast domain would be his. It is probable that at this time visions of untold wealth rolled resplendent before his eyes; the talismanic lamp of Aladdin seemed to be within his grasp; riches, realized power, gratified ambition, haunted his dreams, and in his waking hours spurred him on to the realization of his hopes.

The task before him was an herculean one, but his ingenious fertility of device soon placed his scheme in practical operation. He engaged with him in his undertaking two persons in sympathy with his purposes, Oliver H. Briggs and H.G. Sleeper, and under the firm name of Briggs, Hall, & Sleeper the undertaking was pushed forward. The heirs at law of the original agents, Colby, Chase and Crocker, scattered throughout the United States from Maine to California, and some even in Europe, were ferreted out, their supposed title placed in one man and power of attorney vested in Briggs, Hall & Sleeper to dispose of their vast domain in Georgia. The real estate office of Briggs, Hall & Sleeper was opened with *eclat* at Eastman, Georgia, flaming circulars were distributed, and the people were notified that this immense estate was thrown upon the market, and that persons could now obtain choice farms and homes at remarkably low prices. Purchasers, attracted by the easy terms offered, and caring little about the true ownership so long as they could get good color of title, began to flock to the office of Briggs, Hall & Sleeper, and they for a while did have a thriving business.

The Perpetual Injunction

In the meantime Mr. George E. Dodge was not standing idly by while his property was thus being summarily disposed of. Availing himself to the provisions of the Constitution and laws of the United States, which give jurisdiction to the Federal Courts of controversies between citizens of different States, Mr. Dodge filed a bill in equity in the Unites States Circuit Court, at Macon, Georgia, praying a decree upon the validity of his own title and asking a perpetual injunction against Briggs, Hall & Sleeper, the purchasers of title from them and the Colby, Chase and Crocker heirs. There were seventy-nine defendants to the bill. At the trial Mr. Dodge produced the original contract of association made in 1833, of the members of the old Georgia Lumber Company, the minute book showing the appointment of Colby, Chase and Crocker as their agents to visit Georgia and make the purchase, and a certified transcript of a suit from one of the Superior Courts of the State of Maine, from which it appeared that after the purchase of the lands in Georgia a suit was brought between the members of the association for a settlement, and Colby, Chase and Crocker formally acknowledged that they had purchased the lands for the Company with the Company's money, and a formal settlement between the parties was decreed by that Court more than fifty years ago. The proof made before Judge Emory Speer as Chancellor was overwhelming, and a final decree was rendered by the United States Circuit Court on April 5th, 1886, declaring the title of Mr. Dodge good and valid and forever enjoining Luther A. Hall, his associates and those claiming under him from interfering in any manner with the said lands.

Sailing on a New Track

The failure of this Napoleonic scheme was the turning point in the career of Luther A. Hall. For some time after the granting of the injunction against him, little was heard of Hall, but after two or three years had elapsed, the fear of the Court seems to have receded in the perspective, or perhaps the fact that in the interim Mr. George E. Dodge had sold and transferred these lands to his brother, Norman W. Dodge, may have led to a brief on Hall's part that it was no longer in the power of the Federal Court to punish him for a violation of the decree.

At any rate, in the year 1889, seized with a fresh cupidity towards these lands, he seems to have entered upon a career more daring in its execution and with more reckless disregard of law than even his first ambitious venture. Failing to get possession of the title under which Mr. Dodge claimed, his next scheme was to attack the title which he had before tried to acquire, and, promulgating the document of communism, he advanced the idea that these lands still belonged to the State of Georgia, and championed the right of squatters to occupy them at their pleasure. His second onslaught was, however, promptly met by a petition for a rule filed against him by Mr. Norman W. Dodge in the United States Circuit Court, at Macon, in which he was charged with the inauguration and operation, in violation of the injunction granted against him, of the following scheme in the connection with the land squatters of Dodge, Telfair, Laurens and Montgomery Counties: Hall, it was charged, would furnish free to a squatter a complete but forged chain of title to any lot, or any number of lots he might desire, so long as the value did not exceed two thousand dollars ($2,000) to the squatter, that being the minimum limit of the jurisdiction of the Federal Court. The squatter would be told to erect some cheap shanty on the property and go into possession of the lots, the understanding being that if Mr. Dodge brought suit in the State Court to eject the squatter (which he was sure to do), Hall would defend the suit as attorney, taking half the land, if successful, as his fee. The following letters, the originals of which were put in evidence at the trial, were attached to the petition for the rule, as illustrative of the scheme.

Luther Hall's Letters

The Stuckey Letter

"Eastman, GA., August 24, 1889.
Mr. H.T. Stuckey:

Dear Sir - Enclosed find list of land in the Sixth District. Any of these lots that you can get in possession of I can hold against the world. These lands belong to the State of Georgia, and we are a part of the State. I do not think we should let Dodge have them. I will represent for half of what we make. Have nothing if I am unsuccessful. There are not many lots in this district, and if you wish to look after lots in other districts I will send numbers. Interest your friends in this, but be careful not to talk too much; we will be safer in this matter. As soon as you are in possession of a lot let me know to whom you wish deed made.

Obedient, L.A. Hall"

"Eastman, GA., September 5, 1889.
Mr. H.T. Stuckey:

Enclosed find list as requested; work these lots for all you can. Get into possession of all you can, though we will not put over two thousand dollars worth in one name.

Obedient, L. A. Hall"

The Louis Knight Letters

"Eastman, GA., November 22, 1889.

Mr. Louis Knight:

Dear Sir - Enclosed I send you copies of deeds as I wish. Get up the deeds just like these, except as to the age, and send them as early next week as you can, and I will make it all right with you. Write me day you will send them.
                              L.

P.S. - I will send more soon."

In the original letter to Knight was enclosed also a roll of un-
ruled, dingy white paper and on a small slip of paper were these
words:

> "Use this if you can, as soon as possible, and send
> to me. I have sent for some that is better.
>
> L.A. HALL"

The original of these letters, which fell into the hands of Captain John C. Forsyth, the resident agent of Mr. Dodge, were used
against Hall with overwhelming effect, in connection with the
other testimony, the hearing of which occupied the attention of
the Court on the rule for several days.

Hall was convicted of violating the injunction granted against
him, found guilty of contempt and sentenced to five months imprisonment in Chatham County jail, and was promptly placed
within its iron walls.

Hall in Jail

It would naturally be supposed that the events narrated would
have suggested to Hall the wisdom of abandoning the schemes in
which he had been engaged, but the mortification of his imprisonment and the crushing of his pride, seem rather to have wed-
ded him to the prosecution of endeavors in which he at the same
time hoped for profit, as well as revenge toward those who had
been instrumental in his downfall. He had scarcely been incarce-
rated before he commenced again his operations, by means of
correspondence with his friends on the outside. The original of
two of these letters were given in evidence on the conspiracy trial,
and read as follows:

"In Jail, Savannah, GA., March 24th 1890.

Messrs, Clark & Norman:

"Well, you know I am here a victim to a merciless prosecution for acting in behalf of the people. I have spent all the money which I had defending myself and am here penniless. I am getting on about as well and cheerfully as any man under the circumstances. I wish somebody would run Henry T. Stuckey out of that county. He lied about me and betrayed confidence. It is a question whether the Dodge crowd or the people will rule. They have commenced on me and now they will undertake to do as they please with the people. Encourage the people to stand up for their rights. Let me hear from you and oblige.

L. A. Hall"

"In Jail, Savannah, Ga., March 24th, 1890.

Mr. J.R. Freeman:

Dear Sir - As you are aware, the Court held me in contempt and sentenced me to five months in jail. Tell all the boys to not be scared at all. I will be out to help them after a while. * * * The Judge was willing to fine me, or change from imprisonment to fine, but Sexton and Forsyth would not consent. Wishing you well, I am your friend,

L.A. HALL"

The persistent efforts made by Hall while in jail to continue by correspondence to incite others to take and hold possession of the lands he had been enjoined from interfering with, led Mr. Dodge, through his agent, Captain John C. Forsyth, to present two other petitions for rules against Hall. They were not acted upon by the Court, however, because of the fact that Hall was still serving out the term of imprisonment for which he had been sentenced on the first rule.

On the 1st of September, 1890, Hall's term of imprisonment expired and he was released from custody.

Hall's Canvass for the Legislature

No sooner had Hall returned to his home at Eastman than he announced himself as a candidate for member of the Legislature from the County of Dodge at the ensuing election to be held on the 1st of October, 1890. He addressed his followers in every militia district in the county. The distinct issue presented was, that in his imprisonment by the United States Court he had suffered as a martyr in the cause of the people; that it was a fight between the Dodge Company and the people, and he appealed to them to elect him as a vindication of his course. In one of his public speeches he advised the squatters that whenever Mr. Dodge's agents went upon the lands decreed to be his by the Federal Court, but of which they held possession, to "meet them with shot guns and leave their carcasses for the buzzards to pick, or cram them down gopher holes." Shortly after Hall's release from jail, a countryman of the name of William Strum had purchased a fraudulent title to one of the Dodge lots, and being enjoined from interfering with the land, and disobeying the injunction, he was arrested and fined. James Brophy, one of Mr. Dodge's woodsmen, had assisted the officer in making the arrest. After Hall's release from jail, Strum narrated to Hall this occurrence, and remarked that Brophy had "acted very biggity." Strum afterward testified on the conspiracy case that Hall, in reply, said to him: "You people have your guns, the nights are dark—you can do your own work."

It may be observed here, that although there were a large number of people engaged in crooked land schemes in the counties referred to, that after all they formed but a small minority of the population. The great mass of the country people of these counties are plain, honest, and honorable, and make substantial and law-abiding citizens, and yet, a strong minority of evil disposed persons, when they are given for a time unchecked headway, can give a color of lawlessness to an entire community, county or State. The fact that the mass of the population of Dodge County are law-respecting people, could not be more fully demonstrated than by the fact that on the first day of October, 1890, the good people of the country turned out at the polls, and Luther A. Hall and his pleas of martyrdom were snowed under by an overwhelming majority.

Wright Lancaster

Among the young countrymen of the adjoining County of Telfair, Wright Lancaster, at the age of thirty, had attained considerable local prominence. His father, some years before the events we are about to relate, in a personal difficultly with Edward McRae, ex-Sheriff of Telfair County, had been slain by the latter in self-defense, a circumstance which it appears very much embittered Wright Lancaster and his brother John against McRae, and helped to intensify the ill feeling which they bore against the Dodge Company, in whose employment McRae was afterward engaged. The Lancasters had the general reputation of irascible and turbulent men, but previous to the events to be narrated, they were not supposed to be men likely to engage in a conspiracy to murder.

Wright Lancaster, although small of stature, and with features which but for the thin compressed lips and firm set of the jaw might well be described as of the delicacy of a woman, was endowed with iron nerves and strong mental power. A leader among the country people, he was elected Sheriff of his county, and was serving his first term at the time of Hall's release from jail. Ambitious to accumulate wealth, he had in the spring of 1890 erected and put in operation a saw mill in the lower part of Telfair County on a new railroad recently built through that section. Having no lands of any consequence of his own and little money, and nearly all the timber in reach being on the land which had been decreed to be the lands of Mr. Dodge by the United States Court, he was driven to make such bargains as he could with such squatters as were in possession of any of the Dodge lots under claim of right.

In August 1890, forming an acquaintance of Mr. J. L. Bohannon, of Pulaski County, Georgia, a saw mill man, who was looking for a suitable place to locate a mill, a partnership was formed between them, Bohannon putting in his personal services, some money and saw mill equipments. During Hall's canvass for the Legislature, Wright Lancaster accompanied him on his speechmaking tour, and was conspicuous among those who cheered when Hall made his tirades against the Dodge Company.

Lem Burch

Lem Burch, a farmer, resided about one mile from Lancaster's mill. Not content with a good farm which he possessed, Burch seems to have been seized, some two years before the events we are about to relate, with the general land-grabbing mania, which became epidemic, with the greatly enhanced value of timber lands consequent upon the new railroad and the general development of a country which had hitherto attracted but little attention from the outside world.

There were three lots of land containing two hundred and two and a half acres each, well located in his neighborhood, and containing a magnificent forest of pine timber, upon which he had long fixed a covetous gaze. There were men in his neighborhood in the business of making forged titles, why should he not own these lots? He acted upon the suggestion of his desires. To one of these lots he obtained a deed from Wright Lancaster for twenty-five dollars. This was witnessed before a Notary Public, and laid away as color of title. To two other lots he obtained complete but forged chains of title, running back to the original grantee from the State. These deeds were put in evidence at the trial, and their spurious character was completely demonstrated by the testimony of Mr. O. N. Dana, who for thirty-five years has been engaged in the printing business in the famous publishing house of J.W. Burke & Co. Several of these deeds which at first glance might, from discoloration, be taken for ancient documents, when held up, so that the light might strike through them, exhibited watermarks belonging to manufactures of only recent date, and from the wood-pulp texture of the paper and similar indications it was shown that they were executed long after the time indicated by the dates on the face of the papers. Burch himself stated on the witness stand that he had purchased one chain from Andrew Renew and the other from Lucius Williams, who he said were engaged in the business of furnishing titles to squatters as desired.

After the formation of the partnership between Lancaster and Bohannon in August, 1890, the latter learning that Burch claimed these heavily timbered lots, offered to purchase the timber on them, together with the timber on the three other lots on which Burch lived. The latter, however, asked six hundred dollars a lot for the timber. Bohannon thinking this too high, reported the matter to his partner, Wright Lancaster, who advised him to leave the matter for him to work out, that he knew how Burch had gotten title to the lots and could get them cheap. In the meantime, Mr. A.D. McCrimmen, one of Mr. Dodge's woodsmen, on the part of Mr. Dodge, informed Burch that he must surrender his claim to the three lots belonging to Mr. Dodge, and offered him eight hundred dollars cash for the timber on three other lots, to which it appeared Burch had title. Wright Lancaster, however, obtained from Burch a lease, securing the right to cut the timber on the entire six lots, giving in consideration his notes for one thousand dollars on five years' time.

That Lancaster knew the character of the title he was buying is apparent, also, from the fact that the lease, which was put in evidence at the trial, recited that Burch warranted the title only to the three lots upon which he lived, and not to the other three lots included in the lease.

About this time a man by the name of Bullard, who had gone into possession of two of the Dodge lots in the neighborhood of the Lancasters, by erecting a cabin so as to straddle the dividing line, becoming frightened abandoned his holding, and Wright Lancaster had his brother-in-law, James Moore, moved into the abandoned cabin to maintain possession and claim the timber. Wright Lancaster had by this time gotten himself so deeply involved in the land troubles that he seems to have come to the conclusion that something desperate had to be done to overthrow Mr. Dodge in the successful assertion of his rights, or he himself would be overwhelmed when his trespasses on the Dodge lots were brought to light. Thrown in intimate relations with Luther

A. Hall, practicing in the Court of which he was Sheriff, out of their common grievance, the desire for revenge, the hope that by striking terror into the hearts of Mr. Dodge and his agents the former would be forced to abandon the prosecution of the rules then pending in the Federal Court, desist from further proceedings to carry the decree in favor of his title into execution, and make terms and concessions at their dictation, sprang the most diabolical, cold-blooded conspiracy and murder that has ever blackened the annals of our State.

After Wright Lancaster had obtained the lease from Burch, he had the latter informed that Mr. Dodge's agent had learned of the lease and was going to have Burch put in jail on account of it. The latter, in great trepidation, went to Lancaster and begged for a revocation of the instrument. Lancaster, however, would not consent to it, but suggested to Burch that the way out of his trouble was to be found in the murder of Mr. Dodge's agent, Captain John C. Forsyth; that the consummation of that crime was easy of accomplishment; that he (Lancaster) knew the men who would do the deed. He would send them to Burch's house, and furnish a supply of mutton and otherwise contribute to their support while lying in wait to do the work; they would do the work for six hundred dollars; he would contribute, Hall would contribute, Burch must contribute, and others would do their part.

Charles Clemens

About eighteen miles from the Lancasters, in Telfair County, bordering on the line of Montgomery County, lived a young man some twenty-three or twenty-four years of age, of the name of Charles Clemens. He resided with his father, an old farmer, well to do and respected in the community. Charles and his brother William, however, grew up wild and dissipated, consorted with persons of bad repute, and finally entered upon a career of crime which was ended in disgrace and bowed in sorrow the silvery locks of their aged father. In the year 1888 Charles and William Clemens were indicted for the crime of robbery in the Superior Court of the adjoining County of Coffee. The evidence against them showed that the two young men had visited the home of an old man who was reputed to have hoarded up a considerable amount of money on his premises. One of the young men forcibly held the old man, while the other searched the home, and carried off as booty the sum of twelve hundred dollars in gold. They were tried, convicted and sentenced to six years' imprisonment in the Georgia penitentiary. Their case was appealed to the Supreme Court of Georgia. In the meantime the young men were enlarged on a *supersedeas* bond in the sum the twenty-five hundred dollars, Wright and John Lancaster being among the sureties. In February, 1890, the mandate of the Supreme Court affirming the judgment of the Court below was returned, and Clemens and his brother failing to respond, their bond was forfeited.

The principal witness for the State in the robbery case was a raftsman by the name of Shelton Powell, who pursued his occupation in rafting timber on the Ocmulgee and Altamaha. The principal witness for the defense in the same case was a Negro, if he may be called a Negro, known as Rich Lowry, alias Rich Herring. He belonged to a peculiar mixed race of people who have their principal habitat at a small town or village in North Carolina known as "Scuffletown," from the characteristic disorders of the population. They are said to be a mixed race of White, Indian and Negro blood, and are usually designated as "Scuffletonians." With the decline of the naval store or turpentine business in North Carolina, many of these people drifted into the pine regions of South Georgia, and among them was Rich Lowry, or Rich Herring, as he was more frequently called in Georgia. While Rich's mother was a mulatto, he claimed to be, on his father's side, a nephew of the notorious North Carolina outlaw, Henry Berry Lowry. It is probable that Clemens, through association with Rich, took his first lessons in crimes of blood.

The bond of the two Clemens had been forfeited. It was the duty of Wright Lancaster as bondsman as well as Sheriff of his county to return them to the Court. Arrest and the penitentiary stared them in the face. What could they do to avenge the disgrace which had fallen upon them? How could they escape from the clutches of the law? Was the first step revenge? Who knows?

Shelton Powell, the witness upon whose testimony they had been convicted, was one day peacefully plying his avocation on the river. Slowly his raft, of timbers banded together, was being swept down the Ocmulgee by the onward flow of the waters toward the ocean. Slowly the raftsman treads from side to side, while, bending to the pole that serves as a helm, he guides his raft on the winding current and meanderings of the river. Suddenly a puff of smoke is seen to issue from a cane thicket on the shore, the sharp crack of a rifle is heard, and Sheldon Powell, the raftsman, shot through the back, falls upon his raft, not dead, but a hopeless paralytic for life! Who shot him? It remains a mystery to the State authorities. I was not investigating that, and I, too, must say it is a mystery. But observation as a prosecuting officer leads me to the conclusion that controlling motives furnish clues, which, if followed up, lead almost certainly to the detection of the perpetrator of the crime.

Powell, living upon the charity of neighbors, paralyzed and bed-ridden for life, was in his affliction visited by Charles Clemens. What form of inducement was used we know not, but Clemens in his confession says he promised Powell one hundred dollars if he would give him an affidavit retracting the testimony delivered against him in Court, that he might use it with the Governor in obtaining a pardon. But the money to buy this retraction, to purchase his liberty, to rend the shackles of the law which bound him to a felon's fate, where was it to come from?

The Murderers Lying in Wait

About the middle of September, 1890, Charles Clemens and the Scuffletonian Lowry made their appearance at Burch's house. They had spent the night before with John Lancaster, and he had brought Clemens over in the buggy with him until within a short distance of Burch's, where Clemens got out, and, joining Lowry who had taken a short cut through the woods, the two last mentioned slipped around the back way, while John Lancaster made his appearance at the house and notified Burch of the arrival of his guests.

On this eventful morning the details of the cold-blooded murder of Captain Forsyth were planned, and Clemens and Lowry took up their abode with Burch to carry out the work to which they were assigned. Clemens and Lowry were to be paid three hundred dollars apiece for "doing the work."

The subscribers to the fund were:

Wright Lancaster	$200.00
Luther A. Hall	200.00
Lem Burch	100.00 if he could
Louis Knight	100.00

Louis Knight had just previous to this been ejected at the suit of Mr. Dodge from a lot of land which he held in possession, and had become greatly incensed at Captain Forsyth, who prosecuted the suit as Mr. Dodge's agent. It is probable that it was largely through motives of revenge that he promised to contribute toward carrying out the purpose of the other conspirators.

Burch's Family

In addition to his wife and some younger children, Burch's family consisted of a son, Wyly, sixteen years old, and a daughter, Miss Sabie, about eighteen years of age. Among the regular visitors at Burch's house was Henry Lancaster, a young man of twenty-three or four years of age, and a cousin of Wright Lancaster. He had the reputation of being a wild, reckless and dissipated young man, but for some time had been employed as woodsman in connection with his cousin's mill. Of prepossessing appearance, at least in the eyes of Miss Sabie, who probably knew nothing of his evil nature, it is said that he soon found a tender lodgement in her heart. Whatever may have been the understanding between Burch and Henry Lancaster in regard to family matters, the evidence developed in the conspiracy trial showed that Henry was at the time a constant visitor at Burch's house, and entered fully into the murderous purpose of the conspirators, and that it was from him, after the murder was committed, that the assassins received the money, contributed by the other conspirators, to satisfy their claims.

McCrimmen

Among the employees of the Dodge Company, none possessed in a greater degree the confidence of Captain Forsyth, Mr. Dodge's principal agent, than their woodsman, Mr. A.D. McCrimmen. Still a bachelor at the age of forty-five, a genial unsuspecting countryman, his rotund form and bulky weight which tipped the balance at three hundred and twenty-five pounds, did not prevent him, when the labor of the day for the woodsman was over, to seek the inviting home of farmer Burch, where just at this time roasted lamb and savory mutton-chops seemed to be plentiful. But there are those who hint, even to this day, that the attraction of McCrimmen to farmer Burch's home is best accounted for by reasons of a sentimental character with which he had become inspired in the contemplation of the farmer's daughter. However that may be, certain it is that in conversations with the unsuspecting McCrimmen, who was totally ignorant of their terrible purpose, the conspirators easily posted themselves from time to time of the movements of their intended victim, Captain Forsyth, and the other agents of Mr. Dodge. During the visits of McCrimmen to Burch's house Clements and Lowry concealed themselves in the barn or sought seclusion in the neighboring woods until his departure.

Captain Forsyth

Captain John C. Forsyth, who had for many years been the chief agent of the Dodge Company in Georgia, had so managed the business of his principals, that in spite of the bitterness engendered by the land troubles, and the difficulties incident to his occupation, he was personally held in the highest regard by all classes of the people in the counties where his duties called him, and by his friends he was beloved.

Outside of expressions of animosity made by Louis Knight after he had lost a suit a few weeks before, and Hall's statement made shortly after the institution of the second rule against him in the federal court, that Forsyth, as agent for Mr. Dodge, was persecuting him in the federal court and unless he desisted he would be killed, the evidence on the conspiracy trial showed that even the men who planned and consummated his murder, uniformly expressed their regard for him as a man, and only resolved upon his death as a necessary means to the end to be accomplished, the striking down of the power of Mr. Dodge, which rested upon the enforcement of the decree of the federal court.

Forsyth, with his wife and daughter, a lovely young girl of sixteen summers, resided in a charming home at Normandale, the terminus of the company's railroad, and where their business headquarters in Georgia were established. Normandale, a beautiful little village where enormous lumber mills were established, and which took its name from Mr. Norman W. Dodge, is on the East Tennessee, Virginia and Georgia Railroad. Just six miles southwest of it, across the country, was the home of Lem Burch, where the assassins were lying in wait.

Progress of the Plot

About a week after the arrival of the assassins at Burch's house, Wright Lancaster spent the night there and slept in the same room with Clemens. What transpired between them that night we may never know, but after that visit the murderous plot was rapidly pushed to its tragic end.

It was necessary that Clemens and Lowry, who were not acquainted with Forsyth, should be able to identify him, else the plot might miscarry. The election for member of the Legislature was to take place on the first of October. They had learned from McCrimmen that Captain Forsyth would be at Chauncey on that day. Burch loaded up a wagon with a supply of eggs, butter and country produce, and in company with Lowry set out for Chauncey. Before reaching there the Scuffletonian separated from him and they went into town apparently as strangers to each other. Burch found Forsyth and going up to him made some remarks in the nature of pleasantry and touched him upon the arm. Lowry, who was standing near, understood the signal, the victim was known, and the object of their visit was then accomplished.

The Murder

On the evening of October 7, 1890, about 4 o'clock, Clemens and Lowry set out on their murderous mission to Normandale. Clemens was armed with a Winchester rifle, Lowry carried a double-barrel, breech-loading shot-gun, carefully charged with buck shot. A cold, drizzling rain had set in, and by the time they had neared Normandale the shades of night had fallen upon the landscape, and save as a cheering beam of light streamed out from the open windows of the cottages which formed the little village, there was nothing to relieve the darkness, which was rendered more intense by the lowering clouds, from which the rain would fall in pattering drops. Arriving near the outskirts of the village Clemens took shelter in an abandoned shanty, where he awaited the progress of events, and prepared himself to make good the escape of Lowry in case of pursuit. Lowry hastened on to Captain Forsyth's house, where, climbing over the piazza, he peered into the library window, but there was no one within.

Captain Forsyth, in his dining-room, was seated at the supper table, around which were gathered the members of his family. After telling his wife that court matters would require that he leave for Macon on the early morning train, he arose from the table and sought the comforts of his library. Taking up his paper, lighting a cigar, he seated himself in his easy chair with his back toward the piazza window. Little did he think that he had spoken for the last time with those he loved, that for the last time in this world for him the curtains of the night had shut off the setting sun. The sash being down and the shutter open, at that very instant with cat-like tread, the assassin was stealing toward the easement; the next instant with leering gaze the Scuffletonian glared through the open window at his victim, the snake-like eyes of the savage glanced along the gleaming barrels of his breech-loader, his finger touched the trigger, a load report, a crash of glass, the murder is done and the murderer is gone.

"Tell mamma to come." They were the last words that fell from the lips of the dying man. Shot through the back of the head the murderous charge of buckshot had penetrated the brain and done its deadly work. When, horrified by the loud report, a moment later the agonized wife reached his side, she found the dying man speechless and reclining as if asleep in his chair. One look of recognition, the pressure of the hand he loved so well, and he fell back unconscious. In a few short hours, like the expiring flicker of a candle, the light of his life went out.

Leaving her heart-broken mother to care for her dying father, the heroic presence of mind that would have reflected credit upon a woman, the echo of the fatal shot had scarcely died away before Miss Nellie Forsyth, braving alone the rain and darkness and the certain proximity of the murderous assassins, sped to the nearest physician for assistance, but alas! her father was beyond the reach of help. The neighbors were aroused and every effort was made by them to discover the perpetrator of the crime. The track of the assassin was plainly to be seen, where springing from the veranda into the soft earth of the flowerbeds, he had made his way out of the garden. Bloodhounds were placed upon the trail, but just beyond the outskirts of the village they seemed nonplussed, and the pursuit had to be temporarily abandoned. Having taken off their shoes, Clemens and Lowry had at this point saturated their feet with turpentine, anticipating that if they were pursued by hounds the dogs would be thrown off the scent. With the light of the next day a party of young men took up the trail of the murderers. The ground, softened by the rain, was in a condition to take a well defined impression of each footstep. Just beyond the outskirts of the village the first trail was joined by a second trail leading from the abandoned shanty. The trail of the two men was then followed down the railroad and across the country about five miles to within about one mile of Burch's house, where the posse for some reason abandoned the pursuit.

Captain Forsyth possessed many warm friends in Macon and in other parts of Georgia, and when the news of his mysterious and tragic death was dashed over the wires, it created the most profound sensation. The remains of Forsyth were interred on Saint Simon's Island by the sea. There beneath the spreading live oaks and clinging moss beside the "Marshes of Glynn," which have been immortalized by the sweet verses of Sidney Lanier, sleeps the victim of one of the foulest and most cruel murders that has ever blackened the history of our State.

While from the first announcement of the mysterious murder the dark suspicion that Luther A. Hall was the instigator of the crime seems to have taken possession of the public mind from the strong motives known to exist with him, yet there seemed to be no proof at hand of his complicity, and for a time it appeared that the murder of Forsyth would remain forever an unsolved mystery.

Reaping the Fruits of Their Crime

The successful accomplishment of their first great undertaking without discovery seems to have emboldened Hall to take advantage at once of the consternation created among the agents of Mr. Dodge, by causing a panic among men who knew not but that they were marked out as the next victims for slaughter. Hall publicly announced that he "had the Dodges on the hip now." A few days after the murder the following conversation took place between Hall and two countrymen, in the hearing of Judge Roberts of the State Superior Court. One of them remarked that: "Dodge had better send out some more of his damned agents." The other suggested that "they had a few more shotguns in the county" and Hall replied: "Yes, and he had best send steel houses for them to live in."

Six days after the murder he called separately upon each of two of the local attorneys who had been representing Mr. Dodge at Eastman, and referring to the rules pending against him in the United State Court, in a peremptory manner demanded to know if Mr. Dodge intended *now* to persist in the prosecution of the rules, and stated his desire for their immediate withdrawal. He then addressed the following letter to Messrs, Hill & Harris, the general counsel of Mr. Dodge, having charge of the suits in the Federal Court, the words in italics being underscored by Hall:

> "Eastman, Ga. October 13, 1890
> Messrs, Hill & Harris, Macon, Ga.:
>
> I learned from Judge Speer's remarks that there are two proceedings filed against me in U.S. Court for contempt of Court. Please let *me* know *at once* if these are to be insisted upon, and if not I wish them withdrawn *at once. My friends* are anxious to know

if Mr. Dodge proposes to keep up his war upon me, as Mr. Hilton informed my daughters that it has 'just commenced.'

A reply by return mail will greatly oblige me.

Respectfully, L.A. Hall."

But though Hall and the other conspirators at this time deemed their secret secure, and felt safe in the further prosecution of their diabolical scheme, even then the sword of the avenging angel had been drawn, and God in his providence working upon the conspirators themselves, was bringing to the light the deep and dark secrets of their unholy plot.

Burch Paralyzed

On the night of the murder Clemens and Lowry made their way back to Burch's house, and communicated to him the successful accomplishment of their undertaking, and changing their wet and dripping clothing, they retired to bed. But a guilty conscience and fear of detection soon caused Burch to arouse them and induce them to leave his house. They spent the remainder of the night in an old shanty, or "shack," and the next morning, taking his son with him on a beef hunt, Burch made it convenient to pass the shanty, furnish them with a supply of rations, a small installment of their reward, advised their immediate withdrawal from the neighborhood, and arranged for a future meeting. Clemens and Lowry then left for their respective homes.

On the next day Burch was stricken with paralysis. The horrors of his crime seethed in his troubled conscience like molten iron in water. There he lay for days unable to stir. To add to the terror of his situation, Lowry sent him word that unless he was paid for his bloody work he would murder him and his family, and Burch felt that the Scuffletonian would not hesitate a moment to add another to his long list of bloody crimes. He had borrowed one hundred dollars and had sent it to the assassins by Henry Lancaster, but that could only appease them for a time. As soon as he could get out, Burch endeavored to collect the promised contributions to the fund. Wright Lancaster put him off by saying that he was on Charlie's (Clemens) bond, and would have to pay on it some time as much as he had subscribed, and he would make that all right with Charlie. He had done his part; he had furnished mutton to feed them while they were staying at Burch's house. Burch then begged him to cancel the lease upon his lands that he might use that as collateral to raise funds to pay the assassins, but Lancaster would not hear to that. Then it was Burch in despair told Lancaster: "When you look upon my grave and see my orphan children, you can say to yourself, 'I am the cause of their ruin.'" His next effort was to collect the promised contribution of Louis Knight, but the latter had had the misfortune of having one of his eyes mysteriously "pop out" about the time of the murder, and had no money to contribute or opportunity to raise any.

It was testified by some of the witnesses on the conspiracy trial that on the night of the murder an examination of the piazza of Forsyth's house, from which the fatal shot was fired into the room, revealed the fact that broken pieces of the pane of glass through which the shot was fired were scattered over the floor of the piazza for several feet back from the window, indicating that the person who fired the gun may have received upon his person quite a sprinkling of broken glass, thrown back in the reaction. It was currently rumored that the doctor who attended Knight had taken a piece of glass out of his eye; but the doctor was not found, and there was no evidence upon that point at the trial.

On the 17th of October Burch visited Eastman, and was seen by a merchant of that place to enter Hall's office. In his confession, Burch says that Hall at that time stated he was not able to pay his subscription to the murder fund, but made an appointment for the next week.

On October 23d, Burch and his brother-in-law, Andrew Cadwell, arrived at Eastman by train from Hawkinsville before day in the morning. They went to a restaurant kept by Sam Rogers, and leaving Cadwell there, Burch went out and was absent some time, returning about daybreak. It was at this time Burch visited Hall's house and obtained the hundred dollars subscribed by Hall to the murder fund. Even then, however, the amount raised was far from sufficient to meet the demands of the assassins. Burch then induced Cadwell to endeavor to borrow the money for him. A number of merchants and other persons were approached by Cadwell for that purpose, and he finally succeeded in borrowing one hundred dollars from Judge Roberts. This distinguished Judge dreamed little of the purpose to which it was to be applied. On returning home, the hundred dollars paid by Hall and the hundred borrowed from Judge Roberts was sent by Burch, through Henry Lancaster, to the assassins.

Murder Will Out

About a week before the murder of Captain Forsyth, in a personal difficulty with a man by the name of Clark, Wright Lancaster had received a stab in the neck, which, although not serious, had caused him to be temporarily confined to his house under treatment. During this time Mr. J. L. Bohannon, of Pulaski County, with whom Wright Lancaster had some two months before formed a co-partnership in the mill business, as already stated, went by invitation to stay at the house of James Moore, the brother-in-law of Lancaster, whom the latter had put in possession of the Bullard lots, as before mentioned. Thinking that the interest of Bohannon was the same as that of Lancaster, that he was identified with them, and that it would be perfectly safe to talk to him, Moore, who was a man not particularly blessed with shrewdness, unwittingly confided to Bohannon the secrets of the conspirators, the inside history of the assassination, the parties to it, the price paid for the commission of the crime, the subscribers to the fund, and the still broader purpose of the conspirators to kill and burn, and organize such a reign of terror that Mr. Dodge would be forced to abandon the rights decreed to be his by the Federal Court, and his agents compelled to quit the country. He advised Bohannon to talk so as to let the suspicion of guilt which was attached the Andrew J. Renew remain where it was.

Horrified by the story of the terrible crime which had been imparted to him, and the responsibility of the dangerous secret of which he had so unexpectedly come in possession, Bohannon begged Moore to tell no one that he had imparted the story of the crime to him. He remembered now the private conversations which had for some time before the murder been taking place between Burch and Wright Lancaster. He recalled the strange expression on his partner's face when the latter imparted to him the news of Forsyth's murder, an expression which Bohannon afterwards testified he would carry with him in memory to the grave. And he recalled the strange conduct and conversations of Burch after the murder. Bohannon remained eight or ten days longer at the mill, watching the conduct of the parties until becoming satisfied that Moore's statement was true, and that he was associated with a gang of murderers, he excused himself as if for a temporary absence, and visited his old father, and laid before him the terrible situation in which he found himself, and sought his advice. Acting upon the advice of his father, he then laid the facts before Mr. Oberly, who had taken the place of Captain Forsyth as Mr. Dodge's general agent, and before Mr. Walter B. Hill, of the firm of Hill & Harris, the attorneys of Mr. Dodge at Macon, and the latter then referred the matter to the writer as United States District Attorney. About this time other facts and circumstances leading to the conclusion of the defendants' guilt were brought to my attention. Warrants were issued, and on the 6th and 7th of November, 1890, just one month after the murder, Luther A. Hall, Wright Lancaster, John K. Lancaster and Lem Burch were arrested.

Burch's Confession

Marshall Corbett and his prisoners reached the United States Court House at Macon about dark on the evening of the 7th. The arrest, the knowledge of his guilt, the load upon his conscience, had so preyed upon the mind of Lem Burch, that terror was pictured in every lineament of his features. He complained of feeling ill, and of symptoms indicating a return of the malady from which he had hardly recovered. He was brought temporarily into my office and a physician sent for. From the very first the conviction seemed to possess him that I knew the entire facts of the case. Sinking into a chair, he begged me to tell him if we had captured Lowry. I replied we would have him he might be sure. "Yes, yes," he said, "the United States will get it all. I am a ruined man, without hope in this world or the world to come. My God! My God! How could I have been led into this terrible crime? I have been in a living hell. I am equally guilty with them. I kept the murderers at my house, I agreed to help pay them for the deed, and I did contribute to their payment. I am ruined, ruined, ruined, but I will tell you all." Burch then narrated to me the history of the conspiracy and the parts played in the terrible tragedy by the various actors. His story completely corroborated the confession made by Moore to Bohannon. As his story progressed, with wild-haunted look the man had in his excitement half-risen from his chair, but the strain was too great. As he reached the conclusion, his speech became thick, his arm fell helpless, and he sunk back in his chair paralyzed on one side. He was placed in the hospital cell at the jail. Two days later Charles Clemens was arrested, and he also confessed the part he had taken in the murder, and his story, as far it went, fully corroborated the previous confessions of Moore and Burch. He was, however, but the tool of the conspirators, and was not let into the deeper secrets of the plot. A week later, Louis Knight was arrested and lodged in jail to await trial.

The Pursuit of Lowry

After the murder of Forsyth, Rich Lowry returned to Lansburg, Montgomery County, Georgia, where for a year past he had made his headquarters. He accounted for his absence during the month previous by stating that he had been on a visit to Florida. He deposited two hundred dollars of his ill-gotten gains with an old colored man named Calvin Fleming to keep for him, and sporting a new suit of clothes and fine gold watch, he cut quite a swell among his fellows. In a short time, however, he engaged with a Mr. Louis McDaniel to carry a raft of timber down the Ocmulgee and Altamaha rivers to Darien, and it was but a day or two after he had started down the river before a Deputy Marshal reached Lansburg in search of him. Finding Lowry gone, the Deputy immediately followed him to Darien, and thence back to Jesup, Georgia, by the railroad on the return trip. In the meantime, as afterward testified to by McDaniel, the latter being in Jesup, he repaired to a barber shop for the purpose of being shaved. Someone in the shop was reading a graphic account in the Macon *Telegraph* of the arrest of Hall, Lancaster and Clemens. The Scuffletonian, who had accompanied McDaniel to the barber shop, immediately went out, and in a few minutes returned to collect what money from McDaniel was due him, and took his departure across the country to Lansburg. The Deputy arrived in Jesup but a short time after Lowry had taken his departure. The Deputy taking the next train got off at the nearest station to Lansburg, and hastening to the neighborhood of Lowry's abode, concealed himself to await his arrival. On the next morning Lowry arrived about daylight, and making his presence known to a few trusted friends, the wily scoundrel, instead of stopping at the negro quarters, found himself a convenient retreat, concealed in the thicket of a neighboring branch, and had his money and effects brought to him. The four or five negroes residing at Lansburg, who visited him at this time and who afterwards testified in the conspiracy case, stated that Lowry told them that he had heard at Jesup of the arrest of Clemens, and he knew then they would be after him next; that he had killed seven men, and that if he was arrested for one crime, and he was not convicted for that, he would certainly be for some other. He said that if they should hear of his arrest, they could make sure that his bullet had made one more man bite the dust; that the murder of one man was but a breakfast for him, and to kill a man was nothing more to him than shooting a beef. In bidding his friends adieu, he told them that when they heard from him again he would either be in North Carolina or in jail at Macon. Plunging into the thicket he disappeared, and that is the last authentic account we have of Lowry. A reward of seventeen hundred and fifty dollars has been offered for his arrest, but whether he has concealed himself in one of the impenetrable swamps of Montgomery County, or whether he has found a safe system with his lawless kindred in North Carolina, remains a mystery.

The Indictment

The testimony of the accomplice, Lem Burch, being in my opinion essential for the case of the Government against Hall, the Lancasters, Knight and Clemens, in accordance with the practice in such cases, I obtained the permission of the Court to use him as what is commonly called State's evidence. The case was submitted to the Grand Jury, which returned true bills against Luther A. Hall, Wright Lancaster, John K. Lancaster, Charles Clemens, Louis Knight, James Moore, Lem Burch, Rich Lowry and Henry Lancaster, the two last named being still at large.

The indictment was drawn upon the provisions of sections 5508 and 5509 of the Revised Statutes of the United States, which in substance provides that if two or more persons conspire to injure, oppress, threaten or intimidate any citizen of the United States, because he had exercised, or was at the time exercising, a right secured to him by the Constitution and laws of the United States, they should be punished for the conspiracy by imprisonment in the penitentiary for not more than ten years; and that if in the execution of the purposes of such a conspiracy any other felony is committed, the offender should be punished for such felony by such punishment as is affixed to such felony by the laws of the State in which the crime is committed. The indictment charged in several counts that the conspiracy was formed by the defendants to injure and oppress, threaten and intimidate Mr. Norman W. Dodge because he had exercised the right secured to him by the constitution and laws of the United States, to bring the rules for contempt against Hall and others, before mentioned, and because he was then in the exercise of the right of pressing in the United States Court the two rules against Hall, which were still pending, and was in the general exercise of the right of bringing rules against all other defendants to the original bill violating the injunction of the Court. It further charged that in pursuance of the conspiracy Rich Lowry murdered Mr. Dodge's agent, Captain John C. Forsyth, and that the other defendants were accessories before the fact to the murder.

The Trial

On the eighth day of December, 1890, the defendants were arraigned in the United States Circuit Court at Macon, Judge Emory Speer presiding. Lem Burch pleaded guilty, Wright Lancaster, John K. Lancaster, Luther A. Hall, Louis Knight, and James Moore pleaded not guilty, and Charles Clements standing mute a plea of not guilty was entered for him by direction of the Court. It was, I think, the purpose of Mr. Hugh V. Washington, who has been appointed by the Court to defend Clemens, to let a plea of not guilty be entered for his client, in hopes that the evidence would show that Clemens acted under duress, to such an extent as would at least induce the jury to recommend imprisonment for life instead of the death penalty, a power which is invested in the jury by the Georgia statute, fixing the punishment for murder, but which is not invested in the Court as it should be where a plea of guilty is entered. If that was not his purpose the course pursued by him at least subserved that end.

The other defendants retained in their defense counsel as able as the bar of a Court noted for the brilliancy of its legal talent could afford. They were represented by Major A. O. Bacon, Mr. Washington Dessau, Charles L. Bartlett, of Macon, and Mr. C. C. Smith, of Hawkinsville.

Mr. F.G. duBignon, of Savannah, who had deservedly won for himself, while occupying the position of Solicitor General of the Eastern Circuit of Georgia, the reputation of one of the ablest prosecuting officers in the State, had at my request been appointed by the Attorney General special counsel for the Government to assist in the prosecution of the conspirators.

Owing to the sudden death of his partner, Judge Walter S. Chishom, of Savannah, Mr. duBignon was not able to reach Macon until the second day of the trial, but in the further conduct of the case which lasted for thirty days, the writer owed much to his sound judgment and able assistance.

Three days were occupied in arguments of demurrers and preliminary motions, five days in empanelling the jury, a list of four hundred jurors having been exhausted before a panel was obtained, sixteen days were occupied in hearing the testimony of the witnesses, numbering nearly one hundred and fifty, who were examined for the prosecution and defense. Three days were taken up by the arguments of counsel and the charge of the Court, yet during the entire trial the court room was packed with an eager throng of spectators, who listened with unabated interest to the unfolding of the plot of the conspirators and the unraveling of the evidence of the mysterious murder of Captain Forsyth, the important particulars of which up to that time it had baffled even the ubiquitous newspaper reporters to obtain. At the conclusion of the testimony the Court allotted six hours to the prosecution for argument and eleven hours to the defense.

The case was opened by the writer, who consumed one hour in presenting the law points of the case to the Court and to counsel on the other side, and two hours before the jury on the evidence. I was followed for the defense by Washington, Dessau, Bartlett, Smith and Bacon, all of whom presented able arguments and appeals, which in a different cause might well have shaken the stern purpose of an upright jury to vindicate the law. But the most eloquent and masterly effort in the case was made by Mr. duBignon in conclusion for the prosecution. For three hours he held the attention of the jury and spectators as if spellbound, and at the conclusion of his argument the feeling was almost universal that the death-knell of some at least of the conspirators had been sounded.

The salient points in the evidence were summed up for the assistance of the jury by his Honor Judge Emory Speer, who reviewed the case and laid down the principles of law which were to guide the jury in their deliberations.

The case was given to the jury on Saturday afternoon. The following was the jury panel:

1.	L.P. Askew, Foreman	7.	G. W. Wright
2.	Herman Hertwig	8.	C. D. Pearson
3.	B. C. Kendrick	9.	E. J. Freeman
4.	S. D. Jackson	10.	J. C. Flynn
5.	W. R. Ivey	11.	W. H. Whitehead
6.	R. H. Barron	12.	Oscar Crockett

The Verdict

On Monday afternoon the jury brought in the following verdict:

"We the jury find the defendants, Charlie Clemens, L.A. Hall and Wright Lancaster, guilty as charged, and we recommend them to the mercy of the Court, imprisonment for life; and we find the defendants, John K. Lancaster and Louis Knight, guilty on the conspiracy counts only; and we find the defendant, James

Moore, not guilty." The jury was polled, but each juror in clear accents pronounced the verdict his.

The long and memorable trial was brought to a close, and the tired jurors were once more free men, while the convicted conspirators were confined to the felon's cell. On the next day the Court pronounced the sentence of the law. Luther A. Hall, Wright Lancaster and Charles Clemens were sentenced to imprisonment for life in the Ohio penitentiary at Columbus, Ohio; Louis Knight to ten years, and John K. Lancaster to six years' confinement in the same prison. Just three months from the date of the murder of Captain Forsyth his murderers were consigned to the penitentiary, and a few days later its iron gates closed forever upon the leaders of the great conspiracy.

THE TRIAL

Circuit Court of the United States, Western Division
Southern District of Georgia

vs.

Wright Lancaster, John K. Lancaster, James Moore,
Louis Knight, Charles Clemens and Luther A. Hall.

October Term, 1890

CONSPIRACY, Etc.

Marion Erwin and F. G. DuBignon, Counsel for the
Prosecution.

Bacon & Rutherford,
Dessau & Bartlett,
C.C. Smith and H.V. Washington,
Counsel for the Prisoners.

SPEER, Judge.

CHARGE TO THE JURY

Gentlemen of the Jury:

The prisoners are on trial upon an indictment in which they are charged with a conspiracy to injure, oppress, threaten and intimidate a citizen of the United States of America in the free exercise and enjoyment of a right secured to him by the Constitution and laws of the United States. They are further charged with a conspiracy to injure, oppress, threaten, and intimidate the citizen because of his having exercised such right and privilege so secured. The laws of the United States provided that "if two or more persons conspire to injure, oppress, threaten or intimidate any citizen in the free exercise or enjoyment of any right or privilege secured to him by the Constitution or laws of the United States, or because of his having so exercised the same they shall be fined not more than five thousand dollars and imprisoned not more than ten years, and shall, moreover, be thereafter ineligible to any office or place of honor, profit or trust created by the Constitution or laws of the United States." This section defines the conspiracy with which the defendants are charged.

The laws of the United States, Section 5509 of the Revised Statutes, further provide: "If in the act of violating any provision in either of the two preceding sections, any other felony or misdemeanor be committed, the offender shall be punished for the same with such punishment as is attached to such felony or misdemeanor by the laws of the State in which the offense is committed." The person against whose rights and privileges, their exercise and enjoyment, the conspiracy is charged to have been directed, is Norman W. Dodge, a citizen of the United States and of the State of New York. The rights and privileges, because of which it is alleged that the conspiracy was formed "to injure, oppress, threaten and intimidate" Norman W. Dodge, has the right to sue out of certain contempt proceedings against the parties whose names are mentioned in the indictment, as having violated a certain decree of this Court granted and made upon a bill in equity, filed, presented and sued to final judgment by George E. Dodge, which decree had become a muniment of the title of Norman W. Dodge to large bodies of land, situated in several counties in this district. As we have seen from the indictment, the conspiracy was to injure, oppress, threaten and intimidate the citizen in the exercise and enjoyment of his right, secured by the Constitution and laws of the United States, or, in other words, because he continued to exercise that right. It also charges that the conspiracy was formed to injure the citizen because of his having so exercised his right so secured; in other words, because he had in the past exercised the right so secured.

You will observe, therefore, gentlemen, that the indictment presents the two-fold accusation—a conspiracy to injure because of a present exercise, and of a past exercise, of a right secured by the Constitution and laws of our general government. It is further charged in the indictment that in pursuance of the conspiracy, a description of which you have just heard, that the prisoners committed a felony, to-wit: the crime of murder of John C. Forsyth, the agent of Norman W. Dodge, and under the provision of the statute which I have read, it is in the legal contemplation of the indictment, that if the prisoners, or two of them, are convicted of this conspiracy and the murder in pursuance thereof, they shall be punished by the law of the State of Georgia relative to the crime of murder. I will now ask your attention to a somewhat closer analysis of the legal import of this law and the indictment which charges the prisoners with its violation. "If two or more persons conspire," that is, if two or more persons enter into a conspiracy. Now, what is a conspiracy? It is an unlawful confederacy or combination of two or more persons to do an unlawful act or to accomplish an unlawful purpose. The offense is complete when the unlawful confederacy, combination or agreement is made, and a criminal act done in pursuance of the conspiracy, is not necessary to justify a convation of it. The degree of aggravation of a conspiracy by a criminal act committed in pursuance thereof, is, of course, proportioned to the degree of heinousness of the crime so committed. Now, to apply this definition to the charge in this indictment, if you shall find that two or more of the prisoners entered into an unlawful confederacy or combination to do an unlawful act to accomplish an unlawful purpose, and if you shall further find that such act and purpose is declared unlawful by the statute under which this indictment is framed, you will be justified in finding that the offense of conspiracy as charged in the indictment is complete, notwithstanding you may fail to find that any crime was committed in pursuance of the conspiracy. Such an unlawful agreement for such unlawful purpose would be a crime for which the punishment for conspiracy would attach, notwithstanding that the proof might be silent or insufficient as to an overt criminal act; but if in addition to the unlawful agreement amounting to a conspiracy, you should also find that two or more of the prisoners had committed an additional crime, to-wit: the crime of murder as charged in the indictment, and had committed it in pursuance of the conspiracy, such an additional crime would be an aggravation of the conspiracy, and would be, under the Federal statute, 5509, which I have quoted to you, punishable on conviction, as such offenses are punished by the laws of the State of Georgia.

What, then, will be your first inquiry? Obviously, was there an unlawful confederacy or combination of two or more persons, or, in other words, was there a conspiracy to accomplish an illegal purpose? If so, the act of one of the conspirators is the act of all. Where several persons are proved to have combined together for the same illegal purpose, any act done by one of the parties in pursuance of the original concerted plan and with reference to the common object, is, in the contemplation of law, the act of the whole party, and therefore the proof of such act will be evidence against any of the others who were engaged in the same conspiracy. It is also true that any declaration made by one of the parties during the pendency of the illegal enterprise is not only evidence against himself, but is evidence against the rest of the parties, who, as we have seen, when the combination is proven, are as much responsible as if they had done the act themselves. You will observe, gentlemen, that the act of combination to do wrong, is the keystone, if I may use the expression, in the crime of conspiracy. It is true, that the act of unlawful combination is more dangerous and disturbing to the peace of society than would be the crime, which is the object of the combination, when accomplished by a single individual. It has been declared that the confederacy of several persons to affect any injurious object, creates such a new and additional power to cause injury, as to require special criminal restraints. You can readily appreciate why this is true. A conspiracy will become powerful and effective in the accomplishment of its illegal purpose in proportion to the numbers, power and strength of the combination to affect it. It is also true, that as it involves a number in a lawless enterprise, it is proportionately demoralizing to the well-being and law-abiding characters of the men engaged, and, as a consequence, of the community to which they belong, such is the general idea of a conspiracy.

Now, what is the particular conspiracy charged in this indictment, and what is particular unlawful result, which the Grand Jury, after its investigation, has imputed to these prisoners. It is a conspiracy, as we have seen, to injure, oppress, threaten and intimidate Norman W. Dodge, a citizen of the United States, in the exercise, the free exercise of a right and privilege secured to him by the Constitution and laws of the United States, and because of his having so exercised the same. An unlawful combination to accomplish one or both of these results, the Court charges you, is a conspiracy indictable and punishable under this statute, and it has been so held by the supreme appellate tribunal of our country. Now, what is the right of Norman W. Dodge, on account of the free exercise of which, it is alleged, that this conspiracy was formed to injure and oppress him?

It appears, gentlemen, from the recitals in the indictment, and the evidence to prove them, that on the 18th day of April, 1884, George E. Dodge filed his bill in equity in this the Circuit Court of the United States for the Western Division of the Southern District of Georgia, against Briggs, Hall and Sleeper, and against many other parties, in the nature of a bill of peace to quiet the title of the plaintiffs to large bodies of land in the counties of Dodge, Telfair, Laurens, Pulaski, and Montgomery, and to restrain defendants from unlawful interfering with and trespassing upon the same, and to have certain fraudulent, or pretended deeds, of the respondent delivered up to be cancelled. This bill was pressed to final adjudication on the 5th day of April, 1886. It was defended by Luther A. Hall, among others, both as a respondent and solicitor of this Court, in its equity branch. After final hearing and trial the Court granted a final decree, enjoining the

defendants, Hall and all other defendants, their agents and confederates, from any character of interference with the land in
question. This decree was the final judgment in the Court, and
since it does not appear that any steps were taken to have it reviewed, or reversed, it was in law conclusive. Subsequently to its
rendition, Norman W. Dodge, as it appears from the evidence and
the deeds before you, acquired by purchase the interest of George
E. Dodge in the lands which were the subject-matter of that litigation, and it is true, as it is alleged in the indictment that this decree became and now is a muniment of title. A muniment is a
record, the evidence or writings whereby a man is enabled to defend the title to his estate. You can readily perceive how this is
true of the decree in question. The Court charges you that it settled irrevocably so far as human agency could settle it, the title of
George E. Dodge to the lands in question, and since Norman W.
Dodge purchased from George E. Dodge, it became as strong a
defense to his title as it was to the title of his grantor, George E.
Dodge. Subsequently to the purchase of these lands by Norman
W. Dodge, it became necessary, in his opinion, for him to apply to
this Court by appropriate application, and appropriate proceedings, to enforce that decree upon persons, whom it was alleged,
did not have the fear of the law in their minds, and who, although
enjoined from so doing, were in a lawless manner proceeding to
disregard the injunction of the Court, and the rights it was intended to protect.

It is in evidence before you that Norman W. Dodge, to-wit: on
the 24th of February, 1890, presented to this Court a petition for
attachment against Luther A. Hall, one of the prisoners now on
trial in this particular case. It was charged that Luther A. Hall had
systematically violated and disregarded the injunction of the
Court, and had interfered with the rights of property it was designed to secure. Upon that petition a rule was issued against the
prisoner Hall, and he was tried and judgment rendered thereon.
Subsequently to the date of this judgment, Norman W. Dodge, to-
wit: on the 12th of July, 1890, filed and presented another petition
for attachment against Luther A. Hall because of an alleged additional violation of the decree of this Court heretofore mentioned,
which violation was subsequent to the judgment as rendered on
the first rule. The second petition was filed, the Court took it un-

der advisement, and it has been, since that time, a proceeding pending in this Court. Thereafter, to-wit: on the 8th day of August, still another petition for attachment because of an additional alleged violation of the before mentioned decree was forwarded to the presiding Judge of this Court, who was not then within its local jurisdiction. This petition was returned to the Court without action on the first Monday in October of this year, and is likewise a pending proceeding here. Now, it is alleged in the indictment that Norman W. Dodge, a citizen of the United States, had the right secured to him by the Constitution and laws thereof, to apply for the rules enumerated, for the purpose of enforcing obedience to the decree of a Court of the United States in a matter in which he was interested. And it is further charged that the conspiracy, for which the defendants are on trial, was had, to injure, oppress, threaten, and intimidate him, because of the free exercise of his right to sue for and obtain the rule first issued, and because he was, at the time of the conspiracy, suing for the rules which were then pending. Now, gentlemen, this brings us to the announcement to you of a decision which the Court has already pronounced upon a demurrer presented, argued and considered in the outset of this trial. And the Court charges you distinctly, as a matter of law, that Norman W. Dodge, being authorized by the Constitution of the United States, and the laws made in pursuance thereof, to apply to the Court for proceedings in attachment as for contempt, to enforce obedience to a decree of the Court in which he was interested, such authority conferred upon him a right, secured to him by the Constitution and laws of the United States, and if the prisoners conspired to injure, oppress, threaten or intimidate him in the free exercise or enjoyment of such right, the conspiracy would be complete as defined by the statute, and would, on conviction, subject the perpetrators to its penalty.

We have now seen what is a conspiracy, what is the particular conspiracy charged in the indictment. And you have been instructed that the latter conspiracy is one relative to which, as jurors of this the Circuit Court of the United States, you have the power and the duty to make inquiry, and, on satisfactory proof, of the truth of the charge, to find a verdict. This brings us to the inquiry, what is the nature or character of the proof necessary to support a charge of conspiracy? The first cardinal rule of evidence, to which it is my duty to call your attention upon this subject, has already been referred to. It is this: After evidence showing the existence of the conspiracy is submitted to the jury, the acts of other conspirators may in all cases be given in evidence against each other, if these acts were done in pursuance of the common illegal object. It is also true, that letters written and declarations made by other conspirators are admissible, if they are among the things done in pursuance of the conspiracy. It is also true that declarations of the conspirators may be considered as part of the *res gestre*, that is, part of the things done in pursuance of the conspiracy, although they may not be precisely concurrent with the act under trial. It is enough if they spring from it, and are made under circumstances which preclude the opportunity or idea of a fictitious device or after thought. It is also true that while the declarations of co-conspirators made after the enterprise has ended are not admissible against each other, yet, if they are made in pursuance of the enterprise and tending to the accomplishment of the object for which the conspiracy and overt acts are made in pursuance thereof, was made or were performed, they were admissible. It is also true, gentlemen, that it is not necessary that the conspirators should meet together in order to constitute the unlawful combination. If they have a mutual understanding and act through one or more individuals as a consequence of such mutual understanding, the conspiracy may be complete, and the declarations of the co-conspirators made while the criminal enterprise was pending, are admissible against each other. It is, indeed, not necessary that all the conspirators should be acquainted even, with each other, if they conspire to accomplish the illegal purpose through one common acquaintance, or go-between, the conspiracy may be complete, and in that event, the act of one conspirator is the act of all.

You will perceive that a conspiracy is a joint offense, and you will understand that if several persons jointly conspire to commit a crime, as each man is acting through all the others, or as all are acting equally through one, the degree of guilt is equal, the guilt is equally distributed, and each man is not only equally chargeable with all the guilt, but the law declares that the act of his co-conspirator is his act. He loses his individuality and becomes identified with the crime and the criminal with which, and with whom he is associated, from the very nature of the crime of conspiracy, it is almost invariably secret in its origin. Naturally every precaution is taken when several deliberately unite to commit a crime so injurious to the public welfare. It is rarely, therefore, the case that there is an actual witness to the unlawful combination itself, or of the circumstance attending its origin; it is peculiarly, therefore, a crime where the evidence of motive and of circumstances are valuable as indicating the animating cause of the unlawful combination and the unlawful agreement itself. It is not required, therefore, that the conspiracy or the act of conspiring need be proved by the direct testimony. It is indeed competent to show the conspiracy by showing disconnected overt acts, where the proof also shows that the conspirators were thrown together, or acted through a common medium, and had a common interest in promoting the object of the conspiracy. As I have said, in another place, a common design is the essence of the charge of conspiracy, and this is made to appear when the parties steadily pursue the same object when acting separately, or together, by common or different means, all leading to the same unlawful result. When they do so act, with a common unlawful design the principle on which the acts and declarations of other conspirators, and acts done at different times are admitted in evidence against the persons prosecuted, is that by the act of conspiring together the conspirators have jointly assumed to themselves as a body the attribute of individuality, so far as regards the prosecution of the common design, thus rendering whatever is done, or said, by any one in furtherance of that design, a part of the *res gestre*, and, therefore the act of all. It is always important, in a charge of conspiracy, to show that the alleged conspirators were known intimately to each other, or that they had a common interest in the subject with reference to which the conspiracy was formed. That they were seen conversing together or conferring together. It would be important, also, if it should appear that their intimacy had been criminal and confidential in its character. It is rarely the case that one of the persons engaged in a conspiracy will consent to become a witness to the material fact of the crime. Whenever such person does so consent, if his testimony is in itself reasonable and credible, and if it is corroborated by other evidence as to the material features of the narration, such testimony may become of the most important and satisfactory character.

Of course, in a charge of conspiracy, as in every other criminal charge, the crime must be proven, as laid in the indictment, but it is only necessary to prove material allegations. Thus, if it appear that a particular motive for the conspiracy is alleged in the indictment, if it sufficiently appear from the evidence, and the jury will be justified in finding that such motives did really exist, it will not matter if the conspirators had additional motives, other than that the indictment describes. It will be sufficient for the purpose of the indictment if the motive, which it alleges, is proven, although the conspirators may possibly, or probably have, additional motives.

The crime of conspiracy, like any other crime, must be shown to the satisfaction of the jury, and beyond a reasonable doubt. When I say to the satisfaction of the jury, I do not mean to imply that the jury has the right to demand from the Government absolute and unerring demonstration, mathematical in its accuracy. Proof of this character is rarely attainable in human investigations, disconnected with the exact sciences. All that the law requires is that the jury shall be morally and reasonably satisfied of the guilt of the accused. If, on consideration of all the evidence in this as in any other crime, the juror can say on his oath, "I am satisfied that the defendants did the criminal act with which they are charged, and I have no reasonable doubt about it," a conviction will be justified, and all the purposes of a legal investigation met.

If, however, upon a fair consideration of all the evidence the juror is not satisfied of the truth of the charge, and doubts it upon grounds, upon which he can give a good reason depending on the evidence, or the want of evidence, the prisoner is entitled to the benefit of that doubt and to his acquittal. It is also true in cases of a conspiracy, as in other criminal cases, that the prisoner is presumed to be innocent until the contrary is shown by proof, and where that proof is in whole or in part circumstantial in its character, the circumstances relied upon by the prosecution must so distinctly indicate the guilt of the accused, as to leave no reasonable explanation of them, which is consistent with the prisoner's innocence.

All I have said upon the subject of the degree of satisfaction necessary in a criminal trial, upon reasonable doubt, the presumption of innocence, and explanations of circumstantial evidence consistent with innocence, is as applicable to the crime of murder charged in the indictment as an overt act committed in pursuance of the conspiracy, as to the conspiracy itself. I trust, gentlemen, that you will be enabled to bear in mind all of these general doctrines of the law of conspiracy and these rules of evidence governing its proof. They will be of great service to you when you come to examine the evidence with reference to the law. It is not to be disputed that the topics are somewhat unusual to the average criminal trial, but Courts and juries must rise to the exigency of the responsibilities upon them, and you must, in the discharge of your duty, endeavor to bear in mind, as far as may be possible, the rules which the Court has mentioned and which it anxiously trusts will serve you to ascertain the truth.

Having considered the character of proof usual in cases of conspiracy, we will now advance to the consideration of the proof, offered in this particular case. At this point the Court would remind you that it is the duty of a Judge in a Court of the United States to sum up the evidence for the assistance of the jury. This is not done, as it is sometimes said, to usurp by the Court the province and prerogative of the jury, for there is nothing which the Court can say which will relieve the jurors of the duty of finding the facts for themselves.

The Details of the Crime

Now, gentlemen, with the purpose to aid you in ascertainment of truth, but in no sense to control you, the Court will call your attention to what appears to be the more salient and important portions of the testimony which has been submitted to you. It is in proof that on the night of the 7th of October of this year, 1890, Captain John C. Forsyth was sitting with his family, his wife and children, at the supper table in his home at Normandale, in this district. I allude to the testimony of his daughter, Miss Nellie Forsyth, a young lady apparently some sixteen or seventeen years of age, who appeared as a witness. Capt. Forsyth, after finishing his evening meal, rose from his table, and remarking to his wife that he must go to Macon the next day to attend Court, left the supper room and went into his sitting room, leaving his family at the table. In a few minutes, Miss Nellie, testified that they "heard the noise," by which the Court understood her to mean the report of the gun. She heard her father faintly call, "Tell mamma to come," and she and her mother ran to him. When she saw him he was sitting up in his chair, with his eyes closed, and she first thought that he was asleep, but in an instant she saw the blood on the side of his face, and then the wound in the back of his head. Her mother brought water and tried to staunch the bleeding, but after a few uncertain movements of his hand the dying man fell forward from his chair, and living in a state of utter unconsciousness for two or three hours, breathed his last. Miss Nellie testified that the room was full of smoke—her father had been shot through the glass of the open window. Other witnesses testified in a manner to make plain to the jury the incidents of the assassination of Captain Forsyth. It appeared from this testimony that one of the blinds to the window opening on the front verandah had not been closed. The shot had been fired through the heavy plate glass of the window by the person standing on the verandah. The gun was loaded with buckshot. Buckshot was found in the wound in the head, and some had been driven through into the mouth of the wounded man. The deadly charge from the gun struck the victim on the back of the head and on the left side, and, according to the testimony of Dr. Montgomery, the physician, had been driven through the brain. The charge seemed to have been a very large one. It appeared from the testimony of Mr. Curry and another witness that there were several tracks all made by one man on the soft ground of the flower garden in front of the house. These tracks were made by a man apparently in his socks. He did not have on shoes; and the witness thought he was not entirely barefooted.

On the next morning, a party took up the trail and followed for several miles. It had been raining the evening before, and, according to testimony of Charles Gibbs, they followed it without difficulty. The witness joined the party about a quarter of a mile from Forsyth's house and followed it for five miles on the tram-road. At first there was but one track, but a short distance further on another track came in from the direction of an old shanty on the left-hand side. This track has a shoe print, and having joined the track which had been trailed from Captain Forsyth's, the tracks were traced together a short distance, where it was evident, from the sign, that the party who came in from the direction of the shanty sat down on the tram-road and pulled off his shoes. The tracks were then followed some five miles to the neighborhood of the house of Widow Gillis, a near neighbor to the witness Lem Burch, to whom reference will presently be made. The testimony of Charley Gibbs was not questioned or contradicted in any manner. It does not appear from the evidence that there were any indications as to the identity of the guilty parties on the day after the killing, in the knowledge of the friends of Captain Forsyth.

Sometime after the killing, to-wit: on the fifth day of November, 1890, as we learn from the testimony of Mr. Walter B. Hill, a member of the Bar, who is the general counsel for Mr. Norman W. Dodge, that a Mr. J.L. Bohannon came to him in Macon, and made certain important disclosures, which gave the clue upon which the investigations were made, which led up to the arrest of the defendants, the indictment by the Grand Jury and the trial in which we are now engaged. Bohannon himself was introduced as a witness, and testified that he was down in Telfair County at the time of the death of Captain Forsyth. He was engaged in the saw mill business with Wright Lancaster, one of the prisoners. His home was in Pulaski County, and he had a mill near Hawkinsville; but getting out of timber, and looking for a location for the mill, finding that Lancaster wanted a partner, the witness sold his mill near Hawkinsville and went into business with Lancaster. This was about the last of July. Lancaster informed the witness that he had about twenty lots of timber and could control a great deal more.

The witness testified that after the partnership was formed, and after Lancaster got his timber cut, he told Bohannon to take his mules and get his brother's wagon (Lancaster's brother) and move one of the defendants (Moore) onto certain lands which Lancaster stated he had bought from a Mr. Bullard. He moved Moore to the Bullard land, or rather Moore moved himself. The witness testified also as to a transaction between himself and Burch relative to the lease of certain lots of land from Burch. Burch asked him for $600 a lot and wanted cash.

John Lancaster, another prisoner, told witness to let Wright make the trade; he knew all about it, and could make it much cheaper. Wright told him where Burch got the lands from and how. Wright made the trade and brought the lease and put it in witness's trunk, and it stayed there. Wright stated that he knew how Burch got this land; how he got all of the lots; that he could do more with him, and could make a better trade than the witness. After witness got the lease, Burch saw him and asked him if it was all right. Witness told him it was. Afterwards witness told him that he understood the Dodge Company was going to put him in jail for leasing that land. Burch said they would never live to put him in jail, that he had a rifle and had been practicing with it, and that he would die at the breech of his gun before he would go to jail. It appears otherwise, from the evidence, that one of the lots which Burch leased to Bohannon and Lancaster had been conveyed to Burch by Wright Lancaster, in a deed in evidence dated in 1888. It was one of the lots belonging to Norman W. Dodge, and was embraced in the decree perpetually enjoining Briggs, Hall and Sleeper, their co-defendants, agents and confederates, from any interference therewith. It is also in evidence that a copy of that decree had been read at Burch's house by Tom Curry, one of the agents of the Dodge Company. The Bullard land on which Moore moved was also, in whole or in part, embraced in that decree, and was the property of Norman W. Dodge. The witness testified that he went over and lived a short time with Moore on the Bullard lands.

On the morning of the eighth of October, the witness testified that he was in the commissary at the mill, and he heard somebody out of doors say that Capt. Forsyth was dead. While he was there, he states that Wright Lancaster came and put his hands on both sides of the door, and looked in and said that Capt. Forsyth was dead, and stayed there about a minute. The witness was struck by the expression on his face, thought of it afterwards, and stated that he would never forget it. That day or the next Lem Burch came there and was very much excited talking about Captain Forsyth's death and asked the witness if he was not scared. The witness told him that he was not, and Burch said "You had better be."

Burch stated to the witness: "There is a suspicion resting right here," I said, 'What do you mean by this?' He said, 'Right round this mill,' and he said 'The Dodge Company has offered ten thousand dollars reward, *(I*[Erwin]*now quote from the stenographic report of the testimony),* 'for the murderer of Capt. Forsyth, and they have got ten of Pinkerton's men here. I said, "Where?' and he said, 'Right around this mill,' and I says, 'Why?' I say, 'I would like to see some of them.' I say, 'As far as that is concerned, Wright Lancaster, I just judged from the way he talked,—I say, 'Wright Lancaster slept in the room with me last night, I know he has nothing to do with it.' He says 'Well, Wright Lancaster went from Milan to Chauncey with Hall the day he made that speech,' and he says 'Wright ought never to have done that—that is where he played the mischief, ruined everything.'

Burch was so much excited I suspected him myself as being the murderer of Capt. Forsyth, and I so stated to, I think, Mr. Moore. He told me that if Burch went on in this way 'people would think it was him.'

[Continuing from the stenographic report of the testimony of Mr. Bohannon]

Q. You so stated to Mr. Moore? A. Yes, sir, and I might have to others.

Mr. Erwin: Q. You went to see Mr. Honson in reference to those lots I speak of, Mr. Bohannon, in reference to these Bullard lots. Now did you make any visit to Mr. Honson with Mr. Moore, and if so, state what was the object of the visit. A. I thought the trouble was between Honson and Lancaster and myself, I told Wright that I would go up and buy Honson out, mill and all, and get rid of him, then we could go ahead with the timbers.

Q. Timbers on these lots that you refer to? A. Yes sir. Honson claimed that he had bought them from Bullard and I thought all I had to do was buy Honson out, and my son wanted to put up a shingle mill, and Mr. Moore and myself went up there to see Mr. Honson if I could make a trade with him. I couldn't make a trade with him, he asked me too much for his mill, and besides, he said they were trying to bull-doze him and I thought he insinuated that I was trying to bull-doze him, and I told him I was not. I merely wanted to buy out his mill to settle the difficulty between him and Wright Lancaster.

Q. Did you and Moore start back from that visit? A. We came back together.

Q. State how the conversation came up, if any did occur, between you and Moore, on that visit. A. Coming on back, sir, I felt embarrassed against the Dodge Company somewhat. I thought they were trying to run over those people down there, and from what I heard that I gathered. Mr. Dessau: I don't think that is a proper statement for him to make. By the Court: Never mind the motive which led him to say that, just tell what Moore said. A. I was talking about the killing of Renew, and Mr. Moore told me we better let the suspicion go on like it was, let them think Renew was the man that killed Capt. Forsyth, and asked me if I knew who killed Capt. Forsyth. I told him I certainly did not. And then he told me all about it.

Q. You say he stated all about it to you? Tell us what Moore did state to you. A. Mr. Moore told me that a negro by the name of Rich Lowry, he didn't give his given name, killed Capt. Forsyth. He said Charley Clemens and Lowry were the men that did it. That they had been taken care of by Mr. Burch for several days. He didn't know how many days, and that Burch had them and fed them there until they got a chance to kill him, and he said the dogs are on the wrong track, that these men killed him and went over across the railroad over into Montgomery County, and I said, 'Mr. Moore, who all knows about this?' and he mentioned Wright Lancaster, John Lancaster, Clemens and Lowry, they all knew about it, and Burch, and he said, Burch asked me if it would do to tell you (witness) about it, and I told him I thought it would.

Q. I wanted to ask you whether or not he said they knew all about it before the killing of Capt. Forsyth? A. Yes, sir.

Q. What time was that made? A. I don't know when Burch asked him that, he said Burch asked him if it would do to tell me, and he told Burch he thought it would, and he did tell me. I asked him not to tell anybody that he told me. He didn't ask me not to tell it. I asked Mr. Moore not to tell anybody that he told me. He came to me the next day and told me that the dogs were right as far as Burch's, that those parties did go as far as Burch's and the dogs were on the right track that far, and he said he was not certain but Henry Lancaster wasn't with them, but he didn't know. I think, sir, that is about the conversation that took place between Mr. Moore on that direct line.

Q. Did Mr. Moore tell you—who did he tell you by name were the persons who were concerned in the killing? A. Yes, sir, I stated that awhile ago. I asked him who knew about it, and he told me the names of the parties.

Q. Was the extent of it just simply that they knew of it? A. Yes, sir. They knew all about it. They had it done was my understanding it. They had it done was my understanding, sir. He went on to state further. I told him then, the way Burch is acting this thing will be found out. He said if it is it won't implicate anybody but himself, he says, these parties have not paid any money to it. Other parties have paid the money, six hundred dollars. I asked him how much the negro got. He said he got six hundred dollars.

Q. Do you know anything about any private consultation between any of these defendants and Mr. Burch before or after the killing of Capt. Forsyth? A. They had conversations every time they met, before and after.

Q. Who had conversations? A. Wright and Henry and every one of them. These men all together there. They are all right around the mill.

Q. Do you know anything about Mr. Wright Lancaster having gone over to Mr. Burch's house shortly after the killing of Capt. Forsyth? A. The same day that Burch was so excited at the mill, I spoke to Wright about it myself, he went over to his house, and I heard that he was stricken with paralysis, and had sent for Wright and John to go over and see him. I don't know whether they went or not. I heard they did. The next day I asked Wright what was the matter with Burch, and he said 'Nothing; only he is acting the fool.' [By Mr. Erwin]. I will ask you this, Mr. Bohannon: Did Mr. Moore tell you anything that the negro had stated, this Rich Lowry, about the killing? A. He said Rich Lowry said it was only a breakfast for him to kill Captain Forsyth.

Q. Did he tell you anything further in the connection about their general purpose? A. They were going to keep on until they stopped the Dodge business.

Q. Can you recollect now about the language in that connection? A. They were going to kill them out, they were going to kill the Dodge Company out, until they went away. I went to Mr. Oberly and took him off in a private room, and told him I knew who killed Captain Forsyth, and I wanted to sell him my interest down there, and if he would buy my interest down there, I would tell him the whole thing. He refused to do that. Said he was not authorized to do it, and could not do it, but asked me if I would come to Macon with him. I told him I didn't have a cent in my pocket, and if he would pay my way to Macon, I would come. He went on up to Mr. Hill's office, and I related the same thing to them, that I know, and I wasn't able to lose what I had there and if they would just buy me out that I would put them into possession of all facts and they could go ahead if they saw fit. They refused to do that, they said they had no authority, didn't want what I had, wouldn't hardly have it anyhow."

The witness then stated that he made the disclosures, which afforded the clue to the theory of the prosecution. This concludes the direct examination of the witness Bohannon. He was also closely cross-examined, without, in the opinion of the Court, inducing him to change his direct testimony in any material particular. It is true, however, that this witness has been very fiercely attacked in argument by the defendants' counsel upon two methods of procedure looking to his discredit before the jury. The first of these is by attempted proof of statements contradictory to his testimony under oath. One method of impeaching the testimony of the witness is by proof of contradictory statements in a matter material to the issue. The witness was asked if he did not, on the 18th of October, tell Tom Eason, between Helena and the Ocmulgee River, that "You didn't know, of your own knowledge, or had no information, who was the murderer of Captain Forsyth?" The witness answered that he didn't know and had no recollection of any such statements. Eason testified for the defense that the witness did say in substance what the question imparted. It is for the jury to say whether this is sufficient to discredit the witness. The amount of credit to be given a witness is entirely a question for the jury, but it is proper for the jury to consider all the bearings of the facts in evidence before them, and if they find that the relations between Lancaster and Eason were close and intimate, they will do well to consider carefully whether a mere evasion of the question, the answer to which, if Bohannon's testimony is true, would impute a terrible crime to the friend of Eason, is a circumstance upon which they can afford to discredit the testimony of the witness.

Another attempted contradiction is based upon a question alleged to have been propounded to the witness by B. M. Frizzell. The witness was asked if he did not state to Frizzell in substance that he knew nothing that implicated the Lancasters. This was at the fair in October in this city. The witness replied that he did not say that, but he did tell Frizzell that he had taken out no affidavit against the Lancasters, and it does not appear that any such affidavits were made. Frizzell testified substantially that Bohannon told him that he knew nothing implicating Wright Lancaster. The jury should bear in mind, also, that Frizzell was a lawyer for Lancaster, and came here, according to his own testimony, in part to sound Bohannon. The witness was also asked if he did not say to Mr. W. J. Grace, a young attorney, resident in this city, that there was some money in this matter; that witness and Grace could make it, and urged him to go down there and see if they could not work up the case as detectives. The witness stated that he did not remember any such conversation, but might have talked with Mr. Grace about it.

The Court charges you upon this subject, if you find that there is a contradiction between the witness and W. J. Grace, it is not a matter upon which an impeachment can be based, because it is not material to the issue. He was also asked if he did not, in a conversation with Mr. M.T. Grace, say that he was up here helping to find out who killed Forsyth. The witness did not deny it. The Court does not think this a ground of impeachment. A witness who is impeached by proof of contradictory statements may be sustained by proof of general good character, and the Government in this case has offered proof of the general good character for truth and veracity of J. L. Bohannon.

Mr. W. W. Harrold, who lives at Eastman, in Dodge County, testified that he knew J. L. Bohannon; that his general character for truth and veracity is good, and that he would be obliged to believe him on his oath. Judge W. L. Grice, Col. George W. Jordan, Sr., and Mr. Walker, Dr. Fleetwood, Mr. Henry Waterman and Mr. J. D. Bostick testify with unanimity to the general good character for truth and veracity of the witness. These are citizens of the community in which he lives, and it is the province of the jury to determine what weight is to be given to their opinions of their acquaintance or neighbor. A witness is presumed to be truthful until the contrary is made to appear, and it is the duty of the jury to accept the testimony of a witness which is not in itself improbable or which is not impeached in some of the methods indicated by the law. But, as I have said, the credibility of a witness is entirely for the jury.

With reference to the attack made upon this witness upon the alleged ground that he has bartered his testimony in this case, the jury should bear in mind his evidence and the evidence of Mr. Hill, which is all the evidence on that subject, except the testimony of one of the defendants as to the value of the property he had at the mill. It is important, too, for the jury to enquire whether it be true, that the witness felt obliged to relinquish possession of his property there at the mill, and if so, to determine whether he did this upon imaginary grounds, or upon the grounds he states, that he has been compelled to remain in Macon for his protection. If it be true that shortly after the death of Forsyth, that the witness suddenly left his place of business without any business reasons, and has remained away since that time, and if this was done before the arrest of the prisoners, and if it further appear that he left his property behind him in the possession of Wright Lancaster, it is a circumstance which may, or may not be important, as the jury may or may not believe the motive which he assigns for it. If this was not his motive, why did he leave there, and why has he not returned?

The jury will also bear in mind, that according to the testimony of Bohannon and Hill, and that is all the testimony on this subject, as I have said, except a reference to the value of the property at the mill taken there by Bohannon, Bohannon declined to accept any reward, and only asked that a fair valuation be placed upon his property, if needful, by a disinterested party, and that Mr. Dodge buy it at the price so fixed. This even was not promised him. Nevertheless he gave the testimony which has been read to the jury. It is true, he was assured that Dodge was a just man, with the natural inference that he would be protected from absolute loss. This is a fact for the jury to consider, and it is for them to say to what extent it would show an interest in Bohannon in his

testimony with a view to its discredit. The main inquiry—the vital
question—is, does the jury believe that Bohannon has told the
truth? And if they do, they are authorized to accept his testimony,
notwithstanding there may be circumstances upon which they be
criticized, and notwithstanding that he may have talked idly or
recklessly in the presence of strangers. Such conversations are
always to be carefully scanned by the jury, their surrounding circumstances closely examined before a jury will be authorized to
impute perjury thereon. It is proper for the Court to direct the
attention of the jury to the fact that Bohannon's statement was
made before any arrest was made. It is also true, that after the
arrest of the prisoners, one of them made a statement which,
while it went further than Bohannon's, confirmed the disclosures
which he made in nearly every important particular. I allude to
the statement and subsequent testimony of Lem Burch, one of the
parties indicted, who has been permitted to testify, under an ancient and salutary practice, existing both in this and the mother
country, by which one of a number of persons, charged with a
crime, is permitted to become a witness for the Government to
supply evidence of guilt which could not otherwise be procured. It
does not appear from the evidence that Burch made any confession before he was arrested, and until Bohannon had told the story, and does not appear that Burch knew what Bohannon had
told, and yet the testimony of Burch tallies in large measure with
the original disclosures of Bohannon.

This is also true of the confession of Clemens; in many material
particulars it corroborates Bohannon; and yet, when Clemens
made his confession, it does not appear that he knew anything
Bohannon had stated, although it was told him that Burch had
made a statement. Now, the confession of Clemens is not evidence except as against himself; but, if the jury, in the absence of
any proof of collusion, can discover in the confession of Clemens
indications which tend to show that the original statements of
Bohannon are true, while the confession is not direct proof to
show the guilt of the other prisoners, it may be proof in the event
to sustain the credibility of Bohannon. If it be true, also, that all
the subsequent developments of the investigations tend to verify
and sustain the original disclosures of Bohannon, as reported to
him by Moore, and as he himself observed in the transactions

about the mill, this is important for the consideration of the jury. In estimating the amount of credit to be given to the testimony of Bohannon, you are not authorized, gentlemen, to impute perjury to him, unless you feel it your duty so to do. As I have said, until he is contradicted in matters material to the issue, or otherwise, impeached in some manner pointed out by the law, he is presumed to tell the truth. In weighing this testimony to ascertain its value, it is further your duty to consider all the other evidence in the case as relating to it, and whether it contradicts or supports it. Your first inquiry of course will be, what motive would Bohannon have to swear falsely, especially against Hall and the Lancasters, Moore and Knight? Had he ever quarreled with the Lancasters or either of the other defendants? Were his relations cordial or otherwise with the prisoners? If you had a motive for perjury in the evidence, it should go to his discredit; but if you fail to perceive such a motive, it would be equally strong in favor of his credit.

It is urged in argument that he testified to procure a reward; but you will remember, gentlemen, on that subject, of course as is your duty, the testimony of Mr. Hill that he stated that he would not take a reward, but only desired to be reimbursed what he felt he must lose if he gave his testimony. Even had he testified for a reward, however, that in itself would not necessarily impeach him, but would be a circumstance that the jury should properly estimate as a part of his testimony. If Bohannon really had property interest there, which he felt that he would lose, as a result of his disclosures, there is nothing illegal in his stipulation, or rather in his attempt to obtain a stipulation, before giving his testimony, that he should be protected from loss. The *lena fides* and genuineness of his conduct, is a question for the jury, as likewise is the amount of credit to be given him. If you find from the evidence that, as a result of Bohannon's disclosures implicating nine men in this conspiracy, that proceedings were instituted which resulted in the flight of two of them and confessions of two others, this fact, in itself, is a circumstance which tends to corroborate the truth of his statement to the extent that it is true in part, and it would be then for the jury to say whether it is true in its entirety.

If you find from the evidence that there was no collusion between Bohannon and Burch and Clemens, and that each made disclosures at different times, without conferring with each other, and without probability that they did or could have conferred, and if you further find that their disclosures were substantially the same while the testimony of the two accomplices could not corroborate each other, and while the confession of Clemens cannot be considered as evidence against the other prisoners, yet the unanimity of statements of the three, made without the opportunity of conference, or without proof that they did confer, is a fact which tends to corroborate the three statements so made. I mean to say that the unanimity, if it exists without a conference, if none was had between these three men, may give in the minds of the jury mutual and interchangeable support, each to the others.

Let us now, gentlemen, advance to the consideration of Burch's testimony, and determine, if you can, what effect it should legally and properly have in this investigation. You will remember, gentlemen, the circumstances which attended the hearing of this testimony. The witness was desperately ill, and the Court, from a desire to insure a thorough and certain investigation of the serious case on trial, went with you to his bedside and under circumstances of painful personal inconvenience to Court, jury and counsel, heard this testimony. It was reported by the stenographer, and is before you. You must, however, as I have said before, remember this testimony and make your finding with reference to it for yourselves. What I say or read about it is simply to assist you as far as I can.

You will have the lease from Burch to Bohannon and Lancaster out with you. You will remember that Burch testified that his titles were fraudulent that he got them from Andrew Renew; and from Lucius Williams; one lot he got from Lancaster. The witness testified he had the deeds of these lots made—some to his son, another to his daughter, and another to his wife—to keep from getting into the United States Court. As to lot 58, which he got from Wright Lancaster, he paid him $25.00 for it. He testified that Renew had no interest in the lots—the titles to which the witness got from him. He paid Renew $75.00 for the title, though he knew he had no interest in the lands. He testified that Wright Lancaster told him that he had the best right to the timber.

Lem Burch Testimony

I now read to you from the stenographic report of the evidence: "That he would give me (Burch) a start in that business, he said; and I told him I would see about it, and told him I would see Col. Hall, or somebody, about it. He contended that he would give me one thousand dollars for it, and that was more than I could get than anybody else would give me."

Q. Who was that talking, Wright Lancaster? A. Yes, sir; he would give me one thousand dollars for it; he said he didn't ask them no odds. I told him they could enjoin him and stop him, and he said they would not do it; he went on and spoke about having Forsyth killed, and said trouble had been—the land trouble down there would have been settled if Billy Clemens had not have got killed; that he would have had Billy Clemens to kill him.

Q. Would have had Billy Clemens to kill whom? A. Forsyth; he said that it would have been done—that they were ruining the country, and so on, and said that they knew parties they could get to do it, and he said he knew who he could get to work at it, and they said what they would do it for.

Q. What did they say they would do it for? A. He said that he could have it done for six hundred dollars. In the meantime, I went up to Eastman and saw Col. Hall about the titles.

Q. What time was that, Mr. Burch? A. I think it was when he was at home on bond.

Q. The time he was let out of jail for ten days? A. He said that
[By the Court: Who said?]:

Witness: Col. Hall. When I asked him about the land business —and asked him about the land business—he said that: 'Stick out, everybody—everybody stick out'; that he expected some of them would be killed.

Q. Some of who? A. Of them, the Company; and then he spoke in person of Forsyth, and said he would give one hundred dollars.

Q. One hundred dollars for what? A. For his being killed; he wanted to know how they were doing down there, and so on, and I told him; and then I saw Wright after that, and he said to work it up too; and I told him I was afraid I would get into trouble—that I wanted my lease back; and he said that he would have Forsyth killed; and this here Rich Lowry and Charley Clemens come there to my place to kill him, and stayed there.

Q. How did they come? A. Well, they come to the plum orchard, the first I knew of it; John Lancaster brought my buggy to me, and told me Charles Clemens wanted to see me, and I went down to the plum orchard where he was, and he was knocking along down there, and told me his business, and told me that Wright had sent him, and he knocked around there a day or two; and I seen Rich, and Rich told me that he had. And he said—told me that he would help me to feed him, and told me to kill mutton when I wanted to and he would help me to feed him.

[By the Court: Who told you that?] A. Wright Lancaster. Q. Help feed whom? A. Rich Lowry and these boys.

[By Mr. Erwin]: Told you to kill mutton whenever you wanted to? A. Yes, sir.

Q. To help feed them? A. Yes, sir.

Q. How long did these men, this Rich Herring, alias Rich Lowry, and Charley Clemens stay at your place before the killing of Forsyth actually occurred? A. About three weeks?

Q. About three weeks? A. I think it was about three weeks.

Q. During that time, Mr. Burch, did Wright Lancaster come to your house? A. He come there one time.

Q. Did he stay all night at your house one night or not? A. If my memory serves me right he did.

[By Mr. Erwin]: Mr. Burch, do you know anything about how this Rich Lowry was occupied this year at any time during these three weeks he was stopping at your place? A. I don't think he was.

[When asked to tell the circumstances of the murder, the witness said:] Well, I don't know of nothing that happened at all, only they just taken their guns.

Q. Who took their guns? A. Charley Clemens and Rich Lowry.

Q. Did they go off for any purpose that evening? Do you know whether they stated they were going for any purpose? A. Well, I knowed that they were going there of course; I weren't there, I don't think, when they left.

Q. You were there not long before they did return? A. Yes, sir, the dogs woke me up.

Q. Well, did either Rich Lowry or Clemens make any statement to you as to what they had done when they came back that night? A. They both did; Rich Lowry said that he had killed Forsyth.

Q. Rich Lowry told you that he had killed Forsyth? A. Yes, sir.

Q. What did Charley Clemens say about it? A. He said that he did.

Q. Said who did? A. Said Rich Lowry did; Rich Lowry said himself he did.

Q. Mr. Burch, do you know whether or not there were any inducements offered to Lowry and Clemens to induce them to kill Capt. Forsyth? A. Yes, sir. Q. What was the inducement offered to them? A. Six hundred dollars.

Q. Well, who was to pay the six hundred dollars? A. Well, I paid two hundred dollars, or something over two hundred dollars, and Col. Hall was to pay one hundred dollars, and I let him have a pistol worth about—it cost about sixteen dollars, I reckon.

[By the Court]: Let who have it? A. The negro.

Q. Lowry? A. Yes, sir.

Q. You answered who actually paid the money; my question was whether or not there was any promise to pay them before the killing took place; if so, who made the promise; who was to have paid the money which was paid—the six hundred dollars? A. They were to pay it to me and I was to pay it to him.

[By the Court: No matter who you paid—who paid you?] A. Well, Col. Hall was to pay one hundred dollars, and Wright Lancaster was to pay two hundred dollars, and I was to pay two hundred dollars and no more; Louis Knight was to pay all he could; he never paid anything that I know of; if he did, didn't know it.

[By Mr. Erwin]: Mr. Burch, commencing with Wright Lancaster, how did you know that he was to pay you two hundred dollars to pay the men that killed Capt. Forsyth? A. Well, he told me that he would, and was gwine on snorting around because they hadn't killed him before they did. He said that he had money—money that he was saving for that purpose; and then when it was done he had no money, nor he wouldn't pay none.

Q. Did he give you any reason for not paying the money after the murder was committed—did you go to him for the money? A. Yes, sir.

[By the Court]: Mr. District Attorney, how did he know that Mr. Hall was to pay one hundred dollars, and how does he know that Mr. Knight was to pay anything? You had better show that conspiracy, if you can show it.

[By Mr. Erwin]: Well, Mr. Burch, how did you know that Mr. Hall, Mr. Luther A. Hall, was to pay one hundred dollars to it? A. He told me he would.

Q. Where were you when he told you that? A. I was in his office. Q. Where? A. Eastman.

Q. At this same time? You mean the time when he was out on bond? A. Yes, sir.

Q. Well, I will ask you Mr. Burch, whether or not Mr. Hall at any time, after that time he was out on bond, whether by word of mouth, or by letter, or otherwise, reminded you of what he had said at that time? A. Yes, sir.

Q. How long was it? A. He written me two letters.

Q. Wrote you two letters? A. Yes, sir.

Q. Where were these letters from? A. They were from Savannah. Q. Was that after the ten days he was out on bond? A. Yes, sir.

Q. Mr. Burch, I will ask you whether or not you have these letters? A. I got them.

Q. Do you know what has become of them? A. No, sir; they were destroyed around there, I reckon; I never save no letters.

[By Mr. Erwin: I will state in my place, your Honor, that I expect to prove that matter of loss of the letters, and, under the circumstances, I will ask that we proceed with the examination and make that proof afterwards.]

[By the Court]: Very well, go on.

Q. Now, Mr. Burch, I will ask you what did Mr. Hall say in these letters? A. He written that if matters wasn't attended to before he got back he would have it done himself.

Q. Was there any matter between you and him that was to be attended to other than what you have stated about the killing of Forsyth? A. No, sir.

Q. That is all there was to be attended to? A. Yes, sir.

Q. Did anybody read that letter that you got? A. My daughter did.

Q. Your daughter, Miss Sabie Burch? A. Yes, sir?

Q. Did he state anything else, do you recollect, in either of these letters, about the land troubles in general? A. No, sir; I don't think he did.

Q. Anything about giving any message to other people? A. No, sir.

Q. It was a short letter, then? A. Yes, sir.

Q. There were two letters, you say, you got on the same subject? A. Yes, sir.

Q. Well, now, in regard to Louis Knight, you said that Wright Lancaster told you to see Louis Knight about what he would contribute towards it? A. Yes, sir.

Q. You said that you did see Louis Knight at Milan; I will ask you when you saw him there? A. I could not tell you the date, I saw him there; it was a month or more ago—I can't remember the time I saw him there.

Q. How long before the killing of Capt. Forsyth, do you suppose? A. I suppose it was probably three weeks.

Q. Did you tell Louis Knight that you wanted him to contribute to it? How was it? A. He just said he would do all he could; I knowed he would be able to do as much as any of them.

Q. Did he tell you what he would do all he could towards? A. Yes, sir; of course toward the killing of Forsyth.

Q. Mr. Burch, I will go back again to that interview of yours with Wright Lancaster after the killing of Mr. Forsyth; you said you went to Wright Lancaster afterwards and asked him for the money? A. Yes, sir.

Q. And he would not pay anything. A. No, sir.

Q. Now, did he give you any reason for not paying, or anything of that sort? A. Well, he said he would make that all right with Charley—he was on Charley's bond, and it would have to be paid some time, and he thought he could make that all right.

Q. Charley who? A. Charley Clemens; well, the negro had been sending me word that he would kill me if he didn't get it, and I had been down sick and I weren't able to do anything; I didn't have no money only as I could borrow it; I knew the negro would do it, or I thought it; I begun to beg him for the lease on the timber; I told him he could release it; I told him I would pay it all myself rather than have that negro kill me and some of my folks, and he said that he didn't have it; and then I referred him to what he said about it, and he said he weren't going to pay—that he could make arrangements with Charley; and I says to him—says, 'Wright, whenever you pass my place and see my little orphan children and my grave, I says, 'you can say you are the cause of it;' and he says, 'You are a damn liar,' and he says,'If you say it again, I will pick up a scantling and break your head.'

Q. You mean that you told him that you would be cause if it? A. That he would be the cause of it; I says, 'Whenever you pass my house, and see my little orphan children and my grave'—that was myself who I was alluding to—'you can say that I am the cause of it' and he says, 'You are a damn liar, and if you say it again I will pick up a scantling and break you head'

Q. Mr. Burch, did you have any sickness a day or two after Forsyth's murder? A. I had a stroke of paralysis of Friday—I believe it, I believe it was on Friday.

Q. Capt. Forsyth had been killed on the Tuesday previous? A. I believe he had.

Q. While you were sick, was the time that Mr. Wright Lancaster came over and talked with you? A. No, sir; he did not.

Q. Did he come there later? A. He never come there but one time, and that was in about two weeks—he come there one Sunday evening in about two weeks after I had got sick.

Q. Now, Mr. Burch, after you had that stroke of paralysis—But before I leave that, do you recollect what time of night it was that Clemens and Lowry got back to your house when they announced that Lowry had killed Forsyth. A. I suppose about 11 o'clock at night—I would say probably about 11, as near as I can guess.

Q. Did they sleep all night in your house? A. No, sir.

Q. Did they get up and leave, or how did they do? A. Yes, sir; they left.

Q. Well, what happened about their leaving—what was said? A. Well, I said, I told them I was going down the next morning to hunt a beef, and would be on the road down there *agin* that old shack, and I would see them, and they told me to carry them some rations, and I carried them some rations, and they told me they would stay there in that old shanty that day.

Q. Well, did you see them the next morning? A. Yes, sir.

Q. Did you start off with anybody, when you saw them there—was there anybody with you? A. Wyly was with me.

Q. Wyly, your son? A. Yes, sir.

Q. Did you see them near Turnpike Creek? A. They were, I reckon, about—probably about a quarter of a mile from the Turnpike Creek.

Q. Well, now, Mr. Burch, was there any money paid to them that morning? A. Yes, sir.

Q. How much? A. Well, I am not hardly prepared to tell you exactly; it seems to me like it was that morning—no, sir! no, sir! it was that evening it was paid to them.

Q. How much? A. It seems to me like it was thirty dollars.

Q. Well, what was said about paying this, if anything, about the full amount promised? A. He said that they wanted it right away.

Q. Well, what further was said? Was anything said about paying the balance. A. No, sir; well I don't know as there was, right then, anything said about the trade, because I intended to see them myself.

Q. Was there anything said that morning when you did see them yourself? A. No, sir; there was nothing said—I just handed them the rations and went on.

Q. Was there anything said as to their movements that morning, what they would do with themselves? A. They said that they would stay there in that old shack that day until after they found out how everything was; as soon as they found out how everything was they would go down to Charley's father's.

Q. Well, Mr. Burch, I will ask you right there, before I forget it, how far does this Widow Gillis live from you? A. About a mile.

Q. Did either of those men tell you about how they came back after the murder of Forsyth—what directions were taken? A. No, sir; not that night—I have no recollection of it.

Q. How far do you live from Normandale? A. We have to go there—we go straight through the woods—it is about six miles.

Q. Where did you get the twenty or thirty dollars that you paid to them, the first thirty? A. I borrowed twenty of it from Henry Lancaster; I had the other myself.

Q. Now, Mr. Burch, after you had taken sick, and the balance of that money was not paid, did you send any part of that money to them that was promised to them in the arrangement. A. I did not; I went off and borrowed—I borrowed, I believe it was one hundred dollars; I borrowed one hundred dollars from old man

Jase Lancaster, or Henry did; it was Henry Lancaster who borrowed it for me.

Q. You didn't know this was from Jase Lancaster, except what Henry told you? A. No, sir; but I knew he did as good as if I had seen it.

Q. You borrowed it through Henry Lancaster? A. Yes, sir—from Jase Lancaster; the poor old fellow lacked a heap of knowing what it was for.

Q. Did you make any disposition of that one hundred dollars? A. Before I borrowed that I went up and tried to get some money in Hawkinsville; I could not get none up there, and I got Andy Cadwell to go up there with me, so I came back to Eastman, and Andy borrowed a hundred dollars from Judge Roberts for me.

Q. From Judge Roberts? A. Yes, sir.

Q. Now, Mr. Burch, what time of day or night did you and Andrew Cadwell reach Eastman? A. Well, the train was, I think, two or three hours late—as soon as we got to Eastman, I think, it was probably two hours before day.

Q. Two hours before day? A. Yes, sir.

Q. Where did you and Mr. Cadwell go when you got to Eastman? A. We went down to a blind tiger there; I reckon it was a blind tiger.

Q. Where is this place? A. I could not tell you; it was down there where they got all them blind tigers; we went down there to get something to drink, and we met up with Sam Rogers, and I told them.

Q. Met up with Sam Rogers? A. Yes, sir; I told him I was going off and he could stay around there with Sam until I got back; I slipped off, then, and went up Col. Hall's to get the money.

Q. Where did you go?—was it at Col. Halls office or house? A. It was at his house.

Q. At his house? A. Yes, sir. Q. What time was it that you went? Was that before day? A. Yes, sir.

Q. Well, now, what transpired when you went to Mr. Hall's house? A. I went to the door, and he asked who it was, and I told him, and he come down.

Q. You told him, and he came down? A. Yes, sir, I told him who it was, and he come down.

Q. Came down where? A. Into the sitting room.

Q. Was it light? A. No, sir; it was an hour until day or more.

Q. Was it dark when you came in? A. Yes, sir; well, he had a lamp.

Q. Was anybody in the sitting room with you and him? A. No, sir.

Q. You were by yourselves? A. Yes, sir.

Q. Now, Mr. Burch, you said you got the money from him there? A. Yes, sir.

Q. How much was it? A. One hundred dollars.

Q. Did Mr. Hall fully understand for what that money was being given by him? A. Certainly he did; yes, sir.

Q. Did he talk about it?—what did he say about it then? Well, Mr. Burch, you say—tell me what Mr. Hall said about it that time? Did he make statements in reference to the killing of Mr. Forsyth?—If so, tell me what it was, in reference to the Dodge Company at that time or the Dodges. A. Well, he seemed to be very much displeased, and said that we ought to burn the trestles and bridges, and run them out of there and make them leave the country. Q. He seemed to be very much displeased or pleased? A. Displeased.

Q. Because Forsyth was killed? A. Because it looked like he had to pay the money and they weren't gone; he seemed to be very much displeased about having to pay the money and there weren't more done.

Q. Very much displeased at having pay the money and there was not more done? A. Yes, sir.

Q. And they didn't do what? A. They didn't burn the trestles and run them out from there.

Q. Burn the trestles and run them out? A. Yes, sir.

Q. It was the morning of the circus you got the money from Mr. Hall. A. Yes, sir.

Q. Now, then, you were there on the 16th or 17th of October, when the fair was there; did you see Mr. Hall at that time, in reference to the money? A. Yes, sir.

Q. What conversation did you have at that time in reference to getting it? A. I told him—I asked him if he was ready to pay, and he said he weren't, and told me to meet him down at Court on Monday or Tuesday—on Monday, and he would get it and pay it; and I went out to the river on Monday, and then I thought I would go down on Tuesday or Wednesday, when I got back, and I heard that Court had adjourned.

Q. Then you went back to Eastman on the 23rd, or the day of the circus. A. Yes, sir.

Q. Mr. Burch, we will leave Mr. Hall now, and go back again to Herring and Clemens. How did you send the one hundred dollars you got through Henry Lancaster from old man Lancaster—Mr. Jase Lancaster; how did you get to them that money you say you paid to them? A. Henry carried it to them.

Q. Henry Lancaster? A. Yes, sir.

Q. How did you get to them the one hundred dollars you got from Mr. Hall on the day of the circus—that was the same day, I understand, that you and Andrew Cadwell borrowed one hundred dollars from Judge Roberts? A. Yes, sir.

Q. How did you get that to them? A. Henry carried it. Q. As I understand you, there were two trips made by Henry to pay over that money? A. Yes, sir.

[By the Court]: Did you tell Henry Lancaster where to go? A. They told him where they would meet him at.

[By the Court]: Did you say they told him where they would meet him? A. Yes, sir.

[By Mr. Erwin]: Did Henry tell you anything about it—they were to meet him on the Turnpike Creek; how did you find it out? A. Henry told me.

Q. Mr. Burch, did Henry know about these plans—what was to be done before it was done? A. I don't know whether he did or not; he came from the mill down there, and went off with Rich Lowry, and said—Henry said they went to show them the way to Normandale. Q. That he went to show them the way to Normandale? A. Yes, sir; Henry went with me, if my memory serves me right, when we made the first trip; I ain't positive; I think he did.

Q. Did you know for what purpose he was showing them the way? A. Yes, sir.

[By the Court]: What purpose? A. To kill Forsyth.

[By Mr. Erwin]: Well, Henry was to come and report to you when he carried this money to Rich Lowry and Clemens, and came back; did he make any report as to any conversation between them? A. He came back with this word, that they were going—that the negro was going to kill me if it was not gotten up.

Q. What was gotten up? A. The money.

Q. What money? A. That was to be paid over by me to them for killing Forsyth.

Lem Burch Testimony (Continued)

You will observe, Gentlemen, that Henry Lancaster is charged as a co-conspirator in this indictment; the proof is that he lives in Telfair County, that diligent efforts have been made to arrest him, and that he has, so far, escaped arrest. This is evidence which may tend to show his guilt, and tends to corroborate Burch's story of his complicity with the crime. Burch also testified, on cross-examination, to the conversation with Bohannon, in which Bohannon told him that the Dodges would put him in jail, and he said: "I knew that the way we were shaped up there, everything in the timber business, it would be a mighty easy matter to do it."

[Lem Burch, while confined in jail, was taken with pneumonia and was removed under guard to a boarding house, distant 2 or 3 blocks from the Courthouse. On the second day of the trial, the attending physician pronounced his condition precarious and the chance of recovery doubtful, and the man too ill to be brought to Court. It this emergency, the Court, with the jury, the prisoners, and their counsel, adjourned its setting to the bedside of the sick man. Between fits of coughing and consequent exhaustion which sometimes reduced his voice to a whisper, the testimony of Lem Burch was delivered. This will explain to the reader the occurrence of frequent repetitions in questions and answers, and also the cause of the unfinished and broken sentences which appear in the stenographer's report of the testimony. His testimony continues below.]

Q. Easy matter to do what? A. To put us is jail.[He was also asked]:

Q. Did you see Louis Knight at any time after the murder of Captain Forsyth? A. Yes, sir; I saw him at Milan one time; yes, I saw him twice; I met him around opposite of Mrs. Gillis one time, hunting Sam Williams, I saw him at Milan one evening.

Q. Well, did you talk to him about what he was to contribute to this murder—about paying the amount for having murdered Forsyth? A. I did, that evening.

Q. What did he say to it? A. Well, he was in such a fix with his eye that it looked like he couldn't do anything; he said that he had lost his eye, and said he couldn't do anything.

Q. Well, when Wright Lancaster and you agreed to take this part in the killing of Forsyth, what was the reason he gave, why he wanted Forsyth killed. A. Who, Wright Lancaster? He wanted him killed, and thought it would break up the arrangement and tear everything to pieces, and get him all the timber there was down there. Q. He thought if he didn't get Forsyth killed, that Forsyth or his agents would be able to break up the arrangements with Bohannon and Lancaster, and wanted him killed about these lots of land? A. It weren't only them; my lots weren't nothing.

Q. To other lands? A. Yes, sir.

Q. They wanted lands for the timber for their mill, was that it? A. Yes, sir, and they didn't have any, I don't think.

Q. They didn't have timber for their mill, and if they didn't kill Forsyth, he would keep them from getting it, did you say, was that it? A. I guess it was.

Q. That's from the conversation he had with you was that what you gathered? A. Well, yes, I told you he said they were cutting and ruining the country.

Q. By cutting all the timber to keep other people from getting it? A. By taking all the lands that didn't belong to them.

Q. This was to keep them from taking the lands, was it? A. Yes, sir.

Q. Did you ever hear them say that they wanted him killed because of anything that any particular person had done? A. Not that I have any recollection of.

Q. You don't recollect that they said they wanted him killed because anybody had done anything? A. Not that I have any recollection of.

Q. It was just a general idea, they wanted them killed to keep them from getting the lands they didn't believe belonged to them, is that it? A. Yes, sir.

Q. Thinking about it now as seriously as you can, that is as much of the reason as ever was given by any of them? A. Yes, sir.

Q. You spoke about seeing Mr. Hall in the summer; was it when he was at home, when let out from jail on ten days, was that the time? A. Yes, sir.

Q. That was in Eastman, was it? A. Yes, sir.

Q. You recollect who was present when you saw him? A. I think Elgin Young and E. F. Lee was present with me one time there; I think I saw him two or three or four times, I reckon, that evening when I was there.

Q. There was a large number of people there when he came home, wasn't there? A. There was very few people there that evening.

Q. But, I forgot to ask you, when was it that Wright Lancaster stated this to you about the killing—before Forsyth was killed? A. A great many more times than one.

Q. Well, where? A. Well, pretty much everywhere I'd see him.

Q. It was a constant thing he talked about, was it? A. Yes, sir; he talked about it a great deal.

Q. Talked about having Forsyth killed, and it was all because the Dodges would get the lands and he could not get them for his mill? A. Well, he thought that he had gotten into that business, and he thought if they got him snapped up, he was gone.

Q. Into what business? A. The timber business—land and timber business.

Q. Timber business? A. Yes, sir; land and timber business, where he was running his mill.

Q. What do you mean by snapped up and was gone? A. Taking him up and enjoining him.

Q. When was the first time he ever said to you that he wanted you to take hold of the matter of having him killed? A. It was down there at his mill. He didn't say he wanted me—to have me to take hold of it. He said he was going to have it done; he had two men to do it, and was going to have it done.

Q. Well, when was the first time he ever asked you to have anything to do with it? A. It was along in August, I believe. It seems to me, as well as I recollect—yes, it was behind his old commissary where he was talking; he said that my place was an out of the way place, where he could keep them concealed.

Q. Said what was an out of the way place, your house? A. Yes, sir.

Q. Did he make a proposition to you that you were to take them to your house until they killed Forsyth? A. He said it would be best for them to go there, as they would not be seen there, and keep hid out there.

Q. Yes, and you agreed to do it, did you? A. Yes, sir.

Q. You agreed to do it at that time? A. No, sir; I didn't agree at that time.

Q. At what time did you agree to do it? A. Well, he just sent them there, and Charley told me his business when he come, when he made the proposition that time, that first time behind the commissary.

Q. The time he made this proposition to you behind the commissary, how long did you and he talk together there? A. I suppose we stayed out there, out there on a log—I suppose we talked some fifteen minutes, probably longer.

Q. You didn't tell him you wouldn't do it? A. No, sir.

Q. When you parted, it was understood that you was going to do it? A. He said he was going to send them.

Q. That was in August, you say? A. It seems to me that it was about the first of August.

Q. Tell me where it was you first had a conversation with Louis Knight about this matter? A. At Milan.

Q. I believe you said it was Milan, that is where you had a talk with him? A. I talked with him at Milan.

Q. Did you go—Wright referred you to him, and you told him Wright Lancaster referred you to him? A. Yes, sir.

Q. And you told him you wanted him to pay for having Forsyth killed? A. Yes, sir.

Q. And what was it he agreed to do? A. He said he would do all he could.

Q. Did he intimate how much that would be? A. No, sir.

Q. He was in favor of it, was he? A. I guess he was.

Q. Now, Mr. Burch, did he say anything about whether he wanted Forsyth killed or not? A. Yes, sir.

Q. And that was the time you went to him to know how much he would give? A. Yes, sir; that seems to me, as well as I remember, about three weeks?

Q. Before the killing? A. Yes, sir.

Q. At that time Clemens and Rich Lowry had already been to your house, hadn't they? A. Yes, sir; they had been there.

Q. Been there before that? A. Yes, sir.

Q. Did you see him again at any time at all after the killing—Louis Knight? A. I met him and Sam Williams not far from Mrs. Gillis'.

Q. Mr. Burch, have you ever said to anybody since you have been in Macon that Louis Knight didn't have anything to do with this matter? A. No, sir, I have not; I said that—all I said about it to anybody was that I said Louis Knight would never have known anything about it, I didn't suppose, if I hadn't spoke to him about it. That is exactly what I said.

Q. Who did you say that to. A. I do not know; I can't call it to mind.

Q. Have you said it to more than one person? A. I don't know whether I have or not. Q. Do you remember having said that A. No, sir; I have never said that the—[answer interrupted by coughing.]

Q. Did you say that you didn't suppose Louis Knight would have known anything about it if you hadn't spoke to him about it? A. Yes, sir; that's what I said.

Q.That's what you say now? A. Yes, sir; I said I told the fellows there in jail about it.

Q. Which fellows? A. I told Vaughn, I believe.

Q. Vaughn; who else? A. I think I told the Attorney General one night about it.

Q. [By Major Bacon:] I won't ask anything you said to the Attorney General; I will ask you what you said to other people? A. I told you.

Q. You can't remember anybody besides Vaughn. A. I may have said it to others; I don't remember the others I said it to, there has been too many talking to me—having so much to say that I can't keep up with everything.

Q. Who has been talking to you? I am not talking about the District Attorney? Mr. Burch, when you went to Mr. Hall's house that night, was there any light burning in the house? A. I thought that I could see a light upstairs as I went there.

Q. You mean through the windows upstairs? A. Well, I think—I went up; it seems to me like there was a light burning up there?

Q. Could you see through the glass door—see upstairs inside— could you see through the glass door and see Mr. Hall come down the steps? A. I saw him coming down the steps.

Q. With a lamp in his hand? A. Yes, sir.

Q. You could see that through the glass by the door, could you? A. I guess it was; I don't remember that I saw it through.

Q. What sort of a lamp was it? A. I never noticed it.

Q. Was it a lamp or a candle? A. I never noticed; he set it on the table; I know it wasn't a candle.

Q. What do you call a candle? A. A candle is one of these white things with a wick in it; I never paid no attention to it.

Q. Something like a tallow dip? A. I know what is called an old-time candle; I never seen none of them; they've gone out of fashion.

Q. You never saw a candle, and you saw that night when he came down the steps, Mr. Hall came down the steps, he had a lamp in his hand or a candle? A. I could not say which it was; I told you I never noticed it. I never noticed it all.

Q. You didn't notice down in the room whether it was a lamp or candle? A. I didn't stay but a few minutes.

Q. He had the money in his pocket? A. No, sir; he got up and went back up there and got money.

Q. What kind of money did he pay you? A. Paper money.

Q. Paper money? A. Yes, sir. Q. Went upstairs? A. Yes, sir.

Q. Did he leave the door open of the room you were in? A. Yes, sir.

Q. You saw him go upstairs? A. Yes, sir.

Q. Did he carry the lamp or candle out? A. I don't remember.

Q. You can't recollect whether he left you in the dark or not? A. It seems to me that he did; I won't be positive about it.

Q. You don't recollect definitely whether he left you in the dark or not? A. No, I don't.

Q. Was there any lamp like that hanging in the hall? (referring to a lamp hanging in the room in which the Court was sitting at Mrs. Hogan's boarding house.) A. I never noticed.

Q. You could tell whether you saw any or not, can't you? A. From where I was?

Q. Yes. A. I think he set the light on the hall table there. He didn't have anything like that burning.

Q. Didn't have a lamp like that burning? A. No, sir; Mr. Hall set with the lamp in his land and carried it back upstairs with him when he went back up.

Q. And left you in the dark? A. And he brought it back with him.

Q. Left you in the dark? A. Yes, sir; he weren't gone over a couple of minutes, if that long.

Q. You didn't let him know that you were coming, did you? A. No.

Q. How long before that time was it that you had seen him? A. I seen him when that little fair was going on.

Q. During the fair? A. Yes, sir.

Q. You hadn't seen him since then? A. No, sir; not until that night.

Q. When you went to his house that night? A. Yes, sir.

Q. You knocked at the door? A. Yes, sir.

Q. What did you knock with? A. Knife.

Q. Didn't ring any bell or knock on the door, just knocked with your knife? A. Yes, sir.

Q. How many times did you knock? A. I didn't knock many times before he asked who it was.

Q. Where did he ask from? A. Upstairs.

Q. You hollered out your name to him? A. I told him that it was 'L.B.'

Q. L.B.? A. Yes, sir.

Q. He came down right away? A. Yes, sir.

Q. You think there was a light there before you knocked? A. It seems to me that they had a light upstairs; I won't be positive about it. It seems to me that they did.

Q. Were you ever at his house before? A. I never was inside his house before in my life.

Q. Mr. Burch, who arrested you? A. Mr. Avant, I think, is him.

Q. One of these deputy marshals? A. Mr. Avant, I think, was the one read the warrant; the one that arrested me, Mr. Avant.

[Conclusion of Lem Burch Testimony]

Gentlemen of the Jury, that is the testimony both on the direct and cross-examination of Lem Burch, that is to say, it is, in the opinion of the Court, the most material portion of the testimony. I do not mean by this to intimate that you should not recall all else that he has said, consider it and give it due and proper weight. You must pardon me for dwelling at length on this evidence. No personal weariness of my own, and with all the deference and respect I feel for yourselves, no consideration of your personal weariness, would justify me in withholding from you anything which under the law, is material for your consideration, in this vast and momentous issue. It is true that the evidence of Burch is the testimony of an accomplice, but it is not incompetent on that account. It may be here observed, and in this connection, I use the language of Professor Greenleaf in his well known and valuable treatise on the law of evidence. "That it is a settled rule of evidence that a *particeps criminis*, that is, an accomplice, notwithstanding the turpitude of his conduct, is not, on that account, an incompetent witness." The admission of accomplices as witnesses for the Government is justified by the necessity of the case, it being often impossible to bring the principal offenders to justice without them.

The degree of credit which ought to be given to the testimony of an accomplice is a matter exclusively within the province of the jury. It has sometimes been said that they ought not to believe it unless his testimony is corroborated by other evidence, and without doubt, great caution in weighing such testimony is dictated by prudence and good reason. But there is no such rule of law, it being expressly conceded that the jury may, if they please, act upon the evidence of the accomplice, without any confirmation of his statement, but, on the other hand, Judges, in their discretion, will advise a jury not to convict of a felony upon the testimony of an accomplice alone and without corroboration. And it is now so generally the practice to give them such advice that its omission would be regarded as an omission of duty on the part of the Judge, and considering the respect always paid by the Jury to this advice from the Bench, it may be regarded as the settled course of practice not to convict a prisoner in any case of felony upon the sole and uncorroborated testimony of an accomplice. The Judges do not, in such cases, withdraw the cause from the jury by positive directions to acquit, but only advise them not to give credit to the testimony. But though it is the settled practice in cases of felony to require other evidence in corroboration of that of an accomplice, yet, in regard to the manner and extent of the corroboration required, learned Judges are not perfectly agreed. Some have deemed it sufficient if the witness is confirmed in any material part of the case. Others have required confirmatory evidence that the prisoner actually participated in the offense.

It is perfectly clear that it need not extend to the whole testimony, but it being shown that the accomplice has testified truly in some particulars, the jury may infer that he has in others. I think that the true rule is that the corroborative evidence must relate to some portion of the evidence which is material to the issue, while it need not go to the whole case, yet, in the language of a famous Massachusetts case, the Commonwealth vs. Holmes, decided by Chief Justice Gray, it is true that no evidence can be legally competent and sufficient to corroborate the accomplice which does not tend to confirm the testimony of an accomplice upon a point material to the issue, in the sense that it tends to prove the guilt of the defendant.

It is also true, gentlemen, while the Court is careful to remind you that the credit of this witness is entirely for you, it would be very far from your duty if disregarding what may seem the natural and inherently truthful character of his testimony, you should be hurried away by fierce denunciations, by heated language and by excited epithets imputing infamy to him. On the contrary, with measured and impartial deliberation, like men who have a large interest at stake, you should carefully, anxiously and judiciously scan and weigh the evidence. If the denunciations are not justified by the circumstances of the case, they are "sound and fury signifying nothing," but the verdict of twelve good men is significant, it is imperishable, it is recorded on the permanent records of the Court, and it will live in its effect upon the community in which it is rendered.

To demand of the jury to utterly discredit and to refuse to consider the testimony of a witness, merely because he is an accomplice, is to ask the jury to hold him incompetent as a witness on that account, while, as we have seen, the law does not make him incompetent, and should juries do what the law does not do, many of the darkest and most dangerous crimes would go unpunished for the want of evidence of character. He is, therefore, not incompetent or disqualified as a witness like a man who has been convicted of perjury, but he is a competent witness, and it is for the jury to determine whether under the rule I have given you his testimony is sufficiently corroborated.

Now upon what facts does the Government rely as corroboration of the testimony of Burch. The first inquiry, this being a charge of conspiracy, "Who had a motive to commit it?" Upon this subject the Government calls attention to the fact that the prisoner Hall had been enjoined from interfering with the lands of Norman W. Dodge, that he had a large interest in the attempt to dispossess Mr. Dodge of those lands, that he said to Doughtry that he would have a man in possession of every one of the lots to which Dodge had a weak title by Christmas, that in the letter to Stuckey he enclosed a list of some eighty-nine of these lots, all of which he was enjoined not to interfere with, with a caution to Stuckey to keep the matter quiet, to go into possession, to keep the matter quiet, but to be sure not to get enough of the land to give the United States Court jurisdiction, that he said to Cooper he would put him in possession of any of the lots, and defend his title for half of the land, that on the trial of the rule against him issued for violating the injunction he was convicted and sentenced to five months imprisonment in the Chatham County jail, that on his way to jail he said to Avant that the Dodges had "put in to persecuting him in the United States Court through Forsyth, and if it was not stopped he (Forsyth) would be killed."

It is further in evidence that after that time, two additional rules, one in July and one in August, were presented to the Court, that both of them were sworn to by Forsyth as the agent for the Dodges. These rules, or rather the applications therefore, one of which was filed, and the other not filed because it had been sent to the Judge while he was out of the jurisdiction will be in evidence before you. It is in the testimony of Burch that Hall had said while he was out on the ten days leave that the Court gave him to enable him to prepare for the trial in the other case that he would give one hundred dollars to have Forsyth killed. It is also in evidence that Forsyth had been a witness against Hall in the trial of the first rule on which he was convicted, and Burch testified that he received a letter to him on the subject from Hall in the jail, after the return of the latter to Savannah. Miss Burch, the daughter of the accomplice, whom the jury had before them as a witness, testified that she had seen the letter, and that it was, in substance, "If you do not attend to the matter, I will have it attended to when I return home." And Burch had testified that there was no other matter that he had to attend to for Hall, save the assassination of Forsyth.

It was said by one of the counsel in argument that Miss Burch was under contract to convict these prisoners. There was no such evidence, and nothing that the Court recalls which will justify the inference. It is, indeed, true, that so far as the law and the protection to Burch, because of his testimony, is concerned, it does not make any difference, whether or not, there is a conviction of any or all of these prisoners. The rule which permits an accomplice to become evidence for the Government under promise of protection, would not be tolerated for an instant among any civilized people, if the construction placed upon it by the counsel could be correct.

The result of the trial in which the accomplice testifies is wholly immaterial to his protection. It is also true that in a letter to Freeman, which is in evidence before you, told Freeman to "tell the boys not to get scared, he would soon be out to help them." And he said, in substance, that if it had not been for Forsyth, he would not have been put in jail. The Court charges you, gentlemen, that all of this evidence, if credible by you, is competent and material to the issue as tending to show a motive on the part of the prisoner Hall. It is for the jury to say whether or not it is credible, and it is for them to say whether it is sufficient corroboration of the testimony of Burch to justify them in exercising their power to credit it.

Evidence which tends to show a motive in Hall of strong animosity against Forsyth because of his connection with these rules, or either of them, in the United States Court, is directly material to your inquiry. You also remember what Hall wrote Norman & Clarke: "Stuckey has lied about me, and has betrayed confidence. I wish somebody would run him out of the country." Stuckey had testified on the trial of the first rule. You may, perhaps, gather from Hall's letter to him encouraging him to take possession of some eighty-nine of the Dodge lots, the nature of the confidence. Of course, gentlemen, it is proper for you to bear in mind all that Hall said on this subject in his testimony. He denied utterly the statement to Burch, and the letter from the jail to Burch; in his letter to Freeman he said he alluded simply to his professional services. He denied the statement to Avant. By the humanity of the Federal law, he is permitted to testify in his own behalf, and it is for the jury to attach such weight to his testimony as they think they can safely and properly give to it.

There is other evidence upon which the Government relies as tending to show the animosity of Hall towards the Dodges and their agents. In a public address made at Eastman, according to the testimony of Hamilton Clark, he said to the people that when the Dodges "came on their lands they should meet them with shotguns, and leave their carcasses for the buzzards to pick, or cram them down gopher holes." According to the testimony of McCrimmen, he said in a similar speech, at Milan, that "the Dodges should be sent hellward." According to the statement of Isadore McCormick, he said, at Chauncey, that he was a martyr, and had been persecuted beyond all reason by this great landed monopoly. According to the testimony of Strum, Hall told the witness, who was complaining that one of the Dodges' agents was acting "biggetty." [Hall said:] "The nights are dark, you have your guns, the matter is in your own hands;" or words to that effect. After the killing of Forsyth, according to the testimony of Bright, while complaining of his persecution and imprisonment by the Dodges, he said, "now I have them on the hip."

According to the testimony of the Hon. D.M. Roberts, Judge of the Superior Court, shortly after the death of Forsyth, the witness was talking with Hall on the streets of Eastman when two persons came up, and one of them said "Perhaps the Dodges had better send some more of their d----d agents down here;" the other said: "We have got some more shotguns and buckshot," and Hall replied, according to the testimony of Judge Roberts: "They had better send along some steel houses for them to live in." Now, Gentlemen, this testimony, if true, is likewise material and important to this investigation. Hall complained, if the witnesses are to be believed, because of his imprisonment and alleged persecution. It does not appear that he was imprisoned otherwise or elsewhere than by the United States Court. He showed very strong resentment toward the Dodges in his public declarations, if the testimony is true. It has been urged that to hold him responsible because of these utterances, would be to deny him that free speech which is the heritage of a freeman.

It is perhaps not necessary for the Court to remind the jury that the liberty of free speech is not a license to the encouragement, public or private, of crimes of violence, and the Constitution of the State of Georgia itself, while guaranteeing liberty of speech, declares that any person may speak, write and publish his sentiments on all subjects, being responsible for the abuse of that liberty.

It is proper, however, that the Court should again direct your attention to Hall's testimony on this subject. You will remember how he qualifies, or attempts to qualify the testimony of Judge Roberts. While he admits he advised the people to meet force with force, he denies any encouragement to commit crime in his public speeches. If, however, you credit the witnesses who impute these utterances to him, you may well regard that testimony as material and competent, in the corroboration of Burch, because a bitter and truculent feeling toward the Dodges which would induce Hall to encourage his hearers to commit crimes of violence upon the Dodges or their agents, would be an important element tending to show the motive, and, therefore, the guilt of the conspiracy to murder one of those agents; and if this was done because he had been imprisoned under a rule sued out by Norman W. Dodge in the United States Court, or because such rules then pending, it would be more material, as tending to show a motive for the precise conspiracy charged in this bill of indictment.

With reference to the testimony of Burch, detailing the circumstances under which he got a hundred dollars, as he testifies, from Hall on the 23d of October with which to pay the murderer Herring, the Government relies upon several circumstance of corroboration. They offer evidence to show that Burch and Cadwell had gone to Hawkinsville in an anxious effort to get the money, Burch testifying that Herring had sent him word that if he didn't pay him the money he would kill him. Failing in Hawkinsville, Burch says they came back to Eastman and reached there before day. That he went out to Hall's, knocked on the door with his knife, that Hall called from the upper window and asked who it was. Burch said it was "L.B.," and Hall came down with a lamp in his hand and admitted him. They went into the sitting room and Hall sat down holding the lamp in his hand while he sat there. Burch stated what he came for, and Hall went upstairs and brought the money down, but claimed that Burch and his party had not done enough—they had not burned the trestles and driven the Dodges out of the country. The testimony of Cadwell is that he came there with Burch that morning; that they went to Sam Rogers, who kept a store and boarding house, went upstairs and made a fire. It was before day; that Burch came with him from Hawkinsville; that they hadn't been there long before the witness missed Burch—he was gone about two hours, or rather the witness did not see him for about two hours. L.M. Peacock testified that he resided at Eastman, and saw Cadwell and Burch on the 23d of October. They tried to borrow a hundred dollars from him—Cadwell did—and said he wanted it for a friend who was in town; he said that Burch lived eighteen miles to the south of Eastman, or rather south, and Cadwell southeast.

Sam Rogers testifies that Andy Cadwell came to his house the same morning, he went upstairs and made a fire, that there was a person with Cadwell who he was very well satisfied was Burch; that some of them came down the stairs and went away and were gone about half an hour, or not quite so long. He said it was a half mile from his house to Hall's place.

Now, gentlemen, if the testimony of Cadwell and Rogers be true, it is material and important as tending to corroborate Burch. These parties were in Hawkinsville the day before. They reached Eastman on the train before day. It was necessary to build them a fire at some inconvenience. What motive then, would Burch have had, before day, to disappear from the fireside and be gone for a period as long as that. He says he went to Hall's. Cadwell says he missed him. You will also consider, gentlemen, the intrinsic merit of Burch's statement. He tells you he knocked on Hall's door with his knife after the question is asked him, he says that Hall sat with the lamp in his hand during the interview. These may be trifling circumstances, without importance, but the jury, having their attention called to them, may possibly deem them of that natural character which will negative the idea that the story was concocted. On this subject it is proper to call your attention to the denial of Hall, and to the statement of Hall's daughters, and a servant, that his room was down stairs and that he always slept down stairs. If this be true, it may discredit Burch.

The jury, however, ought to consider all the circumstances which might surround a man in Hall's situation. He was known to be hostile to the Dodges. Their agent, Forsyth, had been shot dead through his window in a lower room of his house, sixteen days previously. Fifteen days previously Renew had been killed by the friends of Capt. Forsyth. The jury will inquire whether Hall could have had any apprehension which would cause him to sleep upstairs. If the testimony of Warren which related to that day is entitled to any credit, there were those who were accusing Hall of participation in the death of Forsyth, and the jury will inquire whether there is any motive which would prompt Hall to stay upstairs instead of in his usual room during that period of excitement.

At this point the Court will call your attention to the testimony of D. T. Warren, who tells you that he met Burch that day. He had not seen him for two years; after some conversation Burch said to him: "What is the news," and Warren replied : "The news is that they are putting the killing of Forsyth on you, and Hall and Knight." His words were: "they have got you and Hall and Knight spotted with the killing of Forsyth; it seems to me that Col. Hall has had trouble enough," and Burch replied that Col. Hall had nothing to do with it, and knew nothing about it, and, pointing to the breech of a gun that was in his buggy, said: "There is the gun that did the work." Great stress is laid upon the testimony of this witness by the defense. The prosecution replies that it is not likely that Burch would have made, in such a reckless manner, a confession of deadly crime to a man whom he had not seen for two years. They call attention to the fact, too, that Burch came there from Hawkinsville, which is on this side of Eastman, and came on the train, and that he did not come in a buggy. You will remember the testimony of Cadwell and Peacock on that subject. If Burch's buggy was in Eastman, how could it get there? These are matters for the jury. If they believe from the evidence that Burch's buggy was not in Eastman, they should discard the testimony of Warren altogether. That, however, is entirely for the jury.

If the jury believes from all this evidence that the testimony of Burch is sufficiently corroborated, or is otherwise entitled to their credit, they are authorized to act upon it. If, however, they do not believe the testimony of Burch, they should discard it and the prosecution must fail. The circumstances of corroboration relied on to corroborate Burch with reference to Wright Lancaster are that he had moved his brother-in-law, Moore, onto the Bullard land, which comprised some of the Dodge lots, that this was a violation of the injunction; that he had deeded one of the Dodge lots to Burch, in violation of the injunction, and that Burch had leased him some of the Dodge lots.

Burch testified that Wright Lancaster sent Clemens to him, that he knew nothing about Clemens or Lowry. It appears from the evidence that Clemens lived in a different part of the county from Burch, that Lowry, or Herring, had been a witness for Clemens in his trial for highway robbery in Coffee County; that John Lancaster brought Clemens to Burch's house; that Clemens slept at Lancaster's the night before. John Lancaster admits carrying Clemens to Burch's house, but explains that he did it merely to carry Burch's buggy, which he had borrowed, back. John Lancaster tells you he could never get along with Burch. It seems, however, that he had borrowed his buggy. He tells you that he knew nothing about the coincidence of Lowry's reaching Burch's at the same time Clemens reached there. It is true that Wright Lancaster was on Clemens bond for robbery, and as his security and also as the Sheriff of the county, could have arrested Clemens, if it be true that he was a fugitive from justice. Burch said Wright Lancaster said he would send Clemens to his house, and John Lancaster did actually carry him there. The theory of the prosecution is that Wright Lancaster had such a hold on Clemens, and through him on Lowry, that he could control Clemens and induce Lowry to commit the murder for pay. It is in proof, by Wyly Burch, that shortly before the murder of Forsyth, that Wright Lancaster came to the house, stayed all night, and slept with Clemens.

Bohannon testified that after Burch's sickness and excitement that Wright Lancaster went up to see him, and when he came back said that "Burch was acting the fool." The flight of Henry Lancaster is a fact which tends to corroborate Burch's statement that he sent the money to the Negro by Henry Lancaster. Bohannon's testimony to the several conferences between Burch and the Lancasters at the mill is of a similar character. Lowry's flight, the testimony of Louis McDaniel, of the two colored men, John Williams and Calvin Fleming, of Montgomery County, the absence of Lowry from his home in Montgomery County for a month, coincident with the time he remained at Burch's, his return home, his new clothes, his gold watch, his two hundred dollars in money, his conduct in Jesup when he learned that Clemens, Hall, Burch, and the others were arrested, his conduct when he returned to Montgomery County, his statement that they had caught Clemens and would be after him next, and his subsequent disappearance, all strongly tend to show his guilt, and to corroborate the testimony of Burch in that respect.

You will also, gentlemen, consider the letter to Hill & Harris, and the conversation with Bishop and Cheney, on the part of Hall, in connection with the statement of Bright "that he had the Dodges on the hip now," and see if the construction which the prosecution attempts to place upon that evidence is justifiable. You will bear in mind the explanation of it that Hall has given. If you believe that Hall was using the murder of Forsyth as a means of forcing or intimidating the Dodges to abandon the proceedings against him, this evidence becomes very material indeed as tending to support the theory of the prosecution. Of course, if it was a mere appeal for discontinuance of these rules, it would have no such significance. In this connection you should bear in mind, that Hall is a lawyer of considerable experience, and you should also consider whether the incidents shortly preceding his application to these gentlemen, the death of Forsyth, and his own public declarations would render it reasonable that he should be appealing to the Dodges or their attorneys for an amicable settlement, or abandonment of the proceedings against him.

The circumstances of corroboration that the Government relies on to connect Louis Knight with the conspiracy, to the testimony of Burch, are the proof offered to show his criminal intimacy with Hall in the forgery of deeds, the fact that he had litigation with the Dodges which he had lost, and the testimony of Curry to the effect that he had charged Forsyth with forgery and perjury. Hall himself testifies that Forsyth told him that Louis Knight was making forged deeds. As a consequence of this (to state the substance of his testimony), he sent the copy of the deeds in evidence to Louis Knight, so that forgeries could be made, so that he might detect other forgeries by comparison before the jury, passing on an issue of forgery. It is in evidence also that in one of the envelopes he sent to Louis Knight there was a quantity of paper to be used for this purpose. The letters were mailed about the 22d or 23d of November, and they contained a request for the immediate return of the forged deeds. Hall testifies that he had no Court in which he practiced, which met at that time, in which he could possibly use these deeds, and the jury can inquire into the reason for his haste in having them returned, to estimate the credit to be given to the statement as to the use he proposed with these deeds. This evidence is only admissible; however, to show the intimacy between Hall and Knight, which is always proper in a case of conspiracy, and being proper, it is material to corroborate the testimony of Burch to show their joint action.

I believe, Gentlemen, that I have called your attention to everything I deem material which it is insisted corroborates the testimony of Burch. Charles Clemens is jointly indicted with the other alleged conspirators, and his position before you is in no sense different, so far as this indictment is concerned. The testimony of Burch is admissible against Clemens, and if you believe that it is otherwise credible, under the rules I have given you, he might well be convicted on that testimony. He has likewise confessed his guilt. If you believe from the evidence that his evidence was voluntary, and admits the crime with which he is charged, and is corroborated as to all the material evidence of that crime, you would be justified in convicting him on the confession so corroborated. He is a person of full age and sound mind, and it is no excuse to him for the commission of crime that he was coerced or persuaded into its commission. Before, however, you can convict Clemens of any crime under this indictment, you must find that he is guilty of the conspiracy as charged in the indictment. You cannot convict him because he may be guilty of murder, or of the crime of murder generally, this Court has no jurisdiction to try or to punish. You will, therefore, be obliged to acquit Clemens altogether, unless you find that he committed the murder in pursuance of the precise conspiracy charged in this bill of indictment. To determine whether he understood the conspiracy to exist, if you believe from the other evidence in the case that it did exist, you may look to his confession, and, if it shows that he entered the conspiracy after it was formed, he is quite as guilty as one of the original conspirators, if such they be. But, I repeat, that if you do not find the conspiracy existed as charged, and for the purpose you should also find that the identical conspiracy existed between himself and others who are not on trial. But the conspiracy must be proven as charged.

At this point I will give you, gentlemen, a request to charge, presented by the Counsel for the prisoners, with a trifling modification.

It is not within the power of the United States to punish for a conspiracy to murder within the State, unless the murder was committed in violation of some one of the United States statutes (92 U.S. Rep. 553). In this case the question of the power of the United States to inquire and punish for the alleged murder of Forsyth, depends upon whether the killing was done in pursuance of conspiracy to intimidate, threaten or injure Norman W. Dodge, as alleged in the indictment,

It needs something more than a proof of mere passive cognizance of fraudulent or illegal action of others to sustain conspiracy. If, therefore, you should find that there was, from the evidence in this case, a conspiracy as charged in this indictment, then in order to convict any person with the conspiracy so as to make such person liable under the indictment, you must find that such person did something more than entertain a mere passive cognizance of such conspiracy. You must find that such person did some act or made some agreement showing an intention to participate in some way in such conspiracy.

With reference to proof of intimacy between the alleged conspirators, you should bear in mind the proof that Hall himself testifies that he had represented Burch in two cases, and that Burch had brought him money while he was in jail. You should bear in mind, gentlemen, all that the defendants have said in their own behalf. They have all been sworn, and they have all denied all incriminatory features of the evidence for the prosecution. Of course, if you believe them, you should acquit them. With the exception of Hall and Clemens, they have all offered proof of general good character. Good character is a fact fit like all other facts proven in the cause is to be weighed and estimated by the jury. Good character of a prisoner may render that doubtful which would otherwise be clear. If the guilt of the accused is proven to the satisfaction of the jury, however, notwithstanding the good character of the accused has been given its due weight by them, it would be their duty to convict the defendants irrespective of such proof of character, for men who have borne a good character, it is the common experience, may and do commit crimes. In determining whether or not all the prisoners who have put their characters in issue are shown to possess good character, the jury must consider all the evidence upon that subject. Several witnesses were introduced by the prosecution to show that Louis Knight was a man of bad character, and one witness, I believe, was introduced to show that Wright and John Lancaster had bad characters.

The jury will bear in mind all that was said on that subject for and against the character of these prisoners, and make such estimate as they think proper in view of the evidence. Evidence of character is not evidence, as a general rule, of the highest and most important character in legal investigations. The Government cannot put the prisoner's character in issue unless the defense thinks proper to do so. It is true, moreover, that because a prisoner may not choose to put his character in issue he is not to be prejudiced in the minds of the jury thereby. Evidence has been offered also both to attack and sustain the general character for truth and veracity of the witness Burch. A witness impeached by proof of general bad character for truth and veracity may be sustained by proof of general good character for truth and veracity. That is a question entirely for the jury. Even though a witness may be impeached, the jury may credit him if they are satisfied that he has told the truth in the particular case at bar.

At this point the Court will read to the Jury Sections 4320, 4321, 4322, 4323 of the Code of Georgia, which reads as follows:

Murder is the unlawful killing of a human being, in the peace of the State, by a person of sound memory and discretion, with malice aforethought, either express or implied.

Express malice is that deliberate intention unlawfully to take away the life of a fellow creature, which is manifested by external circumstances capable of proof. Malice shall be implied where no considerable provocation appears, and where all the circumstances of the killing show an abandoned and malignant heart.

The punishment for persons convicted of murder shall be death, but may be confinement in the penitentiary for life, in the following cases: If the jury trying the case shall so recommend, or if the conviction is founded solely on circumstantial testimony, the presiding Judge may sentence to confinement in the penitentiary for life. In the former case it is not discretionary with the Judge. In the latter it is.

A word of instruction, now, as to the form of your verdict, and I have done. This indictment, as we have seen, is framed under two sections of the Revised Statutes. There are conspiracy counts framed under Sections 5508 R.S. which the Statute provides its own punishment: *viz*: not exceeding ten years imprisonment, etc. There are also counts for a substantive, and additional, felony, framed under Section 5509 R.S., which provides that if a felony is committed in the progress of such a conspiracy, the parties convicted shall receive their individual punishment, according to the punishment fixed for such felony under the laws of the State. This substantive offense is murder. The jury may therefore, as they may believe is proper from the evidence, convict all or some of these defendants, both on the conspiracy counts, and the felony counts, or they may convict all or some of these defendants on the conspiracy counts only, or they may acquit all, or acquit some, and convict the others. A verdict of guilty generally would mean guilty on the conspiracy counts, and on the murder counts, the substantive felony being that of accessory before the fact to murder. The punishment on a general verdict of guilty will be death, unless the jury recommends imprisonment for life. If you find all the defendants guilty both on the conspiracy and felony counts, the form of your verdict will be: "We, the Jury, find the defendants, (naming them), guilty as charged," recommending them mercy or not, as you may believe is proper from the evidence. If you find some of the defendants guilty both on the conspiracy counts only, the form of your verdict will be: "We, the Jury, find the defendants, (naming them), guilty as charged, and we find the defendants, (naming them), guilty on the conspiracy counts only," as you may believe is your duty in view of the evidence. You may find some of the defendants guilty generally, some guilty on the conspiracy counts only, and others not guilty, as you may be impressed. Or you may find all the defendants not guilty.

Gentlemen of the Jury, this has been a case of unusual importance, an investigation of momentous interest, and it is not surprising that in view of the anxiety and zeal of the advocates that topics have been presented to your minds which have no pertinence to the issue on trial, and no appropriateness in the range of mental vision of upright, law-respecting and oath-respecting jurors. Such incidents are so usual in criminal trials that the mind ceases to be startled at their presentation, and yet, they are gravely injurious to the cause of justice. I allude to open and palpable appeals to the sympathy and commiseration of the jury, to pathetic allusions to afflicted families, to misleading references to the conduct of parties whose character and conduct is in no sense involved in the issue on trial, and, in short, to all of those *ad captandum* observations which drop the poison of prejudice into the mind of an unsuspecting juror, and thus palsy and paralyze his best and most honorable efforts in the direction of a stern and inflexible performance of duty.

Perhaps nothing is more dangerous in this direction than observations which tend to create a false impression upon the mind of the jury, that it has become their duty, a point of precedence, to disregard the assistance which the Court with the best, the most anxious, and most earnest desire to aid them to arrive at a just conclusion, has tendered in its instructions. We have much larger latitude in that respect, under the Federal system, than obtains in the Courts of the State. We can sum up the evidence, as I have attempted to do in this case. We may, in strong terms, express opinion on the evidence, as I have carefully refrained from doing in this case. We must, however, in any case, in either event, leave the facts to the free finding of the jury, as I have already done, and again do in this case. It is all done, however, to aid the jury and not to lead them.

Permit me to say that it has been the purpose of the Court in this laborious trial, to give to this evidence a searching scrutiny which the magnitude of the accusation demanded. In that task the Court has witnessed with pleasure and satisfaction the attention, the patience, the impartiality, and the scrupulous regard to duty which has appeared to signalize the action of the jury. The Counsel from their respective and opposing positions of advocacy have left nothing undone or unsaid which could influence your verdict, or enable you to see their respective causes in the fullest and clearest light. The Court has reviewed the entire case in its instruction as best it could, and the issue is now finally committed to you. The vast record is consigned to your fair, patriotic and intelligent *arbitrament,* and may the Omnipotence whose bright attributes are truth and justice now guide your hearts and minds to their righteous ascertainment.

APPENDIX I

Supplemental Confession of Charles Clemens

Deputy Marshals Avant and Kelly, of the Marshal's guard, accompanying the conspirators to the Ohio Penitentiary, report the following supplemental confession made by Charlie Clemens while on the cars between Lexington, Ky., and Cincinnati:

Deputy Avant: "Charlie, why didn't you tell the District Attorney what you told me and John Kelly the day we arrested you?"

"I did not do as my lawyer told me," said Clemens. "I blame myself with it all. My lawyer told me to make a full statement and I refused because they had scared me by telling me that they were going to break my neck. I am talking to you now for the last time I know on earth. I am going to make a statement that I will be willing to face my God with, and it would be useless for me to make a false statement, because I don't expect to receive any benefit from what I say.

"John Lancaster and Louis Knight would have had a life sentence with the balance if the truth had been told on the stand. John Lancaster told me in jail that he owed the balance of his life sentence to me; that he would have been convicted for life if I had told what I knew. There is a list made up, in Burch's handwriting, that was headed 'money subscribed to pay Rich Lowry, Charlie Clemens and Henry Lancaster for services rendered.' I saw the list and it is something like this:

"Lem Burch, $200; Andrew Renew, $200; Wright Lancaster, $200 ; L.A. Hall, $200; Louis Knight, $200; and $800 more from other people."

"Burch showed me that list and said here are the men that are going to pay the money, and every one of them was good. And after that I had packed my grip and was fixing to go home. I had told Burch that I didn't want nothing to do with it, and he sent for Wright and Henry Lancaster, and they come there and stayed there all night, and Wright told me, showing me the list, here are the men that are going to pay the money, and they will stick to you, but if you back out now, after knowing what you know, and after having our confidence, you will be done like Tom Smith was."

Deputy Avant here asked "Did they kill Tom Smith?"

Clemens answered: "I think they did. Burch told me that there was one man there that knew the plans and was to do the work, and he backed out and they had fixed him.

"When I first went there I stayed three days, and I went home, and on Sunday night I borrowed a mule from a neighbor and was going over to my father's, and somebody waylaid me and shot at me three times, and I jumped off the mule and run in the branch. The next morning me and another man went up there and there were two mule tracks, and they looked very much like two mule tracks that Burch and John Lancaster had been riding, like the tracks of the two mules that they rode down to my father's house to see me. Wright Lancaster was the first man that told me that he wanted to get me and Rich Lowry to do the work.

"Lem Burch and Henry Lancaster came after me when they made up the money. Henry Lancaster and Lem Burch came after me and told me that the money was made up, and that Lowry would be there the next day, and for us to come on up to Burch's house. That evening we went up to John K. Lancaster's house, and he carried us, me and Lowry, up to Burch's. I rode in the buggy with Lancaster and the negro walked.

The First Attempt

"Henry Lancaster and Lowry were the first two men that went up to Normandale to kill Forsyth. I was suffering with the rheumatism for about a week in my knee, and during that time either Burch and Lowry or Henry Lancaster and Lowry would go up to Normandale every night. When I got well, me and Lowry went over there. I stopped near Sugar Creek and Lowry went on up to Capt. Forsyth's house, and Forsyth was not at his house, and he went down to the office and there he saw four or five men, and he was not able to tell which one was Forsyth, and he left them, because he did not know which was Forsyth, and came back to me, and we went back to Burch's house.

"Lowry told Burch that there were five or six d——d big fat men in there and he was afraid to shoot for fear he would kill the wrong man, and Burch told him that he was glad that he didn't shoot, for he would not have him to kill McCrimmen instead of Forsyth for anything in the world. He said I will go and show you which one Forsyth is so that you will not make any mistake. The next day Henry Lancaster and Lowry went over to Normandale so Henry could point out Forsyth to him, and they heard that Forsyth had gone out on the tram-road, and they hurried back to Burch's house and Burch, Henry Lancaster and Lowry went over on the Dodge road to waylay Forsyth and shoot him as he came back on the train. They never got to see Forsyth, he was not on the train, or if he was they couldn't get to see him. Burch said to Lowry: 'Well, I will show you the right man so that you will make no mistake,' and he carried him to Chauncey on election day and pointed out Forsyth to him.

He Meant to Kill McRae

"One night Burch came in and said to me, Ed McRae is going to be at Normandale tonight and now is the time for you to get to kill him; so me and Lowry both went together that night to Normandale and went up to the office and neither Ed McRae or Forsyth was in the office, but Oberly and McCrimmen and the bookkeeper were there. They left the office and went up to Forsyth's house and all the rooms were dark, except one upstairs and Lowry crawled up and looked in at the window and he came down and said that he couldn't see anybody.

"If Ed McRae and Forsyth had been there I was going to shoot Ed McRae and Lowry was going to shoot Forsyth." (Here Clemens went on to state all the circumstances connected with the killing of Forsyth on the night that the killing occurred.)

He then went on to state that Henry Lancaster and Burch were collecting up the money and would pay it as they collected it. Louis Knight did not have any money when they went to him as he had not sold any cotton, but told them he would give them his fine black horse, or if they would wait till he sold his cotton then he would pay them the money. They fully expected to collect $1,600 but Burch and Henry Lancaster were to have $1,000, and if Burch hadn't been arrested and if the people hadn't found it out they would have had the money collected up.

Clemens here stated to the deputy marshals as follows: "The list was kept in a little black book about eight or ten inches long, and the book was laid in a tin box and was laying upon the wardrobe. I expect that Henry is right now trying to collect up that money. He will go to them, these parties that are not known in it, and they will pay him to keep him from saying anything about it.

"Burch told the truth as far as he went, but he didn't want to tell on any of his kinsfolk or any of the parties that were to pay him and Henry Lancaster. Me and Rich Lowry was to have the first $600, to be paid by Hall, Wright Lancaster and Lem Burch, and then Henry Lancaster and Lem Burch were to make up the balance as they could.

Louis Knight With Them

"On one occasion before the killing Burch came home and told me and Lowry that we must go to Normandale that night, that he had seen Louis Knight, and that Knight would meet us at a certain point on the road to Normandale and accompany us that night to see if we couldn't do the work.

"A while after dark Lowry and myself went from Burch's house to the place mentioned by Burch, and there we met Louis Knight, and we all went together to Normandale.

"I stopped at the garden gate and Lowry went to the front of the house and Louis Knight went into the yard to the edge of the steps, and had been there some time looking for Forsyth.

"Someone came in and came very near catching Knight, and Knight had to step in the shade of the house at the end of the steps to keep the party from seeing him. We cannot see Captain Forsyth, and we concluded that we had better leave. I had a Winchester, Knight had a double-barrel shot gun and Lowry had a double-barrel gun."

Avant and Kelly say that the whole of this after-confession was told with the upmost coolness and appearance of truth.

9.

Legal Treatise

Roy N. Cowart

Lucius Lazarus Williams and wife Catherine Garrison circa 1880
(Photograph courtesy of Julian Williams)

Legal Treatise

Roy N. Cowart

I am the great-grandson of Lucius Lazarus Williams (Uncle Loosh). My great grandfather was a direct descendant of Joseph Williams, Sr., who died in 1750 in Duplin County, North Carolina. Joseph Williams, Sr., had four sons, Byrd Williams, Aaron Williams, Joseph Williams, Jr., David Williams, and a daughter, Mary Williams. Joseph Williams, Jr., had the following children: Elizabeth Williams, Mary Williams, Rebecca Williams, Phoebe Williams, Nancy Williams, Joseph B. Williams, David J. Williams, and William H. Williams. Aaron Williams had one daughter, Esther Williams. Byrd Williams had two children, John Williams and Lazarus Mathis Williams. John Williams, Byrd Williams' son, married Elizabeth Williams, daughter of Joseph, Jr. They were first cousins. The following children were born of this union, Joseph Goodin Williams, Lucius Lazarus Williams (Uncle Loosh), and Emily Williams.

Lucius Lazarus Williams married Catherine Garrison on December 4, 1852. They had three children, T. Jack Williams, William H. Williams, and Mary Williams. Catherine Garrison Williams died in 1863 during the birth of T. Jack Williams. He then married Margaret McDermott. They had the following children: Carrie Williams, L. L. (Nig) Williams, Steve (Punch) Williams, Clarence Williams, John M. Williams, and Arthur Williams. Mary Williams married Jasper Newton Rawlins and they had one daughter, Irvina Catherine Rawlins, and sons, O. J. Rawlins, L. L. Rawlins, and William (Bill) Rawlins, Jack Rawlins, and Ernest Rawlins. Irvina Catherine Rawlins married James Allison Cowart and they had thirteen children. I, Roy Newton Cowart, am the twelfth of those children.

I give this background so that the reader might know whereof I speak.

I am a practicing attorney in Warner Robins, Georgia. I have been practicing in Warner Robins for forty-one years. My practice involves tax law, business law, estate planning, and real estate law. I have tried many real estate cases involving title to lands which were taken from the rightful owners by the huge kaolin industry in Twiggs, Wilkinson, and Washington counties without just consideration. Many of the kaolin companies were New York or New Jersey corporations and they requested to be tried in the U. S. District Courts. They were transferred from the superior courts to the U. S. District Courts for trial. These cases involved paper titles to the land, heir land without proper paper title, and claims of adverse possession and prescriptive titles.

To understand the title to the lands being questioned in this, it is necessary to explain these different types of rights to land.

A paper title is a title that is documented by deeds recorded in the county clerk's office in the county where the land is situated. These titles go back through each owner of the land to the first owner, the state. The states gave grants to different individuals who applied for the grants and then each subsequent purchaser of the land received a deed from the seller, all of which deeds were recorded properly in the county where the land was situated. They had to be properly witnessed by one witness and a notary public who placed his seal thereon.

The purchaser had to pay a valuable consideration for the purchase or receive a gift from the donor of the land. The land had to be properly described so as to locate it exactly or give a sufficient key from which it could be located. It is very important that the purchaser record his deed in the property county immediately upon receipt of the deed.

If the purchaser did not record his deed and thereafter I checked the records in the clerk's office and found that the seller still owned the property of record, I could go to him, get him to give me a deed to the same property, go record it prior to the other party recording his, and I would have the legal paper title. I must go into possession of the land within seven years after I received my deed. I may abandon my paper title and the other parties may own the land under the doctrine of adverse possession (later discussed). I could go to the local magistrate court and file an eviction proceeding against the party who had the first deed and have him evicted from the land because he did not record his deed and I recorded mine. This is why we refer to the Georgia Recording Statute as a "race statute." The one who wins the race to the clerk's office to record his deed is the one with proper paper title.

Heir property results when a person who has a paper title dies and his or her estate is not administered through the probate court (ordinary court). The heirs live on the property and continue to live on the property through several generations without a deed. We then have to get all of the heirs to sign affidavits concerning the decedents' heirs up through the present, if they can all be found. This is very hard to accomplish in many instances and we have to go through a partition proceeding in court. This is very involved and we have to notify these unknown heirs through newspaper ads, sell the property and the court holds the unknown heirs' proceeds from the sale for his benefit until the time expires for his share of the property to go to the state. The last one of these I handled involved one hundred and sixty-four heirs all over the United States. We were never able to locate many of these heirs.

The third title acquisition is adverse possession, by the twenty years' possession which possession is open, continuous, notorious and exclusive or this possession must not have originated in fraud.

The other possession title arises when you have a deed or writing to the property but the deed was inadequate (not properly witnessed or does not properly describe the property) or the person giving you the deed did not have a perfect paper title. If under this deed or paper you go into possession of the property which is open, notorious, continuous, and exclusive for a period of seven years, you then have legal title against the whole world, even those with a perfect paper title just as you would with twenty years' possession.

The judge who handled the cases [editors note: in the Dodge Land Litigations] hereafter was Judge Emory Speer of the United States District Court in Macon. I feel strongly that I should include in this report a short history about Judge Emory Speer. The setting for his story begins after the Civil War. The two parties identifiable at the time were the Republicans who perpetrated the war. They were hated in the South, as you can imagine. However, they were in power and nationalized the federal courts, giving them jurisdiction they had not had before. They appointed all district attorneys, federal judges, and the like. Most of the politicians elected to office were the southern Republicans and Yankees who had migrated here after the war. The other party, the Democratic Party, was the party of the South. They were mainly those who fought in the Confederate armies.

Speer entered law school at the University of Georgia at the age of sixteen. He graduated from the Georgia law school in 1869. He did fight with the Confederates in the Battle of Griswoldville as Sherman was going through Middle Georgia on his trek to Savannah. After his graduation, Speer became the political editor of the *Southern Watchman* newspaper, published in Athens, Georgia. His trusted friend, John Christy, published the magazine. Christy was a very active Democrat.

Speer then entered politics and realizing that the Republicans were in control and ran things he switched over to the Republican Party. He has been described as an arrogant, opportunistic, cocky man with an iron will and great ambition. Before he switched to the Republican Party, he ran for Congress as an independent and with the solid black vote in his district around Athens, Georgia, was elected. In 1882 Speer was defeated. He then went to President Chester A. Arthur, whom he had supported on a tariff issue, and procured appointment as the U. S. Attorney for the Northern District of Georgia. The particular tariff issue was one levied against all goods sold by the Confederate states. Arthur was defeated in the 1884 presidential race. Just before his term ended, on January 19, 1885, he nominated Speer as U. S. Judge for the Middle Georgia District. Speer's political opportunism got him in trouble, but he was finally confirmed by one vote.

The Dodge land issue had been brought into the United States District Court in Macon in 1884. Judge John Erskine had handled it prior to Speer's appointment. Upon Speer's taking office he took the case and after a five-day hearing issued his ruling.

In 1913 a subcommittee of the House of Representatives investigated Judge Speer to determine whether he should be impeached. Their recommendation was that he be "severely condemned" and their report was adopted by the committee (Congressional Record, House of Representatives, August 26, 1913, vol. 50; The Investigative Committee Hearings Report 1176, 1913-1914). In 1914 the House passed a bill appointing a second judge to serve in the Macon Circuit. This act further provided that when a vacancy occurred in the Senior Judge's (Speer's) position, it would not be filled. (Statutes at Large of the USA, Vol. 38, p. 959, 1914). It was interpreted by many as a slap in the face to Judge Speer for an extra judge to be appointed in his circuit under these circumstances.

The Dodge land grab started in 1868. From then until 1876 the land in question was owned by the Georgia Land and Lumber Company, a New York corporation. This title was changed because fifty percent of the stock of the corporation had to be owned by Georgia residents. Secondly, if title had remained in the corporation, it could not have claimed as a nonresident and could not have had the case in the U. S. District Court. Until 1876 the Dodges made no claim to the land in South Central Georgia. The back title to the land went from the State of Georgia to Peter J. Williams (1833); from Peter J. Williams to Stephen Chase, Abram

Colby and Samuel Crocker (1834); from the heirs of Colby, Chase, and Crocker to Silas P. Butler; Silas P. Butler to various locals.

Dodge contended that the title went from Colby, Chase, and Crocker to Georgia Lumber Company. Such as deed was given but was improperly executed and not entitled to be recorded.

The locals claimed title through tax deeds executed in 1844 to the land in question. They had lived on the land, farmed it, built nice homes on it, and claimed it as their land under these deeds since 1844. No action was taken to counteract the tax deeds held by the locals until 1876 when Federal Judge John Erskine declared the tax deeds void. The locals continued to live on the land until claims were filed to the land in 1884, some eight years later.

No action was taken to evict them from the land until 1884. The judge, Emory Speer, of the U. S. District, Macon, found that the title of George E. Dodge was a valid paper title to the property and ordered the locals to surrender the lands they held to Dodge. He perpetually enjoined the locals from asserting the rival title or in any way interfering with Dodge's possession and ownership of the lands in dispute.

The first question in any valid paper title involves a deed chain which directly goes to the source of title, the state. If there is a break in the chain, then you do not have a perfect paper title. If the break in the chain occurs more than sixty years ago and the owner at the time of the break has not transferred the title to another party, then title is legally in the present owner, the owner who received a deed from the prior owner, or his or their heirs. However, if the title breaks and the owner, at the time of the break, or his heirs convey the land to another, then the second owner has a solid chain from that date forward and that owner has the perfect paper chain of title.

These theses are subject to a claim of fraud against the second owner, if such exists. This fraud would have to be known to the purchaser of the second deed and he must have connived with the seller to get the title to the property. Absent such as showing fraud will not defeat the second owner's title. Keep in mind that the party who gave the two deeds should know that he gave two deeds to the same property to two different entities, which would be fraudulent, but this is not sufficient. The second purchaser must have known of the fraud and participated in the fraud with the seller.

Looking at the Dodge case, Peter J. Williams sold the land in 1833 to Stephen Chase, Abram Colby, and Samuel Crocker. In looking at the title of record, there is no deed out of these three men to any person or entity. They and their company went broke in 1842, totally abandoned the property, went back to Maine, and actual possession parted. (*The Dodge Lands and Litigation*, by J. N. Talley). Talley was appointed Commissioner by Judge Speer to gather evidence in the land case.

There is a mortgage deed from Georgia Lumber Company to the State of Indiana given in July, 1838. However, the Georgia Lumber Company never had title to the property. Therefore, the State of Indiana did not obtain title. Certainly, no one would have lent $3,000,000 to anyone on a tract of land without a title check. A title check would have shown this glowering gap in the chain of title and it could have been easily corrected by requiring Colby, Chase, and Crocker to execute a deed to Georgia Lumber Company. Certainly, that would have given the Georgia Lumber Company a valid deed and the problem would have been solved. However, this did not happen.

Subsequent to this mortgage deed, Silas P. Butler checked the title to this "abandoned land" and found that the ownership of record was in Colby, Chase and Crocker. He tried to find them and discovered that they were deceased. He then did what anyone who wanted to purchase the land would do: he searched and located the heirs of these three men and obtained a deed from these heirs, giving him title. He then ran ads in the local papers offering the land for sale. He sold it to the locals. They thus obtained perfect title to the land. The persons who purchased from Butler were the same parties who had been in possession of the land since its abandonment in 1842.

A review of the case of Dodge v. Briggs, et al., 27 F. 160, finds that Judge Speer acknowledges the following:

    (a) Dodge had to prove his claim based upon his title being perfect and not on the weakness of the local's title.

(b) The chain of title of claimant Dodge was broken twice, to wit: (1) The purported deed from Colby, Chase and Crocker to Georgia Lumber Company was invalid and not recorded; and (2) That a deed dated December 1, 1849, from the State of Indiana to Martin Green conveying the land in question was an invalid deed, another gap in the chain of title.

(c) That the locals were in possession of the lands, cutting the timber and working the trees for turpentine farms (this was the testimony of Dodge as to how he was damaged).

The judge found that George Dodge purchased his first interest in this land in 1876, never before having any interest therein. He further found that Dodge and his predecessors in title had not been in possession after 1842 until Dodge came down to Eastman and opened an office in late 1876 and found the locals were on the land, cutting timber and farming the trees for turpentine.

Judge Speer, however, overlooked all of these facts and spent his time trying to show that Butler, in purchasing from the Colby, Chase and Crocker heirs, was guilty of fraud in that he was trying to establish a title in themselves, slandering the title of claimant Dodge, yet he readily admits that there were two gaps in Dodge's title chain. The judge ruled that the deed of the heirs of Colby, Chase and Crocker was not valid because the other deed out of them to Georgia Lumber Company was an ancient document (discussed later). This may be true if the Georgia Lumber Company deed was recorded, but it never was and to this day has not been recorded. Thus, the deed to Silas P. Butler was a good and valid deed.

Even admitting only for the sake of argument that Colby, Chase and Crocker should have taken the title in the name of Georgia Lumber Company, the fact is that they did not. The local purchasers would not have known this as a fact because it was not on any record. They would not have conspired with Colby, Chase and Crocker to have taken title individually rather in a corporate name. This all happened in 1837, long before Dodge or the locals were involved in this matter.

It is totally unbelievable that a national insurance company lent Georgia Lumber Company $3,000,000 on this land in 1837 without a thorough title search. It is totally unbelievable that the state of Indiana paid that insurance company the $3,000,000 Georgia Lumber Company owed them with money they lent to Georgia Lumber Company without having their attorney check the title. In checking titles, the records are filed by name only and there are no documents listing property by description. If it is not filed by name you do not find it. It is unbelievable that Judge Speer never mentions these actions in his "equitable ruling," yet he charges the locals with full knowledge of all of these facts when they took action to obtain title to the land from the heirs of Colby, Chase and Crocker. It is totally unbelievable that Judge Speer stated that Dodge had in good faith spent all of his money over the years in protecting this land when Dodge, who purchased it in 1876, knew all of these facts at that time (they were on record.) Dodge was no idiot and he had the title checked which showed these glaring gaps in his title. He decided to gamble when he, in fact, could have taken action at that time to correct these gaps in title, just as the locals did. Equity has to be balanced and he who wants equity must do equity. He must legally correct what he can correct before seeking equity. He cannot be negligent in his affairs and expect equity to aid him. It is ironic that Dodge went to the heirs of Peter Williams and obtained quit-claim deeds from them to clear his title, yet Judge Speer never charged him with slandering the title of Silas T. Butler. This had to show, even to a blind man, he recognized his title was no good. Williams deeded his title away, thus his heirs' deed was invalid.

The judge also refers to the ancient document statute for invalid deeds over thirty years of age as being valid deeds. This is true as he points out, but the person relying on an ancient deed protection must be in possession of the property. He tries to cover this assumption on his part by stating that these were "wild lands" and impossible to possess, yet he admits that the locals were in possession, cutting timber, and farming the land for turpentine. Dodge testified to this as a fact and under the law totally prevented the judge from recognizing it as an ancient deed of title.

Keep in mind that the law says that the claimant Dodge must win his case based on his title alone and not on the weakness of the other man's title. The law applied to the facts in evidence in this case clearly show that Judge Speer overstepped the bounds of the law and his ruling was not the law of the land. Judge Speer should have followed the law of the land and sent Dodge and his carpetbaggers back to New York.

The question of adverse possession in the matter of this land is simple. One who enters into possession under a deed that is allegedly invalid (tax deed) and possesses the land openly, notoriously, exclusively and continuously for seven years has a valid title by prescription (adverse possession), good against all the world even though someone else may have had a valid paper title. The other part of this law is that even without a deed if one enters into possession of land and remains in open, notorious, exclusive and continuous possession for twenty years, the possessor has valid title to the land against the whole world.

The judge found that the locals were in possession of the land cutting the timber and farming it for turpentine, yet he overlooked this law in reaching his ruling. Dodge was an interloper as to the title to this land. The judge may have meant adverse possession could be pursued in another action when he made the following statement at the end of his opinion, "[a] number of the respondents claim title from a different source than Colby, Chase and Crocker. With regard to these the court can pass no decree. If there be controversy with these parties it can be settled in appropriate proceedings elsewhere."

It appears to me that this could have been handled as part of this case. A court has authority to settle all issues involved once it takes jurisdiction. This statement at the end of his opinion, without naming the respondents, makes the entire order and the injunction invalid, yet he issued arrest warrants for those who remained on the land for failure to follow his injunction. It is evident that Judge Speer took a Yankee thread and wove George Dodge a title to this land.

My great grandfather, Lucius L. Williams, was charged with failing to obey the injunction of the court in the land title case. He did not believe he was under such injunction, ignored the charges, and was never served with the warrant, though the Federal Marshal tried hard to serve him. Additionally, an employee of Dodge went on Grandpa Loosh's land and began cutting timber. The employee was shot and killed! The federal court issued a murder warrant for my great grandfather's arrest. The Federal Marshal was never able to serve him with the warrant. On May 20, 1895, the Federal Marshal hired two notorious gunslingers, Robert and Cohen Garrison, and deputized them to go with him to arrest Grandpa Loosh. When they arrived, a gun battle ensued and Grandpa Loosh was killed.

I knew one of the sons of my great Grandpa and he visited us in our home often. My oldest brother died at the age of ninety-one this year, and my oldest living sister is 88 years old. The oldest of the family died eight years ago. She would now be 92 years old. They knew all of the children of Grandpa Loosh. The Dodge Land and Lumber Company's actions and the killing of my great grandfather, Lucius Lazarus Williams, was an often repeated story as seen and told by all of the relatives. The story I always heard was that the Dodge Company hired an assassin who, from the roof of the barn, shot my great grandfather as he lay asleep on the piazza of his home on the China Hill Road exactly twelve miles from McRae, Georgia. Our home was located on the China Hill Road about three-fourths of a mile east of the home where my great grandfather Lucius Williams was slain. I have been to his former home many times. The assassin was a nephew of Lucius, Cohen Garrison. The story always told was that my grandmother, Mary Rawlins, daughter of Lucius, went up to this man at the Blockhouse Church near Jacksonville, Georgia, and told him that she had to forgive him for killing her father, according to her religion, but that it was the hardest thing she ever had to do. I always was told that it was a federal marshal who claimed to have killed him, because, otherwise, the Garrison man would have been charged for murder. The federal marshal, John Kelly, was trying to serve a murder warrant from the U. S. Court in Macon. There was no allegation of conspiracy to commit murder, which was required for the U. S. Court to have jurisdiction. The warrant should never have been issued.

The story goes that Cohen Garrison left the country for several years after the killing. When he returned several years later, the grandsons of Lucius Williams decided they would kill Cohen Garrison for his dastardly act against their grandfather. The men were to draw straws to see who would kill Cohen. Tripp Williams drew the shortest straw and was the one to kill him. Tripp would not do it. Another grandson, Bryant Williams, had the next shortest straw and he accepted the job. On Christmas Eve night, 1903, after a service at the Blockhouse church near Jacksonville, Georgia, Bryant Williams shot and killed Cohen Garrison as he walked out of the service. (For a more complete story concerning this matter, see Addie Garrison Briggs' book, *They Don't Make People Like They Used To*). This was the family's story that I was told.

Since the federal marshal admitted he killed Grandpa Loosh in a shoot-out, the sheriff of Telfair County, Georgia, charged the federal marshal with murder and put him in the Telfair County jail. On *habeas corpus* filed by the federal marshal, the case was transferred to the U. S. District Court in Macon, Georgia. The judge who presided over a trial of the issues was Judge Emory Speer. This hearing and evidence was reported in the case of *Kelly, et al. v. The State of Georgia*, 68 Fed. Reporter, 652. From the finding of facts in the hearing, it was determined that there was a shoot-out between John Kelly, Robert L. Garrison, Cohen Garrison (the federal marshal and the two gun-slinging nephews) and Lucius Williams. Lucius was asleep on the porch and when he was accosted by the marshal, he came up shooting, and in the ensuing battle Lucius was fatally injured and died the next day. I refer to the Kelly case for this information and have asked the authors to include this case in their book so that all who read the book can see for themselves. [Editors note: Mr. Cowart refers to *The Dodge Land Troubles* by Jane Walker and Chris Trowell].

It is patently obvious that Judge Speer ignored the evidence of the doctor who testified in the case and the testimony of other witnesses. Judge Speer was the former U. S. Attorney who worked with these marshals and had a very close relationship with John Kelly prior to being appointed judge in 1885. Judge Speer had very strong opinions as to the truthfulness of this marshal. He had a very low opinion of Lucius Williams prior to hearing this case. This is evidenced in his tone expressed in his opinion. Lucius Williams was the sheriff of Telfair County for ten years up to the beginning of the Civil War. He resigned as sheriff and joined the Confederate Army and served as a Captain in the Army. When he returned he was sheriff for another eight years. This judge should have recused himself in this case because of his obvious bias. You can read his opinion in the Kelly case and decide for yourself.

I have researched the cases concerning the criminal cases that followed the ruling in the land case. I have reviewed the revised statutes of the United States #5508 and #5509, enacted into law in 1870 which are the sections cited by the U. S. Courts in taking jurisdiction and trying persons for felonies (murder) and misdemeanors. The U. S. Constitution granted exclusive jurisdiction to the State Courts for the trial of murder and other such felonies.

To change the Constitutional mandate that the State Courts had jurisdiction to try all murder cases, the U. S. Congress would have to adopt an amendment to the Constitution and submit it to all of the states for their local legislatures to ratify. Two-thirds of all the states would have to ratify the amendment. This was never accomplished nor attempted to be accomplished. Instead of following the required law, the U. S. Congress simply adopted an act giving the Federal Courts jurisdiction to try murder cases arising out of certain conspiracies *instanter*. This was certainly an unconstitutional act and should not have been enforced. The Supreme Court has no authority to amend the Constitution by its rulings. However, the Federal Judges and Judge Speer felt they had to follow it. These two sections enacted in 1870 provide as follows:

Section 5508 (revised): If two or more persons conspire to injure, oppress, threaten or intimidate any citizen in the free exercise or enjoyment of any right or privilege secured to him by the Constitution or laws of the United States, or because of his having so exercised the same; or if two or more persons go in disguise on the highway, or on the premises of another, with intent to prevent or hinder his free exercise or enjoyment of any right or privilege so secured, they shall be fined not more than five thousand dollars and imprisoned not more than ten years; and shall, moreover, be thereafter ineligible to any office, or place of honor, profit, or trust created by the Constitution or laws of the United States.

Section 5509 (revised): If in the act of violating any provision in either of the two preceding sections any other felony or misdemeanor be committed, the offender shall be punished for the same with such punishment as is attached to such felony or misdemeanor by the laws of the State in which the offense is committed.

Section 8 of the act passing these revised statutes states as follows:

Section 8: And be it further enacted, that the district courts of the United States, within their respective districts, shall have exclusively of the Courts of the several states, cognizance (jurisdiction) of all crimes and offenses committed against the provisions of this act.

The question of whether or not the U. S. District Court had jurisdiction to issue a warrant to Grandpa Loosh and to try Luther A. Hall, Charles Clemens, Wright Lancaster, John K. Lancaster, Louis Knight and James Moore on the charges of conspiracy to deny Norman W. Dodge his civil right under Revised Statute #5508 and to try all of them for the murder of his agent, John C. Forsyth, as a result of the conspiracy to deny him his civil rights under Revised Statute #5509 is one of the big questions covered in this book.

Judge Speer cites paragraph 1, #2 of Article 3 of the U. S. Constitution which states:

The judicial power (of the U. S. Courts) shall extend to all cases in law and equity arising under this constitution, the laws of the United States...to controversies between citizens of different states.

Norman W. Dodge was a citizen of the State of New York and the people being tried were all residents of the State of Georgia. It, therefore, follows that the Federal Court had the right to try them for conspiracy.

Judge Speer stated that this was a logical provision of the Constitution furnishing a most significant illustration of the importance of right. "The local prejudices against strangers and non-resident property owners, unreasonable as they are, confined as they necessarily must be to a small portion of the people, are sufficient in many cases to deny and utterly destroy the most valuable rights of the non-residents. Therefore, to deny in such cases the right of the non-resident to prosecute his remedies in the Court of the United States would be to deny his rights altogether and to shut and close to him the avenues of public justice." [Ex Parte Yarbrough, 110 U.S. 651]

As to the trial of the murder case against the parties under Revised Statute 5509, attorneys for the accused parties urged that the pendency of this indictment is a grave instance of disrespect to the autonomy of the State and to the Superior Court of Dodge County because the Federal Constitution vested in the state courts the trial for murder. Judge Speer answered saying perhaps it would be sufficient to say that it can never be any reflection upon the state or its courts that the general government will attempt to protect its citizens in the enjoyment of these rights, secured to them by the Constitution and laws of the common country. Further, Judge Speer states that the murder was committed on October 7th and the U. S. Court indicted the accused on November 20th. If warrants has been issued and arrests made by the authorities of the State, the accused would not now be before this Court. U.S. v. Lancaster et al., 44F, 885 and 895.

The Supreme Court of the United States in U. S. v. Reese, 92 U. S. 214-217, held that the rights and immunities created by or dependent upon the Constitution of the United States can be protected by Congress in the legitimate exercise of its legislative discretion as the need shall provide. These may be varied to meet the necessities of the particular right to be protected.

In layman's language, this states that for any rights a person has under the Constitution, Congress may pass laws to protect these rights and may provide a punishment for their violation.

These cases were rulings of the Supreme Court of the United States prior to the Lancaster-Hall cases and Judge Speer was bound to follow their rulings. These revised statutes were repealed by the Congress in 1910. I frankly feel that Judge Speer was unjustly criticized for the handling of the law in these criminal cases. However, if he had not screwed up so badly on the land cases, the Forsyth and Williams murder cases would never have happened. For shame!

Editor's Note: Mr. Cowart's article originally appeared in *The Dodge Land Troubles*, by Jane Walker and Chris Trowell. A report on the Lucius Williams case is included in that book, outlining the killing of Lucius Williams and citing that eighty-one bullets were fired into the house by the assailants on that day.

Additional Material

Idler's Retreat
Smyrna, Tennessee
37167
August 4, 1982

Mr. Stephan Whigham
Ocmulgee Regional Library System
P.O.Box 606
Eastman, GA 31023

Dear Stephan,

Thanks so much for the interview cassette and
the other mementoes, especially the old photo of the Forsythe
house!

Glad you were able to pick up a copy of
LIGHTWOOD!

My Burr Oak publisher still says that he intends
to bring out a paperback of it, but his plans are very
indefinite.

It was a pleasure to meet you and I remember
our exchange with warmth and enjoyment.

Best of luck.

Brainard Cheney

Letter from Brainard Cheney to Stephen Whigham, 1982

Acknowledgements

This book celebrates the work of Brainard Cheney and honors his contribution to the cultural and historical heritage of the Ocmulgee, Oconee and Altamaha River basin area.

The Lightwood Chronicles owes its genesis to a lifelong love of family stories. I first heard of this history from my maternal grandmother and great-grandmother, Wylena Davis and Hattie Clark Hargrove, respectively. Later, my mother, Welda Davis Whigham, joined the conversation with her memories of the old Forsyth House in Suomi. To them, along with my father, John P. Whigham, I owe my love of history, especially that of the Dodge County area. Another valued family member, my great-aunt Dorothy Hargrove Stoeger, keeps the family traditions alive, offering encouragement and assistance through the years.

In later years, I discovered and located resource material such as *The Dodge Lands and Litigation* by Talley and Marion Erwin's *The Land Pirates*. The late Julia Smith, avid local historian, kindly lent me her copies of these items.

The year 1982 saw Dr. Delma Presley orchestrating his Project RAFT, inspired by his admiration for the novels of Brainard Cheney, especially *Lightwood* and *River Rogue*. Dr. Presley was very helpful to me on projects for our local library at the time. Most important, through him I met Brainard Cheney, for which I express my gratitude. Dr. Presley is a retired professor from Georgia Southern University and author of *The Lightard Knot*, a play depicting events from the *Lightwood* story.

In the spring of 1982, Brainard Cheney traveled from Nashville to the Lumber City area to participate in the project. His novel *River Rogue* was republished for the occasion. I met and interviewed Mr. Cheney, videotaping the occasion. He discussed in detail the creation of *Lightwood*. He articulated his affection for his early years growing up along the river, of the people he knew as a boy and young man, and the kindness and sacrifice exhibited by his mother, Mattie Mood Cheney. I consider it an honor and privilege to have met Mr. Cheney and his wife, Frances Neel Cheney.

Also during this same period, my friend from high school days, Mark Wetherington, was completing his Ph.D. focusing his researches on the south Georgia area. Several years later his book, *The New South Comes to Wiregrass Georgia* (1994), appeared. It covers the period from 1860 to 1910, simultaneous with the events in *Lightwood*. Mr. Wetherington kindly shared his information with me. He continues his work, in recent years publishing a second book, *Plain Folks Fight* (2005). I appreciate his friendship and help in answering my many questions over the years.

Mary Ellen Tripp Wilson published her doctoral thesis on the timber industry in south Georgia in 1981. As a Dodge County native and the daughter and granddaughter of lumbermen, the call of the pine forests was close to home. Her scholarly work offers rewarding reading on the subject.

William J. Steele is a long-time railroad aficionado and expert. His article in the 1993 publication, *History of Dodge County 1932-1992,* presents valuable details of the Macon and Brunswick railroad line and also the smaller tram lines in the Dodge and Telfair County areas.

Jane Walker of McRae, Georgia, spent many years researching the history of the Dodge Company. So far she has produced two very well-received novels and an essential work on the subject, *The Dodge Land Troubles,* written with Chris Trowell of South

Georgia College. Their publication will stand unsurpassed for years to come as a quintessential starting point for any research in this subject area. And it is entertaining reading as well.

Roy N. Cowart is a practicing attorney and a native of the Dodge and Telfair county area. He graciously allowed the inclusion of his essay which originally appeared in Jane Walker and Chris Trowell's *The Dodge Land Troubles*. Thank you to him and to my friend, Mrs. Walker.

I would like to thank Muriel Jackson and Thomas Jones of the Middle Georgia Regional Library System for their help and support in providing material on Marion Erwin, Macon citizen. Their Genealogy Collection is a premier resource for historical and family history research in Georgia and the Southeast.

Thank you to my friends Anne Bowen and Chris Woodburn, for their encouragement and advice during this project.

My thanks to Tonya Coleman and Lynn Sheffield, who both provided valuable assistance in preparing the typed manuscript for this work.

My two friends, Hubert Evans and Julian Williams, kindly provided historical photographs for this project. Both of these gentlemen not only profess a love of family and local history—they also work hard to guarantee that it survives. Their personal photographic archives, along with Mr. Williams' outstanding website, keep history alive for the Ocmulgee Region.

Thanks also to my two Whigham cousins, John Allen Whigham and Gary Yawn. Their shared interest in family history and the history of Dodge County enlivens any family gathering. I appreciate their encouragement for this project through the years. And on my mother's side, my cousin Jimmy Davis, Civil War historian and local history expert.

Thank you to the Sewanee Review and Managing Editor, Leigh Anne Couch, for permission to reprint the Caroline Gordon article on Mr. Cheney's novels.

Thank you to the Chattahoochee Review and its very kind Editor, Anna Schachner, for permission to reprint Ashley Brown's 1998 article on Brainard Cheney.

Thank you to the University of Georgia Press for permission to reprint the two John Goff essays.

Appreciation is extended to Ashley Brown's son, Professor Celso d'Oliveira, for his assistance in securing the rights to Mr. Brown's article and for encouragement for this project. He is commended for maintaining awareness of Mr. Brown's wideranging scholarly work in many areas of southern literature and history.

Thank you to Barbara Smith Cook, of McRae for bringing to my attention Brainard Cheney's letter to the Ocmulgee Hotel, and to Ann Clements Clark for permission to use the letter. Mr. Cheney had sent the letter to her mother, Sarah Clements, in 1936.

I appreciate my colleagues throughout the Ocmulgee Regional Library System for their dedicated and hard work as library workers on behalf of all the citizens of the area.

Thank you to my friend, Josh Sheffield, for sharing his expertise as a printmaker and graphic artist. His hard work made this book possible.

I thank my friend, John B. Coffee, for his longstanding friendship and for sharing a mutual interest in the life and times of Eastman and Dodge County and its history. And I raise my hat to our late, mutual friend, Robert Kight, Jr., thanking him for his encouragement and friendship of more than fifty years.

Roy Neel of Nashville, nephew of Brainard and Frances Neel Cheney, deserves special gratitude for allowing the reprinting of *Lightwood* to coincide with publication of *The Lightwood Chronicles*. My respect and admiration also goes out to Mr. Neel, who is known to have paid much attention to Mr. and Mrs. Cheney during their later years.

My brother, Michael Whigham and his wife, Mai, continue to offer friendship and encouragement for these local history projects. Their goodwill cannot be overstated.

My wife, partner and friend, Carolyn, selflessly offers her support and inspiring and pleasant company for this work and much more. Thank you for everything.

Contributors

ASHLEY BROWN is a distinguished professor emeritus of literature and a renowned literary scholar. Dr. Brown maintained a long friendship with Mr. and Mrs. Cheney, as well as Caroline Gordon and Flannery O'Connor, among others. He retired as Professor Emeritus from the University of South Carolina.

BRAINARD CHENEY authored four novels and is the inspiration for the *Chronicles*. Mr. Cheney enjoyed a long career as a journalist and distinguished political advisor and speechwriter in Nashville, Tennessee. He and his wife, Frances (Fannie) Neel, counted Flannery O'Connor, Robert Penn Warren, Allen Tate and Caroline Gordon among their many friends in the literary world of mid-century United States.

ROY N. COWART works in Warner Robins as an attorney. Mr. Cowart practices real estate, tax and family law in central Georgia. His great-great grandfather, Lucius Williams, died in a confrontation resulting from the Dodge Land Wars.

MARION ERWIN served as the Federal Prosecutor in the Forsyth murder trial. Mr. Erwin later moved to New York City where he prospered as a private attorney in the 1890s and into the 1900s.

JOHN GOFF was a geologist and historian. In his fifties, Mr. Goff added the study of placenames, called *onomastics,* to his skills. He traveled the state seeking the origins of placenames, resulting in his entertaining and important work, *Placenames of Georgia.*

CAROLINE GORDON was an outstanding American novelist and literary critic whose works are revered to this day. She won both a Guggenheim Fellowship and an O. Henry award for her work. Born in 1895 in Kentucky, her writing, both fiction and non-fiction, most often addressed Southern literary subjects. Longtime friend and mentor to Brainard Cheney and Mrs. Cheney.

JOSH SHEFFIELD is a musician, graphic artist, and computer expert. He resides in Eastman within striking distance of William Pitt Eastman's home. He created the layout and presentation of *The Lightwood Chronicles*.

DOROTHY HARGROVE STOEGER is a genealogist and family historian. She was born in the Forsyth House. She continues to research and write about her Clark, Hamilton, Hargrove and other ancestors into her 90th year. She lives in Kansas City, Missouri.

WELDA DAVIS WHIGHAM was born in the Forsyth house and grew up in Tampa, Florida. She married and returned to Dodge County, where she retired as a postal clerk and flourished as an antiques dealer along with her husband, John P. Whigham. She passed away in June, 1999.

Lightwood: People, Places and Characters

Disclaimer: The list below represents an honest effort to correlate the fictional characters and places of *Lightwood* with their possible real-life counterparts. The editor makes no guarantee that any of these are correct. Some characters of course are composites.

Coventry County was Dodge County

Lancaster, the town, was Eastman

Pineville was Chauncey and Normandale/Suomi (related towns)

Proudfitt Coventry was William E. Dodge

Captain Ian McIntosh was Captain John C. Forsyth

Micajah Corn drew from Lem Burch (and possibly others)

Jere Corn was modeled on Littleton Burch

Calhoun Calebb derived from Luther A. Hall

Mathias Hurd was similar to Wright Lancaster

Zenas Fears was possibly Ed McRae

Trigger Fowler likely was Rich Lowry (Lowery) (Rich Herring)

Ardel Cone and his situation resembled Andrew Renew

Judge Cassius Crow was Judge Emory Speer

Tump Deacon may have been Cohen Garrison

A Chronology of the *Lightwood* Area

1000	Native Americans settled the area as early as 1000 A.D., Creek Indians, who were mound builders, lived in the Ocmulgee region.
1540	Hernando de Soto journeyed through the area.
1540-1700	Spanish and English trade with the Creek Indians and the few white settlers.
1733	General Oglethorpe and first settlers arrive in the Savannah area.
1773-1774	Explorer and botanist William Bartram travels through Georgia, exploring the Altamaha, Oconee and Ocmulgee River areas.
1785	Treaties with the Creek Indians open up area west of the Oconee River, "the land between the rivers" or the "forks."
1804	Treaties of Fort Wilkinson and Fort Washington with Creek Indians open up the lands west of the Ocmulgee.
1807	Telfair and Laurens counties created.
1808	Pulaski County created from Laurens with county seat at Hartford, on the east side of the river.

1818   Skirmishes with last remaining Indians. Andrew Jackson and soldiers pursue Creek Indians, the Red Sticks.

1822-1823   Town of Hawkinsville established across river from Hartford.

1822-1823   Construction of the Coffee Road authorized, General John Coffee leading the project to completion.

1832-1834   Northern investors purchase land from Peter J. Williams of Milledgeville. Georgia Lumber Company incorporated, consisting of 300,000 acres of virgin timber. Lumber City created in southern Telfair County as base for timber operations. Ocmulgee River used to transport timber to Darien.

1842-1844   Company failed leaving large debts to creditors. For several years the State of Indiana, through its bank, owned the land. Over time, title to the holdings moved to investors in New York. In 1844, Telfair County tax commissioner offers some of the land for sale due to unpaid taxes.

1868   In 1868, William Pitt Eastman partnered with William E. Dodge and assorted investors to buy 300,000 acres of timber land. Timber operations begin, construction of sawmills and tram lines. Company headquarters was located in Normandale (now Suomi), near present-day Chauncey.

1870   Dodge County created by Act of Legislature. Macon and Brunswick Railroad constructed, linking the remote timberlands to the port of Brunswick.

1870   City of Eastman established as county seat at the location of Station Number 13 on the M&B Line. Large numbers of settlers move into the area, creating a 'boom' town.

1877	First ejectment cases brought against landowners, called "squatters." Dispute centered on questions of the "chain of title" held by the Georgia Land and Lumber Company (Dodge Company).
1880-1884	Attorney Luther Hall challenges Dodge Company's chain of title, sells land advertised as "Homes for the Homeless." Taken to court by the Dodges. Hall serves in Georgia legislature.
1886	Dodge Company wins in Federal Court. Begins ejecting "squatters" and engenders conflict.
1889	Luther Hall loses civil case for "long chain of title" and is sentenced to five months in prison for contempt. Upon release, begins new campaign for legislature in 1890 election and loses.
1890	Luther Hall, Sheriff Wright Lancaster of Telfair, and others allegedly conspire to "sabotage" the Dodge Company operations. On October 7, 1890, Dodge Company Superintendent, Captain John Forsyth, is murdered at Normandale.
1890	Conspiracy trial convicts Luther Hall, Wright Lancaster and others in Macon Federal Court for Forsyth's murder.
1890-1923	Litigation finally vacated in a 1923 court ruling.

References and Suggested Reading

Fiction

Cheney, Brainard. *Lightwood*. New York: Houghton Miflin, 1939.
____. *River Rogue*. New York: Houghton Miflin, 1941.
____. *This is Adam*. New York: McDowell, Obolensky, 1958.
____. *Devil's Elbow*. New York: Crown Publishers, 1969.
All four of Brainard Cheney's novels take place in the Ocmulgee River area, in Telfair and Dodge counties. These works draw upon historical and autobiographical sources.

Humphreys, Josephine. *Nowhere Else on Earth*. New York: Viking Penguin, 2000.
Well-researched novel based on the Lumbee Indian/Scuffletown wars waged by Henry Berry Lowry, as told by his wife, Rhoda.

Price, Eugenia. *The Beloved Invader*. Philadelphia: J. B. Lippincott, 1959.
This bestselling historical novel tells the story of William E. Dodge's grandson, Anson Dodge, Jr. The Dodge Mills, on St. Simons Island, figure in the story of Christ Church, where Anson was pastor.

Walker, Jane. *Widow of Sighing Pines*. Fernandina Beach, Florida: Wolfe Publishing, 2002.
Jane Walker used her historical researches into the Dodge Land Wars in this engaging love story between a strong-willed widow and a timber rafting backwoodsman.

Historical References

Bartram, William. *Travels*. New York: Dover, 1955. Edited by Mark Van Doren.
Classic account of William Bartram's trek through the wilds of the southeastern United States from 1773-1778. Includes details of flora and fauna of Georgia at that time.

Briggs, Addie Garrison. *They Don't Make People Like They Used To: Olden Times in Telfair County, Georgia*. McRae, Georgia: Elspeth Enterprises, 1985.
Much of this work centers around the Dodge Land Wars, specifically the killing of Cohen Garrison. Garrison allegedly fired the fatal shot that killed his uncle, Lucius Williams.

Chalker, Fussell M. *Pioneer Days Along the Ocmulgee*. Carrollton, Georgia: F. M. Chalker, 1970.
Unique and entertaining history of the Ocmulgee River, from its origins beneath the State Capitol building in Atlanta to its merging with the Oconee to form the mighty Altamaha River. Creek Indians, DeSoto, early settlers and more are featured.

Cobb, Mrs. Wilton P. *History of Dodge County*, 1932. Published in Washington: WPA Project Publication, 1932.
Mrs. Cobb prepared the History as a WPA Project during the Depression. She relied not only on written documents but on the reminiscences of older citizens who recalled the earliest days of Eastman and Dodge County.

Dodge, Phyllis B. *Tales of the Phelps-Dodge Family*. New York: New York Historical Society, 1987.
Family history of the Dodges, including William E. Dodge, his notable father, David Low Dodge, and others. The work offers detailed insight into William E. Dodge's business career.

Evans, Tad and John D. Willcox. *William Pitt Eastman: Founder of Eastman, Georgia*. Savannah: Tad Evans, 1993.
Insightful biographical study of Eastman's founder with reproductions and illustrations.

Fishman, Gail. *Journeys through Paradise: Pioneering Naturalists in the Southeast.* Gainesville: University Press of Florida, 2000.
Engaging study of several intrepid explorers and naturalists as they traveled through the southeast.

Goff, John Hedges. *Placenames of Georgia: Essays of John H. Goff.* Edited by Frances Lee Utley and Marion Hemperley. Athens: University of Georgia Press, 1975, 2007.
Premier collection of Goff's essays on sites throughout Georgia. An essential Georgia history resource.

Graham, Abbie Fuller. *Old Mill Days: 1874-1908.* St. Simons Island, Georgia: St. Simons Public Library, 1976.
A labor of love and scholarship by St. Simons Island librarian, Ms. Graham. Author Eugenia Price noted that this was one of the first resources she used when preparing her novel, *The Beloved Invader.*

Hudson, Charles. *Knights of Spain, Warriors of the Sun.* Athens: University of Georgia Press, 1997.
Modern update on the route Spanish explorer DeSoto took through Georgia and the southeast in 1539-1542.

Hudson, Joyce Rockwood. *Looking for DeSoto: a Search Through the South for the Spaniard's Trail.* Athens: University of Georgia Press, 1993.
Ms. Hudson's personal account of how she and her husband researched DeSoto's itinerary in the southeastern United States.

Jonza, Nancylee Novell. *The Underground Stream : The Life and Art of Caroline Gordon.* Athens: University of Georgia Press, 1995.
Outstanding biography of Ms. Gordon, close friend of Brainard Cheney, who he called his "literary godmother."

Lowery, Melinda Maynor. *Lumbee Indians in the Jim Crow South: Race, Identity, and the Making of a Nation.* Chapel Hill: University of North Carolina Press, 2010.

Study of the Lumbee Indians in Robeson County, North Carolina. Contains updated research on this intriguing society whose heritage includes Native Americans, runaway slaves and possibly survivors from Jamestown, the famous "lost colony" of English settlers.

Lowitt, Richard. *A Merchant Prince of the Nineteenth Century: William E. Dodge.* New York: Columbia University Press, 1954.
Standard and well-researched biography of Dodge. In its 384 pages, the Dodge Land Wars rate less than two pages.

Lundberg, Patricia Yawn. *In the Piney Woods of Georgia: Pioneers in a Troubled Time.* Milledgeville, Georgia: Old Capital Press, 2007.
Pictures and text relate the Dodge Land Wars story along with material on the Yawn family of Dodge and Telfair counties.

Maynor, Melinda. *Croatan Indians in Bulloch County, 1890-1920.* [Pembroke, North Carolina: UNC Pembroke, 2002].
An early paper from Ms. Maynor (see Lowery) focusing on the Lumbee migrant turpentine workers in Bulloch County, Georgia.

Morrison, Carlton A. *Running the River: Poleboats, Steamboats & Timber Rafts on the Altamaha, Ocmulgee, Oconee and Ohoopee.* St. Simons Island, Georgia: Saltmarsh Press, 2003.
Illustrated history of navigation in the Ocmulgee and Altamaha river basin.

Neel, Leon with Paul S. Sutter and Albert G. Way. *The Art of Managing Longleaf: A Personal History of the Stoddard-Neel Approach.* Athens: University of Georgia Press, 2010.
Scholarly and very readable account of one of the last wild areas of pine forest in Georgia.

Owsley, Frank. *Plain Folk of the Old South.* Baton Rouge: Louisiana State University Press, 1949.
Pioneering statistical study of ante-bellum farmers and planters with a contrarian economic view on slaveholding landowners.

Price, Eugenia. *St. Simons Memoir*. New York: J. B. Lippincott, 1977.
Accessible and informative recounting of Ms. Price's discovery of St. Simons Island and her subsequent historical novels based on its early inhabitants, including the Dodge family.

Ray, Janisse. *Drifting into Darien: a Personal and Natural History of the Altamaha River*. Athens: University of Georgia Press, 2011.
Ms. Ray's personal and socioeconomic history of the great river and timberlands of south Georgia.

Ray, Janisse. *Ecology of a Cracker Childhood*. Minneapolis: Milkweed Editions, 1999.
In this memoir and valentine to the pine woods of south Georgia, Ms. Ray's work presents her love of family and its relation to the ecology and heritage of the area.

Snow, Frankie. *An Archaeological Survey of the Ocmulgee Big Bend Region*. Douglas, Georgia: South Georgia College, 1977.
Pioneering scholarly study of the area's original inhabitants and their geographical distribution throughout the area.

Steele, William J. "Railroads of Dodge County." Excerpt contained in the *History of Dodge County, 1932-1992*. Eastman, GA: William Few Chapter, DAR, 1993.
Excellent article on the railroads and tram roads of early Dodge, Telfair and adjacent counties.

Stephens, C. Ralph, editor. *The Correspondence of Flannery O'Connor and the Brainard Cheneys*. Jackson: University Press of Mississippi, 1986.
Letters with the emphasis on literary pursuits, from 1953 until O'Connor's death in 1964. Essential reading.

Stoeger, Dorothy Hargrove and Wylena Hargrove Davis. *Letters from Sister*. Eastman, GA: Hattie Wylena Group, 2010.
Letters from Wylena Davis covering the Clark, Hamilton and Hargrove families from around 1810 through 1975 in Georgia.

Talley, J. N. *The Dodge Lands and Litigation*. Atlanta: Annual Report of the Georgia Bar Association, 1925.
Address given by Talley summing up the Dodge Land Wars. Mr. Talley was the legal referee concluding more than fifty years of legal wrangling in the case.

Tripp, Mary Ellen. *Longleaf Pine Lumber Manufacturing in the Altamaha River Basin, 1865-1918*. Ann Arbor: University Microfilms International, 1983.
Ms. Tripp's (now Wilson) doctoral thesis on the timber industry in the Ocmulgee area provides insight and background to the Dodge Land issues.

Walker, Jane and Trowell, Chris. *The Dodge Land Troubles: 1868-1923*. Fernandina Beach, Florida: Wolfe Publishing, 2004.
The massive undertaking by the authors addresses not only the Land Troubles but also the history of the Ocmulgee area. With facsimiles of newspaper articles and original essays on the topic, this essential resource covers the period 1800 to 1923.

Way, Alfred Glover, PhD. *Conserving Southern Longleaf: Herbert Stoddard and the Rise of Ecological Land Management*. Athens: University of Georgia Press, 2011.
Dr. Way presents his study of pioneer pine management expert, Herbert Stoddard, of Thomasville, Georgia.

Wetherington, Mark V. *The New South Comes to Wiregrass Georgia*. Knoxville: University of Tennessee Press, 1994.
Wetherington's pioneering study of the wiregrass area of south Georgia and the socioeconomic changes occurring from 1860-1910 augments the history of the Dodge Land Wars area.

Wetherington, Mark V. *Plain Folk's Fight: the Civil War and Reconstruction in Piney Woods Georgia*. Chapel Hill: University of North Carolina Press, 2005.
Enlightening and incisive study of the cultural factors affecting the military service of Civil War soldiers from the wiregrass area of Georgia and their relation to the planter class.

Index

CPSIA information can be obtained at www.ICGtesting.com
Printed in the USA
LVOW071010180613

339082LV00001B/3/P